GERMAN ORDER OF BATTLE
VOLUME THREE

Other titles in the Stackpole Military History Series

THE AMERICAN CIVIL WAR

Cavalry Raids of the Civil War
Pickett's Charge
Witness to Gettysburg

WORLD WAR II

Armor Battles of the Waffen-SS, 1943–45
Army of the West
Australian Commandos
The B-24 in China
Backwater War
The Battle of Sicily
Beyond the Beachhead
The Brandenburger Commandos
The Brigade
Bringing the Thunder
Coast Watching in World War II
Colossal Cracks
D-Day to Berlin
Eagles of the Third Reich
Exit Rommel
Flying American Combat Aircraft of World War II
Fist from the Sky
Forging the Thunderbolt
Fortress France
The German Defeat in the East, 1944–45
German Order of Battle, Vols. 1 and 2
Germany's Panzer Arm in World War II
Grenadiers
Infantry Aces
Iron Arm
Luftwaffe Aces
Messerschmitts over Sicily
Michael Wittmann, Vols. 1 and 2
The Nazi Rocketeers
On the Canal
Packs On!
Panzer Aces
Panzer Aces II
The Panzer Legions
Retreat to the Reich
Rommel's Desert War
The Savage Sky
A Soldier in the Cockpit
Stalin's Keys to Victory
Surviving Bataan and Beyond
Tigers in the Mud
The 12th SS, Vols. 1 and 2

THE COLD WAR / VIETNAM

Flying American Combat Aircraft: The Cold War
Land with No Sun
Street without Joy

WARS OF THE MIDDLE EAST

Never-Ending Conflict

GENERAL MILITARY HISTORY

Carriers in Combat
Desert Battles

GERMAN ORDER OF BATTLE VOLUME THREE

Panzer, Panzer Grenadier, and Waffen SS Divisions in World War II

Samuel W. Mitcham, Jr.

STACKPOLE
BOOKS

Published by
STACKPOLE BOOKS
5067 Ritter Road
Mechanicsburg, PA 17055
www.stackpolebooks.com

This is a revised and expanded edition of HITLER'S LEGIONS by Samuel W. Mitcham, Jr., originally published in one volume by Stein and Day. Copyright © 1985 by Samuel W. Mitcham, Jr.

Cover design by Tracy Patterson

Cover photo courtesy of HITM Archive, www.hitm-archive.co.uk

Printed in the United States of America

10 9 8 7 6 5 4 3 2 1

ISBN-13: 978-0-8117-3438-7 (Volume Three)
ISBN-10: 0-8117-3438-2 (Volume Three)

Library of Congress Cataloging-in-Publication Data

Mitcham, Samuel W.
German order of battle / Samuel W. Mitcham, Jr.
p. cm. — (Stackpole military history series)
Includes bibliographical references and index.
ISBN-13: 978-0-8117-3416-5
ISBN-10: 0-8117-3416-1
1. Germany. Heer. Infanterie. 2. Germany. Heer—History—World War, 1939–1945. 3. World War, 1939–1945—Regimental histories—Germany. 4. Germany—History, Military—20th century. I. Title.

D757.3.M57 2007
940.54'1343—dc22

2007014285

Table of Contents

Introduction

As a young graduate student recently discharged from the U.S. Army, I started writing a book entitled *Hitler's Legions: The Order of Battle of the German Army, World War II* in the mid-1970s and finished it seven years later. Since that time, a huge amount of literature on the order of battle of the German armed forces and their commanders has become available—so much so that *Hitler's Legions* became obsolete. The purpose of this book, and its companion volumes, is to replace the original, to present the order of battle of the German ground forces in World War II, and to trace each division from inception to destruction. I also (insofar as is possible) have listed the divisional commanders and the dates they held command. If they were promoted, killed, or wounded during their tenure, I have included this information as well. I only regret that I was not able to give a short biography of each commander, as I did in *Panzer Legions* and in the endnotes of some of my earlier books.

I would like to thank Chris Evans, the history editor at Stackpole Books, for suggesting this project, and David Reisch at Stackpole for all of his help. I would also like to thank Melinda Matthews, the head of the interlibrary loan department at the University of Louisiana at Monroe, for her usual superb job in tracking down reference material, as well as anyone else who provided useable information for this project. Thanks also go to Paul Moreau and Dr. Donny Elias for all of their help along the way. Most of all, I would like to thank my long-suffering wife, Donna, and my kids, Lacy and Gavin, for all that they have had to put up with during this process.

Dr. Samuel W. Mitcham, Jr.
Monroe, Louisiana

CHAPTER 1

The Panzer Divisions

1st PANZER DIVISION

Composition (1943): 1st Panzer Regiment, 1st Panzer Grenadier Regiment, 113th Panzer Grenadier Regiment, 73rd Panzer Artillery Regiment, 1st Motorcycle Battalion, 4th Panzer Reconnaissance Battalion, 37th Tank Destroyer Battalion, 37th Panzer Engineer Battalion, 37th Panzer Signal Battalion, 299th Army Anti-Aircraft Battalion, 81st Divisional Supply Troops

Home Station: Weimar, later Erfurt, Wehrkreis IX

Formed on October 15,1935, this division initially included the 1st *Schützen* (Rifle) Brigade (1st Rifle Regiment and 1st Motorcycle Battalion), the 1st Panzer Brigade (1st and 2nd Panzer Regiments), the 73rd Artillery Regiment and assorted divisional units. The division consisted mainly of Thuringians, with significant numbers of Saxons and Prussians and (later) draftees from other parts of Germany. The 1st Panzer took part in the occupation of Austria (1938), the Sudetenland (1938), and Prague (1939). It first saw action in the Polish campaign of 1939, when it rolled from the frontier to the suburbs of Warsaw in just eight days. Sent to the west that winter, it attacked across Luxembourg and southern Belgium in May 1940, and fought in the Battle of Sedan, the drive across France, and in the Battle of Dunkirk, before turning south and helping finish off the doomed French Republic. It suffered only 495 fatal casualties in the process.

After this campaign, the 2nd Panzer Regiment was transferred to the newly formed 16th Panzer Division, and the 113th Panzer Grenadier Regiment was incorporated into the 1st

Panzer Division. It spent the fall and winter of 1940–41 in East Prussia, where it was partially equipped with more modern PzKw III and IV tanks. The 1st Panzer Division crossed into the Soviet Union when Operation Barbarossa began on June 22, 1941, with a strength of approximately 155 tanks. It formed part of Army Group North's 4th Panzer Group (later Army) and took part in the annihilation of the Soviet III Armored Corps at Dubysa in June. The 1st Panzer was seriously depleted by casualties, and by August 16 had only forty-four serviceable tanks; nevertheless it took part in the drive on Moscow (it came to within twenty miles of the Soviet capital) and opposed the Russian winter offensive, where it was surrounded and forced to break out. By February 18, the 1st Panzer Regiment had only eighteen operational tanks; most of the regiment was used to form two ad hoc ski companies. The division nevertheless fought in the critical Rzhev salient and helped save the 9th Army, which was nearly surrounded.

In early July, the 1st and 2nd Panzer Divisions surrounded and destroyed or captured 218 Soviet tanks, 592 guns, and 1,300 anti-tank guns near Pushkeri. In a two day period in August, the division destroyed sixty-five superheavy KV-1 and KV-2 tanks and wiped out a Soviet penetration. Greatly reduced by losses, the 1st Panzer was withdrawn for resting and refitting in January 1943. Initially it was sent to Amiens, France, but spent that summer in Greece. Here it was brought up to full strength; by autumn it had a full battalion of PzKw V (Tiger) tanks and about 100 PzKw VI (Panther) tanks. When Italy defected to the Western Allies in September 1943, the 1st Panzer Division played a major role in subduing the Italian 11th Army, which put up little resistance. In October 1943, it returned to the Russian Front, fighting on the southern sector, took part in the Battle of the Kiev Salient and the counteroffensive west of Kiev (November–December 1943).

It also spearheaded the attempt to rescue the XI and XXXXII Corps, which were surrounded at Cherkassy in February 1944. It could not penetrate the last six miles to the pocket but was still successful in saving half the trapped Germans. The next month the 1st Panzer rescued the 96th and 291st Infantry Divisions from the Soviet spring offensive of 1944. Casualties were again heavy and, as of March 14, 1944, the division's panzer grenadier battalions were at 25 percent of their authorized strengths, and the 1st Panzer Regiment had fewer than sixty operational tanks. The division nevertheless remained in the line and fought in the battles of the Dnieper Bend, the north Ukraine, and eastern Poland in 1944. Retreating behind the Vistula, it was transferred to Hungary and was cited for its counterattack against the Russians at Debrecen. Most of the division was trapped and destroyed at Szekesfehervar, Hungary, in December 1944, when the 6th Army collapsed; despite its losses, however, the remnants of the 1st Panzer Division continued fighting on the southern sector of the Eastern Front until the end of the war. The division then extricated itself from the Red Army and surrendered to the Americans at Mauerkirchen in Upper Bavaria on May 8, 1945. The Americans dissolved the division five days later. Most of its soldiers were released and sent home by the end of July.

Commanders of the division included Lieutenant General/General of Cavalry Baron Maximilian von Weichs (assumed command October 1, 1935), Major General/Lieutenant General Rudolf Schmidt (assumed command October 1, 1937), Major General/Lieutenant General Friedrich Kirchner (November 3, 1939), Major General/Lieutenant General Eugen Walter Krüger (July 17, 1941), Colonel Oswin Grolig (August 8, 1943), Colonel Walter Soeth (September 9, 1943), Krüger (resumed command, September 1943), Colonel/Major General Richard Koll (January 1, 1944), Colonel/Major General Werner Marcks (February 20, 1944), Colonel/Major General/Lieutenant General Eberhard Thunert (September 18, 1944), and Colonel Helmut Huppert (April 23, 1945).

Notes and Sources: Baron von Weichs was promoted to general of cavalry on October 1, 1936. Rudolf Schmidt was promoted to lieutenant general on June 1, 1938. Kirchner became a lieutenant general on April 1, 1940. Krüger reached the same rank on October 1, 1942. Marcks was promoted to major general on April 1, 1944. Thunert became a major general on January 1, 1945 and a lieutenant general on May 1, 1945.

Benoist-Mechin: 68; Carell 1966: 24, 79, 336, 398; Chant 1979: 102; Chant, Volume 15: 2057; Chapman: 347–48; Paul Joseph Goebbels, *The Goebbels Diaries*, Louis P. Lochner, ed. and trans., (1948; reprint ed., 1971): 414; Hartmann: 60–61; Keilig: ff.1; Kennedy: 74; MacDonald 1963: 300; Manstein: 488, 526; Otto E. Moll, *Die deutschen Generalfeldmarschaelle, 1939–1945* (1961); Horst Riebenstahl, *The 1st Panzer Division*, Edward Forces, trans. (1990): ff. 1; Seaton: 360, 367; Schmitz et al., Vol. 1: 33–37; Rolf O. G. Stoves, *Die Gepanzerten und Motorisierten deutschen Grossverbände: Divisionen und selfstaendige Brigaden, 1935–1945* (1986): 11–16 (hereafter cited as "Stoves, *Gepanzerten*"); Rolf O. G. Stoves, *Die 1. Panzerdivision, 1935–1945* (n.d.): ff. 1; Tessin, Vol. 2: 29–31; RA: 144; OB 42: 55; OB 43: 198; OB 45: 286; Ziemke 1966: 225–38. For a detailed description of the Balkans campaign, see U.S. Department of the Army Pamphlet 20–260, *The German Campaign in the Balkans (Spring 1941)* (1953).

2ND PANZER DIVISION

Composition (1943): 3rd Panzer Regiment, 2nd Panzer Grenadier Regiment, 304th Panzer Grenadier Regiment, 74th Panzer Artillery Regiment, 2nd Motorcycle Battalion, 5th Panzer Reconnaissance Battalion, 38th Tank Destroyer Battalion, 38th Panzer Engineer Battalion, 38th Panzer Signal Battalion, 82nd Divisional Supply Troops

Home Station: Würzburg, Wehrkreis XIII; later Vienna, Wehrkreis XVIII

Formed on October 15, 1935, this division initially included the 2nd Rifle Brigade (2nd Rifle Regiment and 2nd Motorcycle Battalion), the 2nd Panzer Brigade (3rd and 4th Panzer Regiments), the 74th Artillery Regiment, the 5th Motorized Reconnaissance Battalion and assorted support troops. In 1938, it took part in the annexation of Austria, and its home station was moved to Vienna. By the start of the war, most of the men of the division were Austrians. The 2nd Panzer suffered heavy losses in central Poland in 1939, and took part in the French campaign of 1940, where it formed part of Guderian's XIX Motorized Corps. It fought in Luxembourg, southern Belgium and France, and captured Abbeville on the English Channel in May, thus isolating the main Allied armies in the Dunkirk Pocket and sealing the doom of France. The following month, it took part in surrounding the French Maginot Line armies at Belfort Gap.

Sent back to Poland in September, the division gave up the 4th Panzer Regiment plus other cadres to the newly authorized 13th Panzer Division and added the 304th Panzer Grenadier Regiment to its table of organization. The reorganized 2nd Panzer took part in the Balkans campaign and took Athens along with the 6th Mountain Division. It crossed into Russia in October 1941, and fought at Vyasma and other points on the road to the Soviet capital. Elements of the unit managed to reach as far as Khimki, small river port five miles from Moscow, and elements of the 5th Panzer Reconnaissance Battalion even reported being able to see the Kremlin itself, before they were thrown back by the start of the Soviet winter offensive of 1941–42. Remaining on the central sector, the battered division took part in the defensive fighting in the Rzhev Salient (1942–43), in the Rzhev withdrawal (1943), at the battles of Kursk and Orel, and at Yelnja, Kiev, and Gomel, and the middle Dnieper battles of the winter of 1943–44, where it suffered heavy casualties.

Withdrawn to Amiens, France to rest and refit, the 2nd Panzer was thrown into the Battle of Normandy in June 1944. It took part in the unsuccessful counterattack at Mortain in August and, with only twenty-five tanks left, was surrounded at Falaise in August. Breaking out with losses, it was reformed at Wittlich in the Eifel area of western Germany, where it temporarily absorbed the remnants of the 352nd Infantry Division. On September 1, it had only 1,600 men, twenty-seven tanks (mostly new replacements), and twelve guns. It was sent back to Bitburg and Wittlich in western Germany, where it was partially rebuilt. It was sent back into combat in the Ardennes offensive, where it again suffered heavy casualties. In the last campaign the 2nd Panzer was fighting against the Americans in 1945, and was down to a strength of only four tanks, three assault guns, and 200 men. The survivors of the old division were grouped with Panzer Brigade Thüringen and ended the war defending Fulda in April 1945. It surrendered to the Americans near Plauen in May 1945.

Its commanders included Colonel/Major General/Lieutenant General Heinz Guderian (assumed command October 1, 1935), Major General/Lieutenant General Rudolf Veiel (March 1, 1938), Colonel Vollrath Luebbe (January 16, 1942), Major General Baron Hans-Karl von Esebeck (February 17, 1942), Major General Arno von Lenski (June 1, 1942), Colonel/Major General/Lieutenant General Luebbe again (August 10, 1942), Colonel Karl Fabiunke (August 20, 1942), Lieutenant General Baron Heinrich von Lüttwitz (February 1, 1944), Colonel Gustav von Nostitz (September 15, 1944), Colonel/Major General Henning Schoenfeld (September 21, 1944), Colonel/Major General Meinrad von Lauchert (December 15, 1944), Colonel Oskar Munzel (March 20, 1945), and Colonel Heinrich-Wilhelm Stollbrock (April 4, 1945–end).

Notes and Sources: Heinz Guderian—the father of the blitzkrieg—was promoted to major general on August 1, 1936, and to lieutenant general on February 1, 1938. Rudolf Veiel was promoted to lieutenant general on October 1, 1938. Luebbe was promoted to major general on October 1, 1942, and to lieutenant general on April 1, 1943. Schoenfeld became a major general on December 1, 1944. He was relieved of his command on December 15 (on the eve of the Battle of the Bulge) and was never reemployed. Lauchert became a major general on March 1, 1945. He "quit the war" (i.e., deserted) on March 20.

Blumenson 1960: 295, 422, 505, 549; Blumenson 1969: 42; Carell 1966: 180, 336; Carell 1971: 26–37, 309; Chant, Volume 14: 1859–61; Chant 1979: 96; Chapman: 347–48; Cole 1965: 177–80; Heinz Guderian, *Panzer Leader* (1967 edition): 25–29; Harrison: Map VI; Keilig: 84, 117, 211–12, 236, 309, 354; Kennedy: 74, Map 7; Kursietis: 77–78; MacDonald 1973: 93, 257, 259; Manstein: 482-83; Mellenthin 1977: 199; Munzel; Scheibert: 364; Speidel: 42; Tessin, Vol. 2: 105–8; RA: 220; OB 42: 55; OB 43: 199; OB 45: 286–87. Guderian also wrote the book *Achtung! Panzer!* (published in 1937) which outlined his basic concepts of armored warfare and was considered revolutionary at the time.

A German half-track at the head of a column takes a break during a road march, probably in Belgium, 1944. This column belonged to the 1st SS Panzer Division, whose unit symbol appears on the left front of the vehicle. It is armed with a light anti-aircraft gun to discourage Allied bombers. The right-hand symbol indicates that this unit is part of the divisional trains. HITM ARCHIVE

3RD PANZER DIVISION

Composition (1943): 6th Panzer Regiment, 3rd Panzer Grenadier Regiment, 394th Panzer Grenadier Regiment, 75th Panzer Artillery Regiment, 3rd Motorcycle Battalion, 3rd Panzer Reconnaissance Battalion, 543rd Tank Destroyer Battalion, 39th Panzer Engineer Battalion, 39th Panzer Signal Battalion, 314th Army Anti-Aircraft Artillery Battalion, 83rd Divisional Supply Troops

Home Station: Berlin, Wehrkreis III

Known as the "Bear Division" from its mascot, the Berlin Bear, the 3rd Panzer Division was activated at the Wuensdorf Maneuver Area, Berlin, on October 15, 1935. At that time it included the 3rd Panzer Brigade (5th and 6th Panzer Regiments), the 3rd Rifle Brigade (3rd Rifle Regiment and 3rd Motorcycle Battalion), the 75th Motorized Artillery Regiment, and assorted divisional troops. Its personnel were mainly Prussians. During the years 1937-39, volunteers from the 6th Panzer Regiment had formed the cadres for the 88th Panzer Battalion of the Condor Legion, which had fought on the side of the Fascist General Franco during the Spanish Civil War. The 3rd Panzer Division took part in the *Anschluss* (the annexation of Austria) in 1938 and the Polish campaign of 1939, where it formed part of Guderian's XIX Corps. It attacked from Pomerania to Thorn in northern Poland, and then southeast to Brest-Litovsk.

The 3rd also distinguished itself in Beglium and France in 1940, fighting in the Battle of the Albert Canal and in the battles south of Brussels, as well as the pursuit after the fall of Dunkirk, which ended in the capitulation of France. In late 1940, the division supplied the 5th Panzer Regiment to the 5th Light (later 21st Panzer) Division, and received the 394th Panzer Grenadier Regiment in exchange. Like the other panzer divisions that were similarly reduced in the winter of 1940–41, the Bear Division lost about half its tank strength.

The 3rd Panzer invaded Russia on June 22, 1941, and seized the Koden Bridge on the frontier by a *coup de main.* It took part in the Battle of the Bialystok-Minsk Pocket and the

Dnieper River crossings, before being sent to the southern sector, where it helped trap several Russian armies, comprising 667,000 men, in the Kiev area. It then turned north again and fought in the Battle of Moscow. During the Soviet winter offensive of 1941–42, it acted as a "fire brigade" and, in March 1942, held Kharkov against massive Soviet attacks. With the 4th Panzer Army, the division took part in the Caucasus campaign and suffered heavy losses in the battles around Mozdok. It escaped from the Kuban by crossing the Sea of Azov over the ice after Rostov was threatened in January 1943. It fought in the Battles of Kursk and Belgorod in July and August, and suffered heavy losses in the Kharkov battles of autumn 1943. Remaining in the line despite its casualties, the 3rd Panzer fought in the Dnieper campaign (where it again distinguished itself), at Kiev, and in the retreat through the Ukraine. It fought its way out of encirclement in Rumania, took part in the Hungarian campaign, and was on the southern sector of the Eastern Front when Hitler committed suicide on April 30, 1945. Prior to the actual German capitulation on May 8, the 3rd Panzer Division managed to break contact with the Russians and headed west to Steyr, where it surrendered to the U.S. Army, and thus avoided Soviet prisons.

Its commanders included Lieutenant General Ernst Fessmann (assumed command October 1, 1935), Colonel/Major General Friedrich Kühn (June 1937), Fessmann (returned July 1937), Lieutenant General Baron Leo Geyr von Schweppenburg (October 12, 1937), Major General Horst Stumpff (October 7, 1939), Geyr (October 31, 1939), Stumpff (February 15, 1940), Kühn (September 1940), Lieutenant General Model (November 13, 1940), Major General/Lieutenant General Hermann Breith (October 22, 1941), Colonel Baron Kurt von Liebenstein (September 1, 1942), Major General/Lieutenant General Franz Westhoven (October 25, 1942), Major General Fritz Bayerlein (October 20, 1943), Colonel Rudolf Lang (January 5, 1944), Lieutenant General Wilhelm Phillips (May 25, 1944), Colonel/Major General Wilhelm Soeth (January 1, 1945), and Colonel Volkmar Schoene (April 19, 1945).

Notes and Sources: The 3rd Panzer was one of the three original panzer divisions in the German Army. Kühn was promoted to major general on July 1, 1940. Breith became a lieutenant general on November 1, 1942. Westhoven was promoted to lieutenant general on April 1, 1943. Soeth became a major general on January 30, 1945.

Benoist-Mechin: 241; Bradley et al., Vol. 3: 452–53; Vol. 4: 267–28; Carell 1966: 9, 474, 488, 491, 512, 546–50; Carell 1971: 19, 48,142; Chapman: 347–48; Hartmann: 61–62; Keilig: 23, 89, 191, 340; Manstein: 488, 525; Schmitz et al., Vol. 1: 215–17; Stoves, *Gepanzerten*: 25–31; Tessin, Vol. 2: 173–74; RA: 46; OB 42: 55, 199; OB 45: 287.

4TH PANZER DIVISION

Composition (1943): 35th Panzer Regiment, 12th Panzer Grenadier Regiment, 33rd Panzer Grenadier Regiment, 103rd Panzer Artillery Regiment, 34th Motorcycle Battalion, 7th Panzer Reconnaissance Battalion, 49th Tank Destroyer Battalion, 79th Panzer Engineer Battalion, 79th Panzer Signal Battalion, 290th Army Anti-Aircraft Battalion, 103rd Field Replacement Battalion, 84th Divisional Supply Troops

Home Station: Würzburg, later Bamberg, Wehrkreis XIII (panzer units); Meiningen, later Schweinfurt, Wehrkreis XIII (infantry units)

This peacetime division was formed in 1938 and consisted mainly of Bavarians, with draftees from other parts of Germany and cadres from the 2nd Panzer Division. Initially it included the 5th Panzer Brigade (35th and 36th Panzer Regiments) and the 4th Rifle Brigade (12th Panzer Grenadier Regiment and 34th Motorcycle Battalion). In the summer of 1939, it received the 33rd Panzer Grenadier Regiment from the 13th Motorized Division. In the Polish campaign, it distinguished itself by penetrating from Germany to the outskirts of Warsaw in just eight days, although it could not take the city and lost about half its tanks in the attempt. The next year it spearheaded the invasion of southern Holland, captured Maastricut, took part in the Dunkirk campaign, and helped finish off France in June 1940, pushing as far as Grenoble. That winter it returned to Germany and lost the 36th Panzer Regiment plus some cadres to the 14th Panzer (formerly 4th Infantry) Division.

It was posted to East Prussia in May 1941. As part of Army Group Center, the 4th Panzer crossed into Russia in June and fought at Minsk, Gomel, Kiev, Bryansk, Vyazma, and other bitterly contested points on the road to Moscow. By November, it had only fifty operational tanks left. In December 1941, it attempted to encircle the strategic city of Tula, southeast of Moscow, but failed, suffering heavy losses in the attempt. Remaining on the central sector of the Russian Front until 1944, it fought at Orel (1942–43), in the Kursk and Dnieper campaigns, and tried unsuccessfully to check the Soviet summer offensive of 1944. In November 1944, it was isolated in the Courland Pocket but was evacuated by sea to northern Germany in early 1945. Now in remnants, the 4th Panzer was isolated on the Frischen Nehrung in West Prussia in April 1945. Most of the 35th Panzer Regiment was shipped out aboard the *Goya* on April 16. Unfortunately, it was struck by two Soviet torpedoes just before midnight and sunk in four minutes, taking almost the entire regiment with it. The rest of the division surrendered to the Red Army at the end of the war in May 1945. An outstanding division even by German standards, it was the most heavily decorated of all the panzer divisions.

Its divisional commanders included Major General/Lieutenant General Georg-Hans Reinhardt (assumed command November 10, 1938), Major General Ritter Ludwig von Radlmeier (February 15, 1940), Major General Joachim Stevers (April 6, 1940), Colonel Baron Hans von Boineburg-Lengsfeld (May 15, 1940), Stever (resumed command, May 19, 1940), Boineburg-Lengsfeld again (July 24, 1940), Major General/ Lieutenant General Baron Willibald von Langermann-Erlenkamp (September 7, 1940), Major General Dietrich von Saucken (December 24, 1941), Major General Heinrich Eberbach (January 6, 1942), Lieutenant Colonel Otto Heidkämper (acting commander, March 2, 1942), Eberbach (April 4, 1942), Lieutenant General Edgar Hielscher (June 23, 1942),

Eberbach (resumed command, July 3, 1942), Colonel/Major General Dr. Erich Schneider (November 1942), Lieutenant General von Saucken (May 31, 1943), Major General Hans Junck (acting commander, January 21, 1944), Saucken again (February, 1944), Major General/Lieutenant General Clemens Betzel (February 7, 1944), Saucken again (March 3, 1944), Betzel (May 6, 1944), Saucken (June, 1944), Colonel Hans Christern (December 21, 1944), Betzel (December 28, 1944), Major General Hans Hecker (April 1, 1945), and Colonel Ernst-Wilhelm Hoffmann (April 10, 1945)

Notes and Sources: Reinhardt was promoted to lieutenant general on October 1, 1939. Schneider was promoted to major general on January 1, 1943. Betzel became a lieutenant general on July 1, 1944. Colonel Dr. Karl Mauss reportedly briefly served as acting commander of the division in the fall of 1942. Colonel Hoffmann was commander of the 12th Panzer Grenadier Regiment.

For the story of the *Goya*, see Christopher Dobson, John Miller and Ronald Payne, *The Cruelest Night* (1979). Benoist-Mechin: 241; Bradley et al., Vol. 5: 221–22; Carell 1966: 69, 79, 80, 136–37; Carell 1971: 35, 591–94; Chant, Volume 2: 217; Volume 14: 1931; Chapman: 347–48; Keilig: 32, 44, 131, 160, 197, 292, 333; Manstein: 487, 538; Mehner, Vol. 4: 382; Vol. 5: 329; Vol. 10: 520; Vol. 11: 367; Vol. 12: 458; Schmitz et al., Vol. I: 289–31; Stauffenberg "Papers;" Stoves, *Gepanzerten*: 37–43; Tessin, Vol. 2: 242–44; OB 42: 56; OB 43: 199–200; OB 45: 288.

5TH PANZER DIVISION

Composition (1943): 31st Panzer Regiment, 13th Panzer Grenadier Regiment, 14th Panzer Grenadier Regiment, 116th Panzer Artillery Regiment, 55th Motorcycle Battalion, 8th Panzer Reconnaissance Battalion, 53rd Tank Destroyer Battalion, 89th Panzer Engineer Battalion, 77th Panzer Signal Battalion, 85th Panzer Divisional Supply Troops. The 228th Army Anti-Aircraft Battalion was added in 1942.

Home Station: Oppeln, Wehrkreis VIII

Originally a peacetime division, the 5th Panzer fought well throughout its existence and was six times cited for distinguished conduct in combat on the Eastern Front. Organized in

November 1938, after the annexation of the Sudetenland, the division's troops were mainly Silesians and Sudeten Germans. In August 1939, it consisted of the 8th Panzer Brigade (15th and 31st Panzer Regiments), the 5th Rifle Brigade (13th and 14th Rifle Regiments), the 116th Artillery Regiment, and assorted divisional troops. The division played a minor and "inconspicuous" role in the Polish campaign of 1939 and a "prominent" part in the French campaign of 1940, according to Allied intelligence evaluations. Here it took part in the conquest of Belgium, the destruction of the main French armies around Lille, and the capture of Rouen. It pushed almost to the Spanish frontier before the French surrendered. It remained in France until January 1941, when it was sent to Romania.

Late in 1940, it supplied the 15th Panzer Regiment plus other cadre troops to the newly forming 11th Panzer Division. At the same time, the HQ, 5th Panzer Brigade was transferred to the 3rd Panzer Division. In 1941, the 5th Panzer was involved in the Balkans campaign, fighting in both Yugoslavia and Greece, including a sharp battle with (and victory over) the 2nd New Zealand Division at Molos. Assigned to Army Group Center, the 5th Panzer crossed into Russia in July and took part in heavy fighting all the way to the gates of Moscow. Remaining on the central sector, it faced the Soviet winter offensive of 1941–42, fought in the defensive battles of 1942–43, including Rzhev, the Rzhev withdrawal, Vyasma, Spas-Demjansk, and Gshatsk, and suffered heavy losses near Orel during the unsuccessful Kursk offensive. Meanwhile, the Soviet High Command paid the division perhaps the highest left-handed compliment of the war when it instructed its generals that the best way to deal with the 5th Panzer was to try to avoid it whenever possible.

Later in 1943, it fought in the battles on the middle Dnieper and, in the summer of 1944, it counterattacked against the massive Russian offensive, inflicting considerable casualties on the Soviets. The 5th Panzer was unable to turn the tide and save the trapped elements of the 4th and 9th armies and, with the remnants of Army Group Center, it took part in the retreats across White Russia, Poland, southern Courland, and into East Prussia, where it fought at Koenigsberg, the Samland peninsula and Pillau. Then orders arrived to transport the elite division back to the west. This operation was only partially completed when the Third Reich capitulated. Apparently the larger part of the 5th Panzer Division surrendered to the Soviets near Danzig on May 9, although a sizable part of it capitulated to the British at Bornholm, Schleswig-Holstein.

Commanders of this division included Lieutenant General Heinrich von Vietinghoff gennant Scheel (assumed command November 24, 1938), Lieutenant General Max von Hartlieb gennant Walsporn (October 18, 1939), Lieutenant General Joachim Lemelsen (May 22, 1940), Major General Ludwig Crüwell (June 6, 1940), Major General/Lieutenant General Gustav Fehn (November 25, 1940), Colonel Kurt Haseloff (May 1, 1942), Major General Eduard Metz (September 25, 1942), Colonel Johannes Nedtwig (February 1, 1943), Major General Ernst Felix Fäckenstedt (July 5, 1943), Major General/Lieutenant General Karl Decker (September 7, 1943), Lieutenant Colonel Heinrich-Walter von Bronsart von Schellendorff (December 30, 1943), Decker (resumed command, January 30, 1944), Colonel/Major General Rolf Lippert (October 16, 1944), Major General Günther Hoffmann-Schoenborn (February 19, 1945), and Colonel of Reserves Hans Herzog (April 9, 1945).

Notes and Sources: Gustav Fehn was promoted to lieutenant general on August 1, 1942. Decker was promoted to lieutenant general on June 1, 1944. Lippert was promoted to major general on January 1, 1945. Hoffmann-Schoenborn was severely wounded on April 9 and evacuated back to Germany the next day.

Benoist-Mechin: 304; Bradley et al., Vol. 2: 284–85; Vol. 3: 395–97; Carell 1966: 175, 330; Carell 1971: 309, 591–92; Chant 1979: 53; Anton Detlev von Plato, *Die Geschichte der 5. Panzer-Division, 1939-1945* (1978); Roger Edwards, *Panzer: A Revolution in Warfare, 1939–1945* (1989): 75; Keilig: 64, 85–86, 126, 147, 179, 207, 224, 238; Kennedy: 74; Mellenthin 1977: 176–77; Mehner, Vol. 5: 329; Vol. 6: 545; Vol. 7: 354; Vol. 12: 458; Schmitz et al., Vol. 1: 361–71; Stoves, *Gepanzerten*: 52; Tessin, Vol. 2: 293–94; RA: 130; OB 42: 56; OB 43: 200; OB 45: 288.

6TH PANZER DIVISION

Composition (1943): 11th Panzer Regiment, 4th Panzer Grenadier Regiment, 114th Panzer Grenadier Regiment, 76th Panzer Artillery Regiment, 6th Motorcycle Battalion, 6th Panzer Reconnaissance Battalion, 41st Tank Destroyer Battalion, 57th Panzer Engineer Battalion, 82nd Panzer Signal Battalion, 57th Divisional Supply Troops

Home Station: Wuppertal, Wehrkreis VI

Created as the 1st Light Division, this unit was composed of Westphalians and Rhinelanders. It initially contained the 4th Mechanized Cavalry Regiment and the 65th Panzer Battalion. It took part in the occupation of the Sudetenland (1938) and Czechoslovakia (1939), and fought in southern Poland in September 1939. It was converted to a panzer division that winter, after the High Command pronounced its light division experiment a failure. The 1st Light Division was redesignated 6th Panzer on October 18, 1939. It initially included the newly-formed 6th Rifle Brigade (4th Rifle Regiment and 6th Motorcycle Battalion), the 11th Panzer Regiment (two battalions), the 65th Panzer Battalion, the 76th Artillery Regiment, and assorted divisional units.

Sent to France in 1940, it was smaller than the panzer divisions created earlier and was equipped with about 130 light, Czech-made tanks; nevertheless, it performed very well in the West. At one point, it pushed forward 217 miles in nine days and overran the British 145th Infantry Brigade at Cassel. It took part in the conquest of Flanders and in the subsequent drive to the south, and ended the campaign on the Swiss border. The division was withdrawn to Germany in July. Here it gave up large cadres to form the 16th Panzer Division, but incorporated the 114th Rifle Regiment (formerly the 243rd Infantry Regiment of the 60th Infantry Division) into its table of organization. It was also reinforced to a strength of 239 tanks, but only twelve were German manufactured PzKw IVs—and even these were inferior to the Soviet T-34, KV-1, and KV-2 tanks it would soon encounter.

A German fire team slowly maneuvers through tall grass, date unknown. The man in the foreground may be searching for mines. Both are armed with light machine guns. They are probably Waffen SS men, as indicated by their camouflage uniforms. HITM ARCHIVE

Sent to Russia in 1941, it broke through the Stalin Line and was involved on the drive to and early stages of the Siege of Leningrad. Transferred to Army Group Center, it suffered heavy losses in the Soviet winter offensive of 1941–42. Temperatures fell to minus 22 degrees Fahrenheit and all of the Czech tanks—which featured pneumatic clutches, brakes and steering columns—failed. On December 10, 1941, the division lost its only remaining tank, which the men had dubbed "Anthony the Last." The 11th Panzer Regiment now reorganized as a battalion and fought as marching infantry. By the end of the year, the division had lost almost every one of its motorized vehicles and the soldiers referred to it as "the 6th Panzer of Foot." They had, however, incorporated more than 1,000 Russian *panje* wagons (two-wheeled peasant carts) into their ranks. By the end of January 1942, the division had fewer than 1,000 combat effectives left and only three operational guns. Its nevertheless played a prominent role in keeping the lifeline of the 9th Army in the Rzhev salient open.

In April 1942, after the spring thaw, the 6th Panzer Division was sent back to France to rest and refit. Here the 6th Rifle Brigade was disbanded and the division received the 298th Army Anti-Aircraft Battalion. While out of the line, every man in the division was given a furlough and the panzer regiment was re-equipped with excellent Mark III (PzKw III) tanks, armed with long-barreled 50mm guns. The division also absorbed the remnants of the 22nd Panzer Division. After Stalingrad was surrounded, the 6th Panzer was rushed back to the Soviet Union, where it tried to relieve the 6th Army, but was halted at Bolwassiljewka, thirty miles south of the city, in very heavy fighting. The division lost half of its tanks in the Stalingrad relief attempt. After the retreat from the Volga, the 6th Panzer Division fought in the retreat to the Don, in the Donetz, and in the Manstein offensive that led to the encirclement of Kharkov in March 1943. Later, it fought at Kursk, Belgorod, at Kharkov again, in the Dnieper battles, and in the northern Ukraine, where it was encircled, but broke out. By early 1944, the 6th Panzer Division had destroyed more than 1,500 Soviet tanks. Withdrawn from the line to refit, the 6th was hastily sent to the central sector of the Eastern Front shortly after the Russians surrounded the bulk of the 4th and 9th armies. It helped stabilize the German front in the east before being sent to Hungary, where it fought in the battles around Budapest and knocked out its 2,400th Soviet tank. It fought in the Battle of Vienna and ended the war on the southern sector of the Eastern Front.

During the war, the 6th Panzer Division lost 7,068 men killed, 24,342 wounded and 4,230 missing—35,640 casualties in all. Its peak strength never exceeded 17,000 men and as usually much less. The remnants of the 6th Panzer surrendered to the U.S. Army but were then handed over to the Soviets. Some of the survivors spent the next ten years in Communist prisons.

Commanders of the 1st Light/6th Panzer Division included Major General/Lieutenant General Erich Hoepner (October 12, 1937), Major General Friedrich Wilhelm von Loeper (assumed command August 1, 1938), Major General/Lieutenant General Franz Werner Kempf (October 1, 1939), Major General Franz Landgraf (January 6, 1941), Major General/ Lieutenant General Erhard Raus (September 1, 1941), Landgraf (resumed command, September 16, 1941), Raus again (November 23, 1941), Colonel/Major General von Hünersdorff (February 7, 1943), Colonel Wilhelm Crisolli (acting commander, July 25, 1943), Colonel/Major General/Lieutenant General Baron Rudolf von Waldenfels (August 22, 1943), Colonel Walter Denkert (March 13, 1944), Waldenfels (returned March 29, 1944), Colonel Friedrich-Wilhelm Juergens (November 23, 1944), and Waldenfelds again (January 18, 1945–end). Colonel Max Sperling reportedly served as acting divisional commander in August 1944.

Notes and Sources: Hoepner was promoted to lieutenant general on January 30, 1938. Kempf was promoted to lieutenant general on July 31, 1940. Raus reached the same rank on January 1, 1943. Walter von Hühnersdorff was promoted to major general on May 1, 1943. On July 14, he was mortally wounded during the Battle of Kursk and died on July 17. Waldenfels was promoted to major general on November 1, 1943, and to lieutenant general on June 1, 1944.

Carell 1966: 23–24, 236, 267; Carell 1971: 66, 81–83,123,530; Chapman: 347; Alan Clark, *Barbarossa: The Russian-German Conflict, 1941–1945* (1965): 266 (hereafter cited as "Clark"); Harrison: 141; Hartmann: 63–64; Keilig: 62, 68, 153, 196, 208, 311; Kennedy: 74, 133, Map 7; Manstein: 389, 499; Mehner, Vol. 6: 545; Mitcham 2001: 71–78; Helmut Ritgen, *The 6th Panzer Division, 1937–1945* (1985): ff. 1; Horst Scheibert, *Bildband der 6. Panzer-Division, 1939–1945* (1958), ff. 1; Schmitz et al., Vol. 2: 23–26; Seaton: 327; Tessin, Vol. 2: 31; Vol. 3: 18–22; RA: 100; OB 42: 56; OB 43: 200; OB 45: 289.

7TH PANZER DIVISION

Composition (1941): 25th Panzer Regiment, 6th Panzer Grenadier Regiment, 7th Panzer Grenadier Regiment, 78th Panzer Artillery Regiment, 7th Motorcycle Battalion, 37th Panzer Reconnaissance Battalion, 42nd Tank Destroyer Battalion, 58th Panzer Engineer Battalion, 83rd Panzer Signal Battalion, 58th Panzer Divisional Supply Troops

Home Station: Gera, Wehrkreis IX

Formed at Gera in 1938 as the 2nd Light Division, its men came from Thuringia, which was not noted for the fighting qualities of its soldiery; nevertheless, the 7th Panzer turned out to be an outstanding combat unit. Nicknamed the "Ghost Division" from its unit emblem, it initially included the 66th Panzer Battalion and the 6th and 7th Mechanized Cavalry (later Rifle) Regiments, as well as the 7th Reconnaissance Regiment. It took part in the invasion of Poland and was converted to a panzer division in the winter of 1939–40. During this process, it added the 25th Panzer Regiment (which absorbed the 66th Panzer Battalion) and 7th Rifle Brigade, which controlled the 6th and 7th Rifle Regiments, but lost the 7th Reconnaissance Regiment, which was dissolved. Its former I Battalion became the 7th Panzer Reconnaissance Battalion.

In February 1940, the division was placed under the command of Major General Erwin Rommel, who would become the "Desert Fox." Equipped mainly with captured and inferior Czech tanks, the 7th Panzer smashed its way through Belgium and France, repulsed the major Allied counterattack of the campaign at Arras, and cut off the escape of major French and British forces at Cherbourg. It lost more men than any other German division in the French campaign—2,160 total casualties, of whom 682 were killed. It also lost forty-two tanks. It inflicted a disportionate amount of damage on the enemy, however. It overran the French 1st Armored Division, took more than 10,000 prisoners, destroyed more than 100 French tanks, thirty armored cars and twenty-seven field guns in forty-eight hours, at a cost of thirty-five killed and fifty-nine wounded. Later, it overran the French 31st Motorized Division, the 4th North African Division, and much of the British 51st Highland Division. It captured 97,468 prisoners and captured or destroyed 277 guns, sixty-four anti-tank guns, and 458 tanks and armored cars in the process.

The 7th Panzer Division was engaged in occupation duties in the Bordeaux region until being sent east in the spring of 1941. It crossed into Russia in June with 14,400 men and fought in the battles of the Minsk Pocket, the Dnieper crossings, Smolensk, and Moscow. It suffered such heavy losses in the winter fighting that it was sent back to France in May 1942 to rest and refit. (Between June 22, 1941 and January 23, 1943, the division lost 9,203 men.) In this process, the 7th Rifle Brigade was disbanded. In November of that year, the division took part in the occupation of Vichy France.

Sent to the southern sector of the Russian Front after the fall of Stalingrad, the 7th Panzer defended against heavy Soviet attacks aimed at Rostov in early 1943, and later fought in the Battle of Kharkov. After being repulsed in the Kursk offensive, the 7th Panzer fought in the battles around Kiev and Zhitomir, where it was twice cited for distinguished conduct. In November, the division took heavy casualties in the Kiev withdrawal and fought in the Tarnopol area until March 1944, when it was overrun and the 1st Panzer Army encircled. The remnants of the division broke out, but its losses were ruinous. The division was reduced to a strength of 1,872 men, nine guns, eleven anti-tank guns, and nine tanks. The 7th Panzer nevertheless fought on and opposed the Russian summer offensive of 1944 as a part of Army Group Center, fighting at Minsk, Lida and Memel. Escaping disaster yet again, it was again officially cited for distinguished conduct in August 1944, for its action in the Battle of Raseiniai in Lithuania. It was heavily engaged when the Russian winter offensive of 1944–45 hit the Vistula and was trapped in Danzig as part of Army Group North in early 1945. Evacuated by sea, but without any vehicles or tanks, the 7th Panzer took part in the Battle of Berlin in April 1945. Most of its men managed to escape to Allied lines and surrendered to the British at Schwerin, Schleswig-Holstein, on May 3, 1945.

Commanders of the 2nd Light/7th Panzer included Lieutenant General Georg Stumme (assumed command October 1, 1938), Rommel (February 2, 1940), Major General/Lieutenant General Baron Hans von Funck (February 7, 1941), Colonel Wolfgang Gläsemer (August 16, 1941), Major General Baron Hasso von Manteuffel (August 23, 1943), Major General Adalbert Schulz (January 16, 1944), Colonel/Major General/Lieutenant General Dr. Karl Mauss (January 30, 1944), Colonel Gerhard Schmidhuber (acting commander, May 2, 1944), Mauss (returned, June, 1944), Colonel Hellmuth Maeder (acting commander, October 1, 1944), Mauss (November, 1944), Colonel Max Lemke (acting commander, January 4, 1945), Mauss (January 23, 1945), and Colonel Hans Christern (March 23, 1945).

Notes and Sources: Rommel was promoted to lieutenant general effective January 1, 1941. Funck was promoted to lieutenant general on September 1, 1942. General Schulz was killed in action near Schepetowka on January 28, 1944. Dr. Mauss (a dentist in civilian life) was promoted to lieutenant general on October 1, 1944. He was reportedly wounded on January 4, 1945, and was seriously wounded by shrapnel on March 25.

Werner Brehm, *Mein Kriegstagebuch, 1939–1945: Mit der 7. Panzer-Division, 5 Jahre in West und Ost* (1953); Carell 1966: 80, 334, 623; Carell 1971: 39, 66, 208, 510; Chapman: 347; Keilig: 99, 201, 214, 219, 339; Kennedy: 74 and Map 10; Manstein: 298–99; Hasso von Manteuffel, *Die 7. Panzer-Division im Zweiten Weltkrieg* (1986); Mellenthin 1977: 211; Mehner, Vol. 7: 354; Vol. 12: 458; Mitcham 2001: 79–86; Plocher 1943: 335; Rommel, *Papers*; Friedrich von Stauffenberg, "Panzer Commanders of the Western Front," unpublished manuscript in the possession of the author; Tessin, Vol. 2: 106–7; Vol. 3: 60–62; OB 42: 57; OB 43: 201; OB 44: 289–90. For the story of the 7th Panzer's campaign in France, see Desmond Young, *Rommel: The Desert Fox*, New York: 1965 (hereafter cited as "Young").

8TH PANZER DIVISION

Composition: 10th Panzer Regiment, 8th Panzer Grenadier Regiment, 28th Panzer Grenadier Regiment, 80th Panzer Artillery Regiment, 8th Motorcycle Battalion, 59th Panzer Reconnaissance Battalion, 43rd Tank Destroyer Battalion, 59th Panzer Engineer Battalion, 59th Panzer Signal Battalion, 59th Divisional Supply Troops

Home Station: Cottbus, Wehrkreis III

This unit was formed in 1938 as the 3rd Light Division. At the time it included the 67th Panzer Battalion, the 8th and 9th Mechanized Cavalry Regiments, and the 8th Reconnaissance Regiment. It fought in Poland in 1939, and in the winter of 1939–40 was converted to a panzer division. During this reorganization, it lost one of its two reconnaissance battalions (which was sent to the 10th Panzer Division) and its reconnaissance regimental staff, but gained the East Prussian 10th Panzer Regiment and the newly formed Staff, 8th Rifle Brigade, which controlled the 8th Rifle Regiment and the 8th Motorcycle Battalion. Equipped mainly with inferior Czech tanks, the division was part of Reinhardt's XXXXI Motorized Corps in France and suffered heavy losses in the Battles of the Meuse Crossings, which were initially far from successful in this sector. The French, however, were eventually forced to retreat and were swamped by the onrushing panzers. The 8th Panzer Division took part in the destruction of the French 1st and 7th Armies in May 1940, and in the final conquest of France in June.

The division remained in France until March 1941, when it was sent east, and in April took part in the Balkans campaign, where it was lightly engaged. In June 1941, it invaded Russia as part of Manstein's LVI Panzer Corps and was heavily engaged in sweep through the Baltic States and in the drive on Leningrad, fighting in the battles of Dvinsk, Luga, Lake Ilmen, and Novgorod. By mid-July, the division's tank strength had been reduced from 175 to 80. It nevertheless helped check Stalin's Winter Offensive of 1941–42 in the Volkhov sector, south of Leningrad. In 1942, it fought in the defensive battles of Army Group Center (including Kholm, Orel and Smolensk) and was transferred to the southern sector in 1943, after the Kursk attacks failed. That autumn it sustained heavy losses in the withdrawal from Kiev. It was more or less continuously in combat in 1944, fighting in the northern Ukraine, in southern Poland, and in Slovakia, including the battles of Zhitomir, Tarnopol and Brody. The 8th Panzer was sent to Hungary in December and fought near Budapest until January 1945, when it was sent north to Czechoslovakia. It ended the war on the central sector of the Eastern Front and surrendered to the Soviets at Deutsch-Brod on May 9, 1945.

Commanders of the 8th Panzer Division included Major General/Lieutenant General Adolf Kuntzen (assumed command, November 10, 1938), Major General/Lieutenant General Erich Brandenberger (February 21, 1941), Major General Walter Neumann-Silkow (acting commander, April 15 to May 25, 1941), Brandenberger (returned to command, May 25, 1941), Major General Werner Huchner (acting commander, December 8, 1941), Brandenberger (January 29, 1942), Major General Joseph Schroetter (June 20, 1942), Colonel von Wagner (November 14, 1942), Brandenberger (returned November 27, 1942), Major General/Lieutenant General Sebastian Fichtner (January 17, 1943), Lieutenant General Friedrich von Scotti (acting commander, June 1943), Fichtner (returned, July, 1943), Lieutenant Colonel Albrecht Kleinschmidt (September 3, 1943), Colonel Dr. Karl Mauss (September 9, 1943), Colonel/Major General Gottfried Froelich (September 20, 1943), Colonel/Major General Werner Friebe (acting commander, February 1944), Froelich (returned, July 20, 1944), and Colonel/Major General Heinrich Georg Hax (January 22, 1945–end).

An infantry light machine-gun crew is ready to fire. The case on the back of the gunner contains his gas mask. The man to the left is the assistant gunner. HITM ARCHIVE

Notes and Sources: Kuntzen, Brandenberger, and Fichtner were promoted to lieutenant general on April 1, 1940, August 1, 1942, and August 1, 1943, respectively. Froelich was promoted to major general on December 1, 1943. He was relieved of his command on January 22, 1945, by General Balck, the commander of the 6th Army, for irresolute leadership. Friebe was promoted to major general on June 1, 1944. Hax was promoted to major general on April 1, 1945. He was a Soviet prisoner from 1945 to 1955.

Bradley et al., Vol. 4: 95–97; Vol. 5: 217-18; Carell 1966: 21–22; Chapman: 347–48; Keilig: 89, 97, 131, 193; Kennedy: 74 and Map 7; Manstein: 182; Mehner, Vol. 6: 545; Mellenthin 1977: 214; Mitcham 2001: 87–92; Salisbury: 95; Schmitz et al., Vol. 2: 119–27; Stoves, *Gepanzerten*: 66–67; Tessin, Vol. 2: 175; Vol. 3: 99–100; RA: 46; OB 42: 57; OB 43: 201; OB 45: 290–91.

9TH PANZER DIVISION

Composition (1942): 33rd Panzer Regiment, 10th Panzer Grenadier Regiment, 11th Panzer Grenadier Regiment, 102nd Panzer Artillery Regiment, 9th Motorcycle Battalion, 9th Panzer Reconnaissance Battalion, 50th Tank Destroyer Battalion, 86th Panzer Engineer Battalion, 81st Panzer Signal Battalion, 287th Army Anti-Aircraft Battalion, 60th Panzer Divisional Supply Troops

Home Station: Vienna, Wehrkreis XVII

In 1938, after Germany annexed Austria, Hitler formed the 4th Light Division in Vienna. It initially included the 33rd Panzer Battalion and the 10th and 11th Mechanized Cavalry Regiments. The division took part in the invasion of Poland in 1939. That winter it was converted to an armored division and was redesignated 9th Panzer on January 3, 1940. It fought in the Western campaign of 1940, in which it played a major role in knocking the Netherlands out of the war in six days, despite the fact that it was equipped with Czech tanks. After Dunkirk, it was part of Panzer Group Guderian in the pursuit operations that finished off France, and was near Lyon when the French surrendered. It covered more ground than any other division in the Western campaign. It returned to Vienna in July.

The next year, the 9th Panzer took part in the blitzkrieg through the Balkans, fighting in both Greece and Yugoslavia. It was then sent to Romania to prepare to invade the Soviet Union. As part of Army Group South, the division swept through the Ukraine and was involved in the encirclement of Kiev, where 667,000 Soviet soldiers were captured. It remained on the southern sector, facing the Soviet winter offensive of 1941–42 and taking part in the offensive that resulted in Stalingrad. The following year the 9th Panzer was transferred to Army Group Center, where it was engaged in the Battle of Kursk and the subsequent retreats. Returning to the southern sector, it was in heavy combat in the retreat to the Mius, in the Battles of Stalino, Zaporozhye, Krivoy Rog, Odessa, and in the Dnieper battles.

By January 1944, it was down to a strength of thirteen tanks. Its infantry and artillery units were also very much reduced. Sent to Nimes in southern France to rebuild, it absorbed the 155th Reserve Panzer Division and engaged in training for a time. Eventually it was posted to an area on the Rhone River northwest of Marseilles, and by the time the Allies landed it had a strength of more than 150 tanks and assault guns and 12,768 men. The 9th was soon sent to Avignon, and in early August was rushed to the disintegrating 7th Army in Normandy, just in time to be encircled at Falaise. It broke out of the pocket, with ruinous losses, and by late August had a strength of only one infantry battalion, one artillery battalion, and five operative tanks. Remaining in the line, it took part in the Battle of Aachen and other Siegfried Line fighting, where it lost another 1,000 men—about two-thirds of its remaining combat strength. It was sent into Army Group B's reserve around the end of September and rehabilitated once more, receiving 11,000 replacements and 178 armored vehicles, at least twenty-two of which were late-model PzKw VI "Tiger" tanks. Soon it was back at the front, fighting in the Geilenkirchen-Aachen sector. It launched a spoiling attack against U.S. forces in the Peel Marshes in November, before going into OKW Reserve.

In December the 9th Panzer played a prominent role in the Battle of the Bulge but suffered heavy losses when Hitler refused to allow a timely retreat. Despite repeated heavy casualties, the division's morale never flagged. It distinguished itself once more in the Eifel fighting of early 1945 and again in the Battle of the Erft River in February, when it was down to a strength of twenty-nine tanks and sixteen assault guns. Still, in late February, it launched a spirited but unsuccessful counterattack against the U.S. bridgehead on the Rhine at Remagen. By this time it had only 600 men and fifteen tanks left. On March 5, 1945, the 9th Panzer was attacked by strong Allied forces and finally collapsed; its commander, Major General Baron Harald Gustav von Elverfeldt, was killed in action. Most of the remnants of the once-proud division were forced into the Ruhr Pocket, where they surrendered to the Americans in April. One small battle group under Major Halle, the divisional adjutant, escaped the American encirclement and joined the 11th Army in the Harz Mountains. On April 26, 1945, OB West ordered that the 9th Panzer be disbanded and its survivors be transferred to other units.

The commanders of the 4th Light/9th Panzer included Major General/Lieutenant General Dr. Alfred Ritter von Hubicki (assumed command April 1, 1938), Major General Johannes Baessler (April 15, 1942), Colonel Heinrich-Hermann von Huelsen (July 25, 1942), Major General/Lieutenant General Walter Scheller (July 28, 1942), Colonel/Major General Erwin Jolasse (July 22, 1943), Colonel Dr. Johannes Schulz, Ph.D. (October 9, 1943), Colonel Walter Boemers (December 1, 1943), Jolasse again (returned, January 1943), Colonel Max Sterling (acting commander, August 10, 1944), Major General Gerhard Mueller (September 2, 1944), Elverfeldt (September 16, 1944) and Colonel Helmuth Zollenkopf (March 6, 1945). Major General Friedrich Wilhelm von Mellenthin was acting divisional commander from December 28, 1944 until February 1945, because General von Elverfeldt had been wounded in a fighter-bomber attack.

Notes and Sources: Hubicki was promoted to lieutenant general on August 1, 1940. Scheller was promoted to lieutenant general on January 1, 1943. Jolasse was wounded on September 16, 1943. He was promoted to major general on October 1, 1943, resumed command of the division on November 27, 1943, and was wounded again on August 10, 1944. Zollenkopf was captured in the Ruhr Pocket on April 18, 1945.

Blumenson 1960: 422, 501; Bradley et al., Vol. 1: 168–69; Carell 1966: 125; Carell 1971: 26–34; Chant, Volume 14: 1855; Volume 16: 2133; Chapman: 347–48; Harrison: 240, 244, Map VI; Carl Hans Hermann, *68 Kriegsmonate: Der Weg der 9. Panzerdivision durch zweiten Weltkrieg* (1975); Keilig: 18, 81, 152, 297, 316; Kennedy: 74, Map 7; MacDonald 1963; 69, 74, 95, 242–44, 567; MacDonald 1973: 34, 163, 191, 221, 370; Manstein: 52; Mehner, Vol. 4: 383; Vol. 5: 329; Vol. 7: 354; Mellenthin 1977: 155; Scheibert: 479; Stauffenberg MS; Tessin, Vol. 2: 243–44; Vol. 3: 136–39; OB 42: 57–58; OB 43: 202; OB 45: 291; Ziemke 1966: 241.

10TH PANZER DIVISION

Composition (1942): 7th Panzer Regiment, 69th Panzer Grenadier Regiment, 86th Panzer Grenadier Regiment, 90th Panzer Artillery Regiment, 10th Motorcycle Battalion, 90th Panzer Reconnaissance Battalion, 90th Tank Destroyer Battalion, 49th Panzer Engineer Battalion, 90th Signal Battalion, 90th Divisional Supply Troops

Home Station: Stuttgart, Wehrkreis V

This division was activated in Prague on April 1, 1939, as a composite unit, made up of a number of previously established active duty formations from throughout Germany. Some of these were transferred from the 20th and 29th Motorized Divisions and the 3rd Light Division. The 10th Panzer was forming in Prague in the autumn of 1939, but was thrown into the Polish campaign before this process was completed, and for that reason it was in reserve during much of the operations. That winter, it completed its organization and, as of April 1, 1940, included the 10th Rifle Brigade (69th and 86th Rifle Regiments, each with two battalions); the 4th Panzer Brigade (7th and 8th Panzer Regiments, with two battalions each); the 90th

Artillery Regiment; and the usual divisional troops (see above). The 10th Motorcycle Battalion was added in early 1941, and the 302nd Army Anti-Aircraft Battalion joined the division in 1942.

The 10th Panzer Division played a vital role in the French campaign. As part of Guderian's XIX Motorized Corps it broke through the French lines at Sedan and penetrated all the way to the English Channel. After being involved in the mopping-up operations in the West, it remained in France until March 1941, when it was recalled to Germany. The 10th Panzer was sent to Russia in June 1941, and fought in the battles of the Minsk Pocket, Smolensk, Vyasma (Vjasma), and the Battle of Moscow. It was heavily engaged against the Russian winter offensive of 1941–42 and held Juchnow (near Rzhev) against repeated attacks. The division suffered such heavy losses that it was sent to the Amiens area of France in May 1942, to rest and rebuild. Here its brigade headquarters were disbanded, because casualties had shrunk the division to the point that they were unnecessary. Still there when the Allies landed in North Africa, the division took part in the occupation of Vichy France in November 1942, and was then rushed to Tunisia as fast as transport became available. Elements of the division were primarily responsible for Eisenhower's failure to take Tunis in late 1942. The 10th Panzer also provided the U.S. Army with some of its most embarrassing moments of World War II, when it routed elements of the U.S. II Corps at Kasserine Pass; however, when the Axis front collapsed in May 1943, the division was trapped. It surrendered on May 12 and was never rebuilt.

Its commanders included Major General Georg Gawantka (May 1, 1939), Lieutenant General Ferdinand Schaal (July 15, 1939), Major General/Lieutenant General Wolfgang Fischer (August 2, 1941), Colonel Guenther Angern (August 8, 1941), Fischer (returned, August 27, 1941), Colonel Nikolaus von Vormann (November 19, 1942), Fischer (returned December 1942), and Major General/Lieutenant General Baron Friedrich von Broich (February 1, 1943).

Notes and Sources: General Gawantka died of natural causes on July 15, 1939. Fischer was promoted to lieutenant general on November 1, 1942. He died on February 1, 1943, when his command vehicle struck a land mine and blew off both his legs and an arm. Broich was promoted to lieutenant general on July 1, 1943, even though he had been captured when Tunisia fell.

Benoist-Mechin: 68; Carell 1966: 80; Chant, Volume 16: 2232; Chapman: 347–48; Keilig: 91, 292; Kennedy: 74 and Map 7; Manstein: 34, 488; Mehner, Vol. 6: 545; Albert Schick, *Die Geschichte der 10. Panzer-Division, 1939–1943* (1993); Schmitz et al., Vol. 2: 241–46; Tessin, Vol. 3: 170–71; OB 42: 58; OB 45: 292; Louis Windrow, *The Panzer Divisions* (1985): 8. Also see W. G. F. Jackson, *The Battle for North Africa, 1940–43*, New York: 1975, for a more detailed description of the 10th Panzer's campaign in Tunisia.

11TH PANZER DIVISION

Composition (1943): 15th Panzer Regiment, 110th Panzer Grenadier Regiment, 111th Panzer Grenadier Regiment, 119th Panzer Artillery Regiment, 61st Motorcycle Battalion, 231st Panzer Reconnaissance Battalion, 231st Tank Destroyer Battalion, 231st Panzer Engineer Battalion, 341st Panzer Signal Battalion, 277th Army Anti-Aircraft Battalion, 61st Panzer Divisional Supply Troops

Home Station: Garlitz, Wehrkreis VIII

The 11th Panzer—a Silesian unit—was formed on August 1, 1940, from the 11th Motorized Infantry Brigade (which had fought in France) and the 15th Panzer Regiment of the 5th Panzer Division. It first saw action in the Balkans in April 1941, and captured Belgrade, along with the SS Motorized Division Leibstandarte Adolf Hitler. It crossed into Russia with Army Group South, fought at Zhitomir, Uman, and Kiev, and was sent to Army Group Center for the Battle of Moscow. It held the Gshatsk (Gzhatsk) sector from January to May 1942, against Stalin's winter offensive. Returned to the south in June, it fought at Orel and Voronesh, on the Don and in the Donetz, and took part in the drive to the Volga. It was not encircled in the Stalingrad Pocket in November 1942, although it did suffer heavy losses from the Soviet winter offensive of 1942–43, in the Stalingrad relief effort, and in the subsequent retreats. The 11th Panzer played a major role in halting the Russians east of Rostov and thus kept the escape route of Army Group A opened. The division fought at Kharkov in March 1943, at Kursk in July, and suffered heavy losses at Krivog Rog in the fall of 1943. It was surrounded, along with several other divisions, at Cherkassy in February 1944. It broke out, but with such appalling losses in life and equipment that it had to be almost completely rebuilt.

It absorbed the remnants of the 416th Grenadier Regiment of the 123rd Infantry Division (which had also been smashed on the Eastern Front) and was sent to the Libourne area of southern France, where it absorbed the personnel of the 273rd Reserve Panzer Division. The 11th Panzer remained in the West and was stationed at Toulouse for a time. In July 1944, it conducted delaying operations up the Rhone Valley against the Allied forces that had landed in southern France. It fought in Alsace, took part in the defense of the Belfort Gap, and in the subsequent withdrawal to the Saar, before being sent to the Ardennes in December 1944.

By the time the Battle of the Bulge began, the division had only 3,500 men left, and only 800 of these were infantry, despite the fact that it had absorbed the remnants of the 113th Panzer Brigade in late September. After the failure of this, Hitler's last offensive in the West, the 11th Panzer Division was reinforced and sent into the Battle of the Saar-Moselle Triangle and again suffered serious losses. The following month it tried to overrun the U.S. bridgehead at Remagen but was down to a strength of 4,000 men, twenty-five tanks, and eighteen pieces of artillery, and was repulsed; nevertheless, it was one of the strongest panzer divisions left on the Western Front. Field Marshal Kesselring, the OB West, ordered it transferred to Army Group G on the southern sector of the front in March, so it escaped encirclement in the Ruhr Pocket and fought until the end of the war. The remnants of this veteran combat division,

A column of Panzer Mark V "Panther" tanks in an unknown village. The use of vegetation as camouflage was widespread by 1944, due to Allied air superiority. HITM ARCHIVE

which had distinguished itself in a dozen battles, surrendered to the U.S. 90th Infantry Division near Wallern Bavaria, on May 2, 1945.

Commanders of the 11th Panzer included Major General Ludwig Cruewell (assumed command August 1, 1940), Colonel Guenther Angern (August 15, 1941), Major General Baron Hans-Karl von Esebeck (August 24, 1941), Major General Walter Scheller (October 20, 1941), Major General/Lieutenant General Hermann Balck (May 16, 1942), Lieutenant General Dietrich von Choltitz (March 3, 1943), Major General Johann Mickl (May 11, 1943), Colonel/Major General/Lieutenant General Wend von Wietersheim (August 8, 1943), Colonel Friedrich von Hake (May 7, 1944), Major General Baron Horst Treusch von Buttlar-Brandenfelds (January, 1945), and Wietershem again (May 3, 1945).

Notes and Sources: Balck was promoted to lieutenant general on January 1, 1943. Wietersheim was promoted to major general on November 1, 1943, and to lieutenant general on July 1, 1944.

Blumenson 1960: 535; Carell 1966: 118, 330, 649; Carell 1971: 47, 123; Clark: 261; Cole 1950: 217, 237, 450, 527; Harrison: 244, Map VI; Hartmann: 64; Keilig: 60, 84, 227, 348, 370; MacDonald 1973: 118. 126, 142, 221, 345, 467; Manstein: 389, 526; Mellenthin 1977: 183; Schmitz et al., Vol. 3: 17-28; G. W. Schrodek, *Die 11. Panzer-Division "Gespenster-Division"—Bilddokumente, 1940–1945* (1984); Stoves, *Gepanzerten*: 85; Tessin, Vol. 3: 200–203; OB 42: 58; OB 43: 202; OB 45: 292.

12TH PANZER DIVISION

Composition: 29th Panzer Regiment, 5th Panzer Grenadier Regiment, 25th Panzer Grenadier Regiment, 2nd Panzer Artillery Regiment, 22nd Motorcycle (later 2nd Panzer Reconnaissance) Battalion. 508th Tank Destroyer Battalion, 32nd Panzer Engineer Battalion, 2nd Panzer Signal Battalion, 303rd Army Anti-Aircraft Battalion (added 1942), 2nd Divisional Supply Troops

Home Station: Stettin, Wehrkreis II

The 2nd Infantry Division—the forerunner of the 12th Panzer—was created at Stettin in the Reichsheer organization of 1921. Its personnel were Prussians. In 1934–35 it was reorganized to include the 5th, 25th, and 92nd Infantry Regiments, under the codename *Artillerieführer II.* In 1936–37, it was again reformed, this time as a motorized infantry division. In the summer of 1939, its 92nd Motorized Infantry Regiment was attached to the 60th Motorized Infantry Division, a separation that was made permanent in 1940. Meanwhile, the 2nd Motorized fought in northern Poland (1939), and in France (1940), where it was part of Wietersheim's XIV Motorized Corps during the "Dash to the Channel." In the fall of 1940, it was reorganized as a panzer division, and was officially redesignated 12th Panzer Division on January 10, 1941. Later that year, it fought in Russia, taking part in the Minsk encirclement, the crossing of the Dnieper, and the Battle of Smolensk, as well as the Battle of Mga on the northern sector.

Hit hard by the Soviet winter offensive of 1941–42, it was withdrawn to Estonia to rest and refit. Soon back in action, the 12th Panzer took part in the battles south of Leningrad in 1942, including Lake Ladoga and Nevel, before being sent to the central sector of the front. It fought at Vitebsk in February and at Kursk in July 1943, and later in the battles of Gomel and of the middle Dnieper and Dneister. Transferred back to Army Group North in January 1944, it arrived too late to prevent the Soviets from breaking the Siege of Leningrad, but it did distinguish itself in the retreat across the Baltic States. That summer it tried to prevent the encirclement of the 4th and 9th armies, but it failed and was driven into the Courland Pocket in September. It fought in the six battles of the Courland Pocket, where it served as a "fire brigade" for Army Group North (later Courland). Much of it surrendered to the Red Army in May 1945. As a special sign of favor, on the orders of the commander-in-chief, Army Group Courland, part of the division was evacuated back to the west on the last ships, so that it avoided Soviet captivity.

The commanders of the 2nd Infantry/12th Panzer Division included Lieutenant General Fedor von Bock (1931–34),

Major General/Lieutenant General Hubert Gercke (October 1, 1934), Major General/Lieutenant General Paul Bader (April 1, 1937), Major General/Lieutenant General Josef Harpe (October 5, 1940), Major General/Lieutenant General Walter Wessel (January 15, 1942), Colonel/Major General/Lieutenant General Baron Erpo von Bodenhausen (March 1, 1943), Colonel Gerhard Mueller (May 28, 1944), Bodenhausen (resumed command July 16, 1944), and Colonel Horst von Usedom (April 12, 1945).

Notes and Sources: Colonel Hans-Joachim Kahler briefly served as acting divisional commander in early 1944, but the dates are not clear. Gercke, Bader, Harpe and Wessel were promoted to lieutenant general on April 1, 1935, January 1, 1938, January 15, 1942, and January 1, 1943, respectively. Bodenhausen was promoted to major general on May 1, 1943, and to lieutenant general on November 1, 1943. He was named commander of the L Corps (also in the Courland Pocket) on April 12, 1945, and committed suicide on May 9, rather than surrender to the Soviets.

Carell 1966: 26, 69, 80; Carell 1971: 591–94; Keilig: 16, 39, 104; Kennedy: 10B, 74, Map 7; Kursietis: 92–93; Lexikon; Manstein: 131–32, 538; Mehner, Vol. 4: 383; Vol. 6: 545; Vol. 12: 458; Salisbury: 275; Scheibert: 382; Schmitz, Vol. 3: 60; Stoves, *Gepanzerten*: 88-89; Tessin, Vol. 2: 100; Vol. 3: 202–4; OB 42: 58–59; OB 43: 208; OB 45: 293–94; Ziemke 1966: 258.

13TH PANZER DIVISION

Composition (1943): 4th Panzer Regiment, 66th Panzer Grenadier Regiment, 93rd Panzer Grenadier Regiment, 13th Panzer Artillery Regiment, 43rd Motorcycle (later 13th Panzer Reconnaissance) Battalion, 13th Tank Destroyer Battalion, 13th Panzer Engineer Battalion, 13th Panzer Signal Battalion, 275th Army Anti-Aircraft Battalion (added 1942), 13th Panzer Divisional Supply Troops

Home Station: Magdeburg, Wehrkreis XI

The 13th Panzer was initially formed in October 1934, as Infantry Command IV. It became the 13th Infantry Division on

October 15, 1935, and included the 33rd, 66th, and 93rd Infantry Regiments. In the winter of 1936–37, it was converted to a motorized infantry unit and in the summer of 1939 gave up the 33rd Infantry Regiment to the 4th Panzer Division. The 13th Motorized Infantry—now a two-regiment unit—took part in the conquests of Poland and France, distinguished itself in both campaigns, pushed across Belgium to Calais in May 1940, and to Lyon in June. It returned to Germany in July and was converted into a panzer division in the autumn of 1940. It spent the winter of 1940–41 in Romania, was sent to Silesia in May 1941, and crossed into Russia with Army Group South in June. The division was very heavily engaged, almost from the beginning. It fought in the battles of Lubin and Uman, in the Stalin Line breakthrough at Hulsk, in the drive on and encirclement of Kiev, in the Battle of the Chernigovka Pocket, and in the capture of Rostov.

By November 1941, its divisional commander and two of its regimental commanders were suffering from nervous exhaustion. After helping halt the Soviet winter offensive of 1941–42 on the Mius River, the 13th Panzer took part in von Kleist's drive on the Caucasus oilfields in 1942, where it crossed the Terek River and pushed to within fifteen miles of Grozny. Most of the division escaped isolation in the Kuban before the Russians retook Rostov, although part of it was cut off and had to be evacuated later via the Crimea. By this time, it had only eighteen operational tanks left. Reunited under the command of the resurrected 6th Army, the 13th Panzer was reinforced with a battalion of Panthers, new model PzKw IVs and several excellent self-propelled tank destroyers. It fought in the lower Dnieper battles in the Ukraine, where it fought near Kharkov and Zaporozhye, and only had seven tanks left when it was surrounded at Melitopol, along with the 336th Infantry Division and the 15th Luftwaffe Field Division. Outnumbered more than 7 to 1, the 13th Panzer led the ensuing breakout on August 30, 1943, and reached German lines on September 2. The battered division remained in the line and covered the retreat from Stalino. It then fought its way back to the Dnieper, fought in the Battle of the Nikopol Bridgehead, and in the subsequent retreat to Krivoy Rog.

The 13th Panzer was partially rebuilt in early 1944, and was rushed back to the front, whereit took part in the Cherkassy relief attempt in February and the retreats to the Bug and Dniester (Dnestr). It suffered heavy losses when the Romanians defected in September 1944. The division had only 40 tanks left when the battle began and lost almost all of them. Withdrawn to reform in October, the 13th absorbed the 110th Panzer Brigade and was back in action on the southern sector of the Eastern Front in November. Most of the division (3,000 men and seventeen PzKw IV and Panther tanks and thirty-five self-propelled guns and eight assault guns) was encircled at Budapest in December and was destroyed when the German garrison tried unsuccessfully to break out of the city on February 11, 1945. The remnants of the division (300 to 500 men) were reformed under the command of Lieutenant Colonel of Reserves Wilhelm Schoening. This kampfgruppe was used to form the nucleus of Panzer Division Feldherrnhalle 2, which was activated on February 2, 1945. This division was unofficially referred to as the 13th Panzer Division, but it was not. The 13th Panzer officially ceased to exist in March.

Commanders of the 13th Infantry/Panzer Division included Major General/Lieutenant General Paul Otto (assumed command, October 1, 1934), Lieutenant General Moritz von Faber du Faur (August 21, 1939), Otto (resumed command, September 7, 1939), Lieutenant General Friedrich-Wilhelm von Rothkirch und Panthen (November 1, 1939), Major General Walter Duevert (June 14, 1941), Colonel/Major General Traugott Herr (November 29, 1941), Colonel Walter Kühn (October 1, 1942), Major General/Lieutenant General Hellmut von der Chevallerie (November 1, 1942), Colonel Wilhelm Crisolli (December 1, 1942), Chevallerie again (May 15, 1943), Colonel/Major General Eduard Hauser (September 1, 1943), Colonel/Major General Hans Mikosch (December 23, 1943),

Colonel Friedrich von Hake (May 18, 1944), Lieutenant General Hans Troeger (May 25, 1944), and Colonel/Major General Gerhard Schmidhuber (September 9, 1944).

Notes and Sources: Paul Otto was promoted to lieutenant general on January 1, 1937. Because of combat fatigue and nervous exhaustion, Walther Duevert had to be relieved of his command on November 29, 1941, cutting short a brilliant career, because he never fully recovered. Traugott Herr was promoted to major general on April 1, 1942. He was seriously wounded on November 1, 1942, and did not return to duty until June 25, 1943. Hellmuth von der Chevallerie was promoted to lieutenant general on May 1, 1943. Eduard Hauser was promoted to major general on December 1, 1943. Troeger was captured in Bulgaria on September 9, 1944 and was handed over to the Russians, who did not release him until 1955. Schmidhuber was promoted to major general on October 1, 1944. He was killed in action during the Budapest breakout on February 11, 1945.

Benoist-Mechin: 133; Bradley, et al., Vol. 3: 229–30; Vol. 5: 196–98, 345–47; Carell 1966: 300–301, 533; Carell 1971: 153, 537; Chant, Volume 15: 2057; Chapman: 347–48; Friedrich von Hake, *Der Schicksalsweg der 13. Panzer-Division, 1939–1945* (1971); Dieter Hoffmann, *Die Magdeburger Division—Zur Geschichte der 13. Infanterie-und 13. Panzer-Division, 1935–1945* (1999); Keilig: 17–18, 59, 76, 130, 137, 227, 250, 285, 303, 349; Kennedy: 74; Manstein: 398; Mehner, Vol. 3: Seite 5; Vol. 4: 382; Vol. 5: 330; Vol. 6: 545; Vol. 11: 351; Mitcham 2001: 109-18; Schmitz et al., Vol. 3: 85–96; Seaton: 197–98 (citing Franz Halder, *Kriegstagebuch,* Volume III: 319, 483, 500); Gerhard von Seemen, *Die Ritterkreuzträger, 1939–1945* (1976): 53, 307 (hereafter cited as "Seemen"); Stoves, *Gepanzerten*: 94; Tessin, Vol. 3: 263–64; 266–68; Thomas, Vol. 2: 279; RA: 172; OB 42: 59; OB 43: 201–3; OB 44: 283; OB 45: 294.

14TH PANZER DIVISION

Composition (1943): 36th Panzer Grenadier Regiment, 108th Panzer Grenadier Regiment, 4th Panzer Artillery Regiment, 64th Motorcycle Battalion, 40th Panzer Reconnaissance Battalion, 4th Tank Destroyer Battalion, 13th Panzer Engineer Battalion, 13th Panzer Signal Battalion, 276th Army Anti-Aircraft Battalion (added 1942), 4th Panzer Divisional Supply Troops

Home Station: Dresden, later Zittau, Wehrkreis IV

Formed at Dresden as the 4th Infantry Division in the Reichswehr organization of 1921, this division included the 52nd, 103rd, and 108th Infantry Regiments by 1935. It fought well in Poland and in the French campaign of 1940, where it followed up the decisive tank breakthrough at Sedan. In August of that year it was sent to the Koenigsbrueck Troop Maneuver Area and reorganized as the 14th Panzer Division, receiving the 36th Panzer Regiment from the 4th Panzer Division but giving up the 52nd Motorized Infantry Regiment to the 18th Panzer Division. The other two rifle regiments also had to give up their III Battalions. The following spring, the 14th Panzer Division was involved in the Balkans campaign and took part in the Russian invasion later that year. It fought in the drive across the Ukraine, the Battles of Kiev, Kholm, Dnepropetrovsk, the Chernigovka Pocket (on the Sea of Azov), and in other battles on the southern sector, where it suffered serious losses. After the Russian winter offensive of 1941–42 had been checked, the division fought at Kharkov in May and in the drive across the Don and to the Volga. It was surrounded with the 6th Army in Stalingrad in November 1942, and was destroyed there in January 1943.

The 14th Panzer Division was resurrected in Brittany, France, in the summer of 1943 and returned to southern Russia in time to take part in the Battle of Kiev that autumn. In more or less continuous retreat after that, it fought at Krivoy Rog, Kirovograd, and in the Dnieper battles, and suffered such heavy losses in the withdrawal from that river that it had to be rebuilt in the summer of 1944. That September it was sent to the northern sector of the front and was soon isolated in the Courland Pocket. After Berlin fell, elements of the 14th Panzer (along with parts of the 11th Infantry and 12th Panzer Divisions) were returned to Germany on the last available shipping before Army Group Courland capitulated, and thus it escaped Russian captivity. These units were selected because they had been the "firefighters" of the army group when the Russians tried unsuccessfully to crush the pocket six times in the winter of 1944–45.

Commanders of the 4th Infantry/14th Panzer Division included Major General/Lieutenant General Erich Raschick (October 1, 1934), Major General/Lieutenant General Eric Hansen (assumed command November 10, 1938), Major General Heinrich von Prittwitz und Gaffron (October 1, 1940), Major General Friedrich Kühn (March 22, 1941), Major General Ferdinand Heim (July 1, 1942), Colonel Baron Hans von Falkenstein (November 1, 1942), Major General Johannes Baessler (November 16, 1942), and Colonel/Major General Martin Lattmann (November 26, 1942), who surrendered the division at Stalingrad. Colonel Günther Ludwig briefly served as acting divisional commander in January 1943. Commanders of the second 14th Panzer Division were Colonel/Major General Friedrich Sieberg (April 1, 1943), Colonel Karl-Max Graessel (October 29, 1943), Colonel/Major General/Lieutenant General Martin Unrein (November 5, 1943), Colonel Werner Mummert (September 6, 1944), Colonel Oskar Munzel (September 15, 1944), Unrein (returned November 25, 1944), Colonel Friedrich-Wilhelm Jürgen (February 1, 1945), Graessel (February 24, 1945), and Colonel Walter Palm (March 20, 1945).

Notes and Sources: The 4th Field Replacement Battalion was part of the division until January 1940, when it was transferred to the 164th Infantry Division and became the I/440th Infantry Regiment. Raschick and Eric Hansen were promoted to lieutenant general on August 1, 1936, and August 1, 1939, respectively. Lattman was promoted to major general on January 1, 1943. Friedrich Sieberg became a major general on June 1, 1943. He was mortally wounded on October 29, 1943, and died in the Kirovograd hospital on November 3, 1943. Unrein was promoted to major general on January 1, 1944, and to lieutenant general on July 1, 1944.

Bradley et al., Vol. 3: 412–13; Vol. 5: 105–6, 240–42; Carell 1966: 301, 490, 495, 564, 599; Rolf Grams, *Die 14. Panzer-Division, 1940–1945* (1957), ff. 1; Keilig: 85, 125, 191, 323, 352; Kennedy: 10B, 74; *Kriegstagebuch des OKW*, Volume II: 1453; Manstein: 482, 487; Mellenthin 1956; 225; Mehner, Vol. 5: 330; Vol. 9: 396; Vol. 12: 458; Nafziger 2000: 39; Schmitz et al., Vol. 3: 125–27; Stoves, *Gepanzerten*: 95–100; Tessin, Vol. 2: 236; Vol. 3: 298–99; Thorwald: 288; RA: 72; OB 42: 59; OB 43: 204; OB 45: 295.

15TH PANZER DIVISION

Composition: 8th Panzer Regiment, 115th Panzer Grenadier Regiment, 33rd Panzer Artillery Regiment, 33rd Panzer Reconnaissance Battalion, 33rd Tank Destroyer Battalion, 33rd Panzer Engineer Battalion, 33rd Panzer Signal Battalion, 276th Army Anti-Aircraft Battalion (added in 1942), 33rd Panzer Divisional Supply Troops

Home Station: Kaiserslautern, Wehrkreis XII

This unit was formed in Darmstadt on April 1, 1936, as the 33rd Infantry Division of the peacetime army. It initially included the 104th, 110th, and 115th Infantry Regiments. It served on the Saar sector in 1939–40, fought in Belgium and France in 1940, and was reorganized as a panzer division in the fall of 1940. It added the 8th Panzer Regiment to its table of organization but gave up the 110th Infantry Regiment to the 112th Infantry Division. Its horses were transferred to Wehrkreis IX and were incorporated into the 129th Infantry Division. It was officially redesignated 15th Panzer Division on November 1, 1940.

In the spring of 1941, it was sent to Libya to form one of the two divisions of Erwin Rommel's Afrika Korps. That summer it gave up the 104th Panzer Grenadier Regiment to the 5th Light Division, which was reorganizing as the 21st Panzer Division. The 15th Panzer fought in all the campaigns on the North African Front except the first: it arrived too late to be on hand when Rommel captured Benghazi in April 1941. The division took part in the unsuccessful attacks on Tobruk in April and May 1941, helped defeat the British relief attempts aimed at Tobruk that summer (Operations Brevity and Battleaxe), and was severely mauled in heavy fighting in Operation Crusader (November 18–December 7, 1941). Down to a handful of tanks, it retreated into Libya. Reinforced by shipments of panzers from Europe in January 1942, the 15th Panzer fought in Rommel's Second Cyrenaican campaign and helped retake Benghazi. Later in 1942, it was involved in the battles of the Gazala Line, the capture of Tobruk, and the invasion of Egypt. It was checked and virtually destroyed in the El Alamein battles. By the time Rommel retreated in early November 1942, the 8th Panzer Regiment had lost all of its tanks and its regimental commander was dead; the 33rd Panzer Artillery Regiment had only seven guns left. The 15th Panzer retreated through Egypt, Libya, and into Tunisia. There it turned to attack again, at the Kasserine Pass. Finally checked, the division was destroyed in the final collapse in North Africa on May 13, 1943.

The commanders of the 33rd Infantry/15th Panzer Division included Major General Ritter Hermann von Speck (assumed command March 1, 1938), Major General Rudolf Sintzenich (April 29, 1940), Major General Friedrich Kühn (October 5, 1940), Major General Heinrich von Prittwitz und Gaffron (October 1, 1940), Colonel/Major General Hans-Karl von Esebeck (April 13, 1941), Major General Walter Neumann-Silkow (May 26, 1941), Major General Gustav von Vaerst (December 9, 1941). Colonel Eduard Crasemann (May 28, 1942), Major General Heinz von Randow (July 15, 1942), Vaerst again (August 25, 1942), and Colonel/Major General/Lieutenant General Willibald Borowietz (November 18, 1942). Colonel von Herff probably served as acting divisional commander from April 10 to 13, 1941, but this has not been confirmed.

Notes and Sources: General von Prittwitz was killed in action by an anti-tank shell near Tobruk on April 10, 1941. Esebeck arrived at division headquarters and took command of the 15th Panzer on April 13. He was promoted to major general two days later. He was seriously wounded by a shell splinter near Tobruk on May 13. Major General Walter Neumann-Silkow was mortally wounded on December 6, 1941, and died on December 9. Major General von Vaerst was wounded on May 28, 1942, and did not return to action until August 25. At the Battle of Alma Halfa Ridge he was acting commander of the Afrika Korps, and his division was briefly commanded by Colonel Waltenberger (August 31–early September 1942). Borowietz was promoted to major general on January 1, 1943 and to lieutenant general on July 1, 1943. He was killed in an accident in Clinton, Mississippi on July 1, 1945, as a prisoner-of-war.

A. J. Barker, *Afrikakorps* (1978): 139; Bradley et al., Vol. 2: 157–59; Vol. 3: 375–76; Keilig: 46–47, 84, 263, 327; Kursietis: 97; Lexikon;

A Panzer Mark IV (PzKw IV) leads a column down a dirt road. HITM ARCHIVE

Mehner, Vol. 3: 24; Vol. 4: 383; Vol. 5: 330; Tessin, Vol. 4: 9–11; Vol. 5: 24–25. Also see Carell 1960; Irving 1977; Jackson; Mellenthin 1956; and Young. Also see OB 43: 204 and OB 44b: B5.

16TH PANZER DIVISION

Composition: 2nd Panzer Regiment, 64th Panzer Grenadier Regiment, 79th Panzer Grenadier Regiment, 16th Panzer Artillery Regiment, 16th Motorcycle Battalion, 16th Panzer Reconnaissance Battalion, 16th Tank Destroyer Battalion, 16th Panzer Engineer Battalion, 16th Panzer Signal Battalion, 274th Army Anti-Aircraft Battalion (added 1942), 16th Panzer Divisional Supply Troops

Home Station: Münster, Wehrkreis VI

Formed in October 1934 under the codename "Commandant of Münster," it became the 16th Infantry Division on October 15, 1935. The unit was made up mainly of Westphalians, with some East Prussians interspersed. It initially included the 60th, 64th, and 79th Infantry Regiments. It was in the Saar in 1939, and thus missed the Polish campaign, but the division did well in France the following year, where it fought at Sedan, supporting the German armor. That summer, it returned to Germay and was converted into a panzer division, receiving the 2nd Panzer Regiment from the 1st Panzer Division and supplying the 60th Infantry Regiment (now motorized) to the 16th Motorized Infantry Division, which was then being formed.

The new panzer division was in action on the southern sector of the Russian Front from July 1941. It was almost continuously engaged, fighting in the Ukraine campaign, the Battle of Kiev, the Donets battles, against the Russian winter offensive of 1941–42, and in the drive across the Don and to the Volga. During the Bacaklesa encirclement (May 17–22, 1942), the 16th Panzer Division captured 31,500 Russians and sixty-nine tanks and 224 other vehicles. It was, however, seriously depleted by casualties in the street fighting in Stalingrad in September and October 1942. As of mid-November 1942, the division had only 4,000 men left. It was ordered to pull out of the line and withdraw to the Donetz to refit. It was in the middle of this maneuver on November 19, 1942, when Stalin's massive offensive struck. The main thrust cut across 16th Panzer's line of march, cutting the division in half. The division staff, 79th Panzer Grenadier Regiment, most of the 64th Panzer Grenadier Regiment, and the 16th Panzer Artillery Regiment were cut off in the Stalingrad Pocket when the pinchers closed on November 23. The rest of the division—including the 2nd Panzer Regiment; the 16th Tank Destroyer Battalion; the I/64th Panzer Grenadier Regiment; and the 16th Panzer Engineer Battalion—managed to escape to the west. Under the command of Colonel Rudolf Sickenius, it fought on as a separate battle group. The rest of the division remained surrounded with 6th Army in the Stalingrad Pocket, and was forced to surrender there on February 2, 1943.

A second 16th Panzer Division was formed in the spring of 1943 and sent to the Taranto sector of Italy in June. It was built around the soldiers who had escaped the Stalingrad debacle and those who had recovered from wounds suffered in 1942—3,400 men in all, as well as 600 Russian volunteers or "hiwis." The new division also absorbed the 890th Motorized Grenadier Regiment and assorted GHQ troops from the 7th Army. Its unit numbers remained the same as in the old division. Shifted to Salerno just before U.S. General Mark Clark's 5th Army landed on the mainland of Italy, the 16th Panzer at first absorbed the full weight of the invasion and inflicted heavy casualties on the Allied landing forces, but it lost two-thirds of its own tank strength in the heavy fighting. It continued in the line and fought delaying actions north of Naples until late 1943, when it was returned to the Eastern Front just in time to take part in the counteroffensive against Kiev. The 16th Panzer suffered heavy losses at Kiev and in the withdrawal across the northern Ukraine. It also tried unsuccessfully to relieve the pocket at Cherkassy. In the fall of 1944 the 16th Panzer was engaged west of the Vistula. It fought in the retreat through Poland and was at battle group strength in east Germany and Czechoslovakia (around Lauban and Brno [Brunn]) when

Hitler shot himself on April 30, 1945. The division managed to disengage from the Russians and broke into three groups: one infiltrated through the mountains and forests and reached Karlsbad, Germany, where it surrendered to the U.S. 3rd Army; one was forced to surrender to the Red Army at Troppau on May 18; and the third reached Pilsen and capitulated to the Americans. This last group, however, was promptly handed over to the Soviets.

Commanders of the division included Major General/Lieutenant General Gerhard Glokke (assumed command October 1, 1934), Major General Gotthard Heinrici (October 1, 1937), Major General Heinrich Krampf (February 1, 1940), Major General/Lieutenant General Hans Valentin Hube (May 17, 1940), Major General/Lieutenant General Günther Angern (August 15, 1942), Lieutenant Colonel Dr. Woermann (late January 1943), Colonel Burkhart Mueller-Hildebrandt (February 1943), Colonel/Major General Rudolf Sieckenius (March 5, 1943), Colonel/Major General Hans-Ulrich Back (November 8, 1943), Colonel/Major General/Lieutenant General Dietrich von Mueller (August 1944), Colonel Theodor Kretschmer (acting commander, December 1, 1944), von Mueller (returned, February 28, 1945), Dr. Albrecht Aschoff (April 1, 1945), and Colonel Kurt Treuhaupt (April 19, 1945).

Notes and Sources: Glokke was promoted to lieutenant general on October 1, 1936. Hube was promoted to lieutenant general on April 1, 1942. General Angern committed suicide in late January or early February 1943, to avoid Soviet captivity. Sieckenius was promoted to major general on June 1, 1943. Back was promoted to major general on February 1, 1944. Mueller was promoted to major general on November 9, 1944, and to lieutenant general on April 20, 1945. Unknown to Berlin, he had been captured by the Red Army on April 19.

Bradley, et al., Vol. 1: 75–76; Vol. 5: 256–58; Blumenson 1969: 86; Carell 1966: 488, 586; Hartmann: 66; Kameradschaftsbund 16. Panzer-und-Infanterie-Division, *Bildband der 16. Panzer-Division* (1956): ff. 6; Keilig: 12, 16, 59, 109, 133, 184, 234; Kursiestis: 98; Manstein: 515; Mellenthin 1956: 225; Mehner, Vol. 8: 556; Vol. 12: 458; Schmitz et al., Vol. 3: 225–35; Stauffenberg MS; Tessin, Vol. 6: 30–37; RA: 100; OB 42: 60; OB 43: 205; OB 45: 295; Wolfgang Werthen, *Geschichte der 16. Panzer-Division, 1939–1945* (1958); Ziemke 1966: 225.

17TH PANZER DIVISION

Composition: 39th Panzer Regiment, 40th Panzer Grenadier Regiment, 63rd Panzer Grenadier Regiment, 27th Panzer Artillery Regiment, 17th Motorcycle (later Panzer Reconnaissance) Battalion, 27th Tank Destroyer Battalion, 27th Panzer Engineer Battalion, 27th Panzer Signal Battalion, 297th Army Anti-Aircraft Battalion (added 1942), 27th Panzer Divisional Supply Troops

Home Station: Augsburg, Wehrkreis VII

The 27th Infantry Division—forerunner of the 17th Panzer—was created in Augsburg on October 1, 1936, and initially included the 40th, 63rd, and 91st Infantry Regiments. Its personnel were Swabians who fought extremely well in Poland and France. The division was converted to the 17th Panzer on November 1, 1940; at the same time it gave up its 91st Regiment to the 4th Mountain Division. The newly formed Staff, 17th Rifle Brigade controlled its rifle regiments and motorcycle battalion until it was separated from the division in 1944, and was used form Headquarters, IV Panzer Corps.

In June 1941, the 17th Panzer struck into Russia with Army Group Center, fighting at Brest-Litovsk, the Minsk encirclement, in the Dnieper crossings, at Smolensk, and in the Battle of Moscow. It destroyed 100 Russian tanks in a single day—July 9, 1941—at Orsha, during the Dnieper crossing operations. That winter it was pushed back to Orel and remained there until December 1942, when it was transferred to the southern sector of the front. Although it was poor shape (it only had thirty tanks left and all of its armored cars had been destroyed), it took part in the attempt to relieve Stalingrad, but was itself encircled and had to fight its way out. It nevertheless acquitted itself very well, destroying twenty-one Soviet tanks in a single day in temperatures of minus 22 degrees Fahrenheit. By Christmas Eve 1942, the 17th was down to a strength of eight tanks and one anti-tank gun, and one of its regiments was commanded by the lieutenant.

It was taken out of the line shortly thereafter and was partially rebuilt. It received fifty new tanks and the 297th Army Motorized Anti-Aircraft Battalion, which later became the 27th (Flak) Tank Destroyer Battalion, which was added to its table of organization on January 12, 1943. Sent back to the front almost immediately, it took part in Manstein's Kharkov counteroffensive in March, it fought at Kursk (July), and in the subsequent retreats from the Donets, the Dnieper bend, and the northern Ukraine. In March 1944, it was encircled with the 1st Panzer Army, but again broke out. It took part in the retreat across eastern Poland and, in September 1944, was still resisting west of the Vistula. In late 1944, the 17th Panzer Division was reorganized again—this time as a regimental-sized *Kampfgruppe*. The Staff, 39th Panzer Regiment, was used to form the 108th Panzer Brigade, and the division was left with a single tank battalion. The seriously depleted and understrength 63rd Panzer Grenadier Regiment was dissolved and used to form the III/40th Panzer Grenadier Regiment—a bicycle unit. All of the division support units were reduced to companies, and the 27th Panzer Artillery Regiment became the 27th Panzer Artillery Battalion. The 17th Panzer Division nevertheless opposed the Russian drive west of the Vistula River in the winter of 1944–45, fought in the disastrous Battle of the Baranov Bridgehead and at Goerlitz, and ended the war in the Deutsch-Brod pocket east of Prague. It surrendered to the Russians near Olmuetz on May 11, 1945.

Commanders of the 27th Infantry/17th Panzer Division included Major General/Lieutenant General Friedrich Bergmann (January 1, 1937), Lieutenant General Hans-Jürgen "Dieter" von Arnim (October 5, 1940), Major General Ritter Karl von Weber (June, 1941), Lieutenant General Wilhelm Ritter von Thoma (July 18, 1941), Colonel/Major General Rudolf-Eduard Licht (November 11, 1941), Major General/Lieutenant General Fridolin von Senger und Etterlin (October 10, 1942), Lieutenant General Walter Schilling (June 17, 1943), Colonel/Major General/Lieutenant General Karl-Friedrich von der Meden (June 22, 1943), Colonel Albert Brux (September 1944), and Major General Theodor Kretschmer (February 1, 1945).

Notes and Sources: Jürgen von Armin was wounded in action on June 26, 1941, and replaced by Ritter von Weber. Weber was wounded in the Battle of Smolensk on July 18, 1941, and died two days later. Senger was promoted to lieutenant general on May 1, 1943. Schilling was killed in action at Doljenhaja on July 20, 1943. Meden was promoted to major general on October 1, 1943, and to lieutenant general on July 1, 1944. Colonel Brux was captured by the Russians on January 19, 1945. The author was unable to discover who commanded the division from then until February 1, 1945. All four of the regimental commanders in the 17th Panzer Division in November 1942 were killed in action during the next two years.

Bradley et al., Vol. 1: 97–99, 334–35; Vol 3: 67–68; Carell 1966: 42, 80, 344, 651; Carell 1971: 89, 525; Guderian: 131, 140, 144; Hartmann: 68; Keilig: 30, 187, 220, 299, 364; Kennedy: 74, Map 7; *Kriegstagebuch des OKW*, Volume I: 1146; Kursiestis: 98–100; Manstein: 134, 498–99, 515; Mehner, Vol. 5: 330; Vol. 12: 458; Seaton: 330–31; Tessin, Vol. 6: 61–65, 251–52; Vol. 9: 57; RA: 116; OB 42: 60; OB 43: 205; OB 44: 285; OB 45: 296; Windrow: 10; Ziemke 1966: 225.

18TH PANZER DIVISION

Composition: 18th Panzer Regiment, 52nd Panzer Grenadier Regiment, 101st Panzer Grenadier Regiment, 88th Panzer Artillery Regiment, 18th Motorcycle Battalion, 88th Panzer Reconnaissance Battalion, 88th Tank Destroyer Battalion, 209th Panzer Engineer Battalion, 88th Panzer Signal Battalion, 88th Panzer Divisional Supply Troops

Home Station: Leisnig, Wehrkreis IV

The 18th Panzer was formed on October 26, 1940, as a result of Hitler's decision to create new armored divisions by weakening older panzer and motorized divisions. The 18th Panzer received the 52nd Motorized Infantry Regiment from the 4th Infantry Division and the 101st Motorized from the 14th Infantry Division. By the end of the year, the 18th Panzer included the newly formed 18th Rifle Brigade (52nd and 101st Rifle Regiments and 18th Motorcycle Battalion); the newly created 18th and 28th Panzer Regiments (two battalions each);

the 88th Panzer Artillery Regiment; and assorted divisional troops. The 28th Panzer Regiment was transferred to the 3rd Panzer Division in March 1941; however, enough of it was left behind to form III/18th Panzer Regiment.

The new division first saw action in Russia, crossing the Bug in underwater tanks originally designed for Operation Sea Lion (the invasion of Britain). It spent the rest of 1941 fighting in a number of battles, including the Minsk encirclement, Smolensk, the Dnieper crossings, Kiev, Roslavl, Bryansk, Moscow, and Orel, all on the central sector of the Russian Front. It also opposed the Soviet winter offensive of 1941–42, near the Soviet capital. Casualties were heavy. During the first sixty days of the campaign, it lost almost 6,000 men—more than one-third of its pre-invasion strength. By July 9, the division had only eighty-three operational tanks—39 percent of its strength just three weeks before. By late July, only twelve of its panzers were operational, compared to 212 on June 21. The division nevertheless acquitted itself very well in the winter fighting of 1941–42.

On June 15, 1942, the division was reorganized and lost several units, including the 18th Panzer Regiment, which was disbanded. The division's only remaining tank unit was redesignated 18th Panzer Battalion. Its table of organization and equipment strength was reduced from more than 17,000 men to about 14,000. This was all academic, however; its actual strength was less than 7,000. The division, however, did receive one new unit: the 292nd Army Anti-Aircraft Battalion.

In the summer of 1942, the much-reduced division was sent to the southern sector of the Eastern Front, where it took part in the initial advances on Stalingrad, but it was soon returned to Army Group Center, with which it fought in the defensive battles of 1942–43. The 18th Panzer Division was virtually destroyed in the Battle of Kursk. It went into the battle with 5,432 combat effectives but lost 4,028 men in the next ten days. The division commander disbanded his supply and rear area units and sent their men to the front. By mid-September, the division had four panzer grenadier battalions, but they

A German commander in a half-track confers with a tank commander. Note the camouflage netting. HITM ARCHIVE

only averaged 130 men each. In autumn 1943, the 18th was fighting around Kiev, and in the fall suffered such heavy losses in the counteroffensive west of Kiev (in the Bryansk, Orscha and Vitebsk sectors) that it had to be disbanded on September 29, 1943. Low morale was a factor in this decision. Its Headquarters and its artillery were used to help form the 18th Artillery Division.

Commanders of the 18th Panzer included Major General/Lieutenant General Walter Nehring (assumed command, October 26, 1940), Major General/Lieutenant General Baron Karl von Thuengen-Rossbach (January 26, 1942), Colonel/Major General Albert Praun (July 1942), Thuengen (returned August 24, 1942), Major General Erwin Menny (September 15, 1942), Thuengen (returned at the end of 1942), and Colonel/Major General Karl Wilhelm von Schlieben (April 1, 1943).

Notes and Sources: Nehring was promoted to lieutenant general on February 1, 1942. Praun became a major general on August 1, 1942. Thuengen-Rossbach was promoted to lieutenant general on January 1, 1943. Schlieben reached the rank of major general on May 1, 1943.

Omer Bartov, *The Eastern Front, 1941–1945: German Troops and the Barbarisation of Warfare* (1986): 11, 18–21, 35; Carell 1966: 14–15, 68–69, 80, 196; Carell 1971: 26; Keilig: 223, 302, 346; Mehner, Vol. 4: 383; Vol. 5: 330; Wolfgang Paul, *Die Truppengeschichte der 18. Panzer-Division, 1940–1943 (mit 18. Artillerie-Division, 1943–1944 und Heeres-Artillerie-Brigade 88, 1944–1945)* (1989); Stoves, *Gepanzerten*: 120–24; Tessin, Vol. 6: 93–95; RA: 72; OB 42: 61; OB 43: 206; OB 45: 297.

19TH PANZER DIVISION

Composition (1943): 27th Panzer Regiment, 73rd Panzer Grenadier Regiment, 74th Panzer Grenadier Regiment, 19th Panzer Artillery Regiment, 19th Motorcycle (later Panzer Reconnaissance) Battalion, 19th Tank Destroyer Battalion, 19th Panzer Engineer Battalion, 19th Panzer Signal Battalion, 272nd Army Anti-Aircraft Battalion (added April 29, 1943), 19th Panzer Divisional Supply Troops

Home Station: Hanover, Wehrkreis XI

This division was formed on October 2, 1934, during Hitler's first military expansion and initially included the 59th, 73rd, and 74th Infantry Regiments. It was codenamed Artillery Leader VI until October 15, 1935, when it became the 19th Infantry Division. It fought in the Polish campaign of 1939 (where it suffered heavy losses at Bzurs in southern Poland) and in Belgium, against the British Expeditionary Force. It was stationed in Paris and then western France until October, when it returned to Germany and was reorganized as a panzer division. It added the 27th Panzer Regiment but gave up the 59th Infantry Regiment to the 20th Panzer Division. Sent to Russia in 1941, it fought in the Bialystok, Minsk and Smolensk encirclements, at Nevel, and in the Battle of Moscow. Losses were so heavy that two of its three panzer battalions had to be disbanded. It nevertheless remained on the central sector in the defensive battles of 1942 and was sent to the critical southern sector in late 1942.

In January 1943, it escaped to Army Group Don after the 8th Italian Army, which it had been supporting, collapsed. The division took part in the Donets battles of early 1943, the Kharkov counteroffensive of March 1943, and the Kursk offensive of July 1943, and suffered heavy casualties in these battles and in the subsequent retreats. It was fighting near Kiev in November 1943, at Zhitomir in December, and was heavily engaged in the withdrawal through the northern Ukraine in March 1944. It formed part of General Hube's "Floating Pocket" in March and April. Rushed north after Army Group Center was crushed, the 19th and two other panzer divisions surprised and destroyed the III Soviet Tank Corps north of Warsaw and thus halted the Russian summer offensive of 1944. It was cited for this action. In autumn 1944, the 19th Panzer was resisting west of the Vistula. Now at battle group strength, the division retreated through southern and eastern Poland, fought in the Baranov Bridgehead battles on January 1945, and the subsequent retreat through Warthegau, Silesia and southern Germany, and ended the war in the Deutsch-Brod pocket east of Prague.

Commanders of the 19th Infantry/Panzer Division included Major General/Lieutenant General Günther Schwentes (assumed command March 1, 1938), Major General/Lieutenant General Otto von Knobelsdorff (February 1, 1940), Colonel/Major General/Lieutenant General Gustav Schmidt (January 1, 1942), Colonel/Major General/Lieutenant General Hans Kaellner (August 18, 1943), and Major General Hans-Joachim Deckert (March 1945). Colonel Walter Denkert was acting divisional commander from March 28 until May 1944.

Notes and Sources: Schwantes was promoted to lieutenant general on June 1, 1938. Knobelsdorff reached the same rank on December 1, 1940. Gustav Schmidt was promoted to major general on April 1, 1942, and to lieutenant general on January 1, 1943. He was killed in action after he led a sizable part of the division into an ambush near Beresowka on August 7, 1943. At least one source reported that he committed suicide after he was captured. Kaellner became a major general on November 1, 1943, and a lieutenant general on June 1, 1944.

Benoist-Mechin: 133; Bradley et al., Vol. 3: 44–45, 77–79; Carell 1966: 67, 151; Carell 1971: 39, 66; Keilig: 51–52, 66, 68, 161, 175, 304, 318; Kennedy: 74. Map 7; Otto von Knobelsdorff, *Geschichte der niedersächsichen 19. Panzer-Division, 1939–1945* (1958); Manstein: 397; Mehner, Vol. 4: 383; Mellenthin 1977: 208; Tessin, Vol. 6: 114–19, 253; RA: 172; OB 42: 61; OB 43: 206; OB 44: 286; OB 45: 297; Ziemke 1966: 340.

20TH PANZER DIVISION

Composition (1943): 21st Panzer Regiment, 59th Panzer Grenadier Regiment, 112th Panzer Grenadier Regiment, 92nd Panzer Artillery Regiment, 20th Motorcycle Battalion, 92nd Panzer Reconnaissance Battalion, 92nd Tank Destroyer Battalion. 92nd Panzer Engineer Battalion, 92nd Panzer Signal Battalion, 295th Army Anti-Aircraft Battalion, 92nd Panzer Divisional Supply Troops

Home Station: Jena, Wehrkreis IX

Formed at Erfurt on October 5, 1940, when Hitler weakened the existing panzer divisions, this Hessian unit received the 59th Panzer Grenadier Regiment from the 19th Infantry Division, as well as a battalion of infantry and a battalion of artillery. It received its motorcycle battalion from the 33rd Infantry Division. The 21st Panzer Regiment drew its troops from the 7th and 35th Panzer Replacement Battalions at Vaihingen (Wehrkreis V) and Bamberg (Wehrkreis XIII), respectively. Other units came from GHQ formations. By winter, the division included the 21st Panzer Regiment (three battalions); the 20th Rifle Brigade (59th and 112th Rifle Regiments [two battalions each] and the 20th Motorcycle Battalion); the 92nd Artillery Regiment (three battalions); and assorted divisional troops. The division first saw action on the central sector of the Eastern Front, took part in the Minsk encirclement, took Vitebsk by coup de main (July 10), stormed Ulla and fought in the Battle of Smolensk (July 16–August 5). In late August it fought in the Battle of Mga and took the city, which was a major junction on the Moscow-Leningrad Railroad. Later that year, it suffered heavy losses in the Battle of Moscow and in the Soviet winter offensive of 1941–42.

Reorganized in March 1942, two of its tank battalions, an infantry battalion and its motorcycle battalion had to be dissolved due to heavy losses. The Headquarters, 20th Rifle Brigade was taken from the division in early 1943 and used to form Staff, 20th Bicycle Brigade. The Staff, 21st Panzer Regiment (which had been upgraded to a brigade headquarters, despite the fact that it only controlled one tank battalion) was also taken from the division and sent north, where it became HQ, Panzer Division Norway. The 20th Panzer Division, meanwhile, remained on the central front from 1942 to 1944, taking part in the defensive battles of 1942 and the Kursk offensive, and in the battles around Gshatsk, Orel, Toropez, Bryansk, Vitebsk, Nevel, Bobruisk, and Kholm. In June 1944, it was encircled by the massive Soviet offensive and had to fight its way out, with ruinous losses. Transferred to Army Group South Ukraine (a supposedly quiet sector), the 20th Panzer again suffered heavy casualties when the Romanians defected and the front collapsed. In November 1944 the division (or what was left of it) was in East Prussia, and the following month was transferred to the Hungarian sector. After fighting in Austria, the burned-out division was sent to Silesia. It was overrun by the Red Army in April 1945, and was pushed into Bohemia, and it ended the war surrounded in the Deutsch-Brod pocket in May 1945.

Divisional commanders of the 20th Panzer included Major General/Lieutenant General Horst Stumpff (November 13, 1940), Major General Ritter Wilhelm von Thoma (October 10, 1941), Major General Walter Duevert (July 1, 1942), Colonel/Major General/Lieutenant General Baron Heinrich von Lüttwitz (October 10, 1942), Lieutenant General Mortimer von Kessel (December 12, 1943), and Colonel/Major General Hermann von Oppeln-Bronikowski (end of October, 1944). Thoma gave up command of the division on or about May 25, 1942. The acting divisional commander between then and July 1 is not listed in the appropriate records.

Notes and Sources: Schwantes became a lieutenant general on June 1, 1938. Stumpff was promoted to lieutenant general on February 1, 1941. Heinrich von Lüttwitz was promoted to major general on December 1, 1942, and Oppeln-Bronikowski reached the same rank on January 1, 1945.

Carell 1966: 42, 78, 80; Carell 1971: 22, 24, 278, 580; Keilig: 167, 212, 247, 340; Kursietis: 103; Mehner, Vol. 3: Seite 7; Vol. 5: 330; Vol. 6: 546; Stoves, *Gepanzerten*: 138; Tessin, Vol. 6: 138-39, 162; Thomas, Vol. 1: 359; Vol. 2: 132; OB 43: 206–7; OB 44: 286; OB 45: 298; Windrow: 10–11.

21st PANZER DIVISION

Composition (Africa): 5th Panzer Regiment, 104th Panzer Grenadier Regiment, 155th Panzer Artillery Regiment, 3rd Panzer Reconnaissance Battalion, 39th Tank Destroyer Battalion, 200th Panzer Engineer Battalion, 200th Panzer Signal Battalion, 609th *Fla* [light anti-aircraft] Battalion, 200th Panzer Divisional Supply Troops

Home Station: Berlin, Wehrkreis III

Formed as the 5th Light Division in late 1940, its divisional headquarters was the former Staff, 3rd Panzer Brigade, which came from the 3rd Panzer Division. Its panzer regiment, recon battalion, tank destroyer battalion and one battalion of its artillery regiment also came from the 3rd Panzer. Sent to North Africa in April–May 1941, it joined the famous Afrika Korps, took part in the drive to Egypt and fought in the unsuccessful efforts to take Tobruk. That summer it received the 104th Panzer Grenadier Regiment from the 15th Panzer Division and was redesignated 21st Panzer Division effective August 1, 1941. It fought in the Battleaxe and Crusader campaigns (where it lost most of its tanks), the retreat from Cyrenaica in 1941, and the subsequent counterattack which retook Benghazi (January 1942). It then again showed its excellent fighting abilities in overrunning the Gazala Line, in the capture of Tobruk, and in the sweep into Egypt. Checked at El Alamein and Alam Halfa Ridge, it was virtually destroyed in the Second Battle of El Alamein in October and November 1942, having only twelve tanks left when the order came to retreat. Withdrawing across Libya, it did not panic and turned to help administer the U.S. Army a notable defeat at Kasserine Pass. It was finally destroyed in the fall of Tunisia in May 1943.

A second 21st Panzer Division was formed in Rennes, France, in mid-1943. It was built around the 931st Mobile Brigade (a bicycle unit). It included a number of Afrika Korps veterans but was equipped with unreliable light tanks, mostly of foreign manufacture. Initially it was designated Mobile Division West but was renamed the 21st Panzer Division on July 15. It was, however, the only panzer division in France to be rated as unfit for service on the Eastern Front. The composition of the second 21st Panzer Division included the 22nd Panzer Regiment, the 125th and 192nd Panzer Grenadier Regiments, the 21st Panzer Reconnaissance Battalion, the 220th Panzer Engineer Battalion, the 200th Panzer Signal Battalion, and the 305th Army Anti-Aircraft Battalion.

The new 21st Panzer Division was sent to Hungary in April 1944 (when that country seemed ready to defect from the Axis), but was hurried back to Normandy in May. It was the only panzer division to counterattack the Allies on D-Day (although it struck hours later than it should have) and more than fifty of its second-rate tanks were destroyed by the British, while inflicting little damage on the invaders. Although its panzer regiment was smashed, its grenadiers fought doggedly in front of Caen for weeks. At battle group strength, the 21st Panzer nevertheless saved the 326th Infantry Division from being overrun by the British in late July. It was encircled at Falaise in August but broke out with heavy losses. When the Normandy campaign began on June 6, 1944, the 21st Panzer Division had 12,350 men, 127 tanks, and forty assault guns. When it finally retreated across the Seine at the end of August, it had lost all of its armored vehicles and assault guns, and had only 300 combat effectives left. After the retreat through France, it was sent back to Lothringen (Lorraine) and hastily rebuilt, absorbing the 112th Panzer Brigade and many low-quality replacements. It was assigned to Army Group G, where it served as a "fire brigade" on the southern sector of the Western Front. It fought in the Saar and, in January 1945, was involved on the drive on Strasbourg and the fighting in northern Alsace, before being sent to the Eastern Front in February. By this time, it had only one tank battalion left. The division fought in the unsuccessful defenses of Lauban, Goerlitz and Cottbus, and ended the war in the Halbe Pocket near Berlin, where the bulk of the 9th Army was destroyed. Most of its survivors ended up in Soviet prisons, although a few managed to escape and join the 12th Army, which surrendered to the Americans in May.

Commanders of the 5th Light/21st Panzer included Major General Baron Hans von Funck (assumed command early 1941), Major General Karl Boettcher (February 1, 1941), Lieutenant General Johannes Streich (February 7, 1941), Major General Baron Johannes von Ravenstein (May 20, 1941), Lieutenant Colonel Gustav-Georg Knabe (November 28, 1941), Boettcher again (November 29, 1941), Colonel Alfred Bruer (early 1942), Colonel/Major General Georg von Bismarck (February 19, 1942), Major General Hans von Randow (September 1, 1942), Colonel Baron Kurt von Liebenstein (October 25, 1942), Colonel/Major General Hans Georg Hildebrandt (January 1, 1943), Colonel/Major General Heinrich-Hermann

A StuG assault gun (left), armed with a long-barreled gun, and a half-track personnel carrier. HITM ARCHIVE

von Huelsen (March 15, 1943), Colonel/Major General/Lieutenant General Edgar Feuchlinger (July 1943), Colonel Helmut Zollenkof (December 25, 1944), and Major General/Lieutenant General Werner Marcks (January 10, 1945). Major Generals Oswin Grolig and Franz Westhoven and Colonel Hans von Luck also deputized for Feuchtinger briefly at various times for short periods in 1944.

Notes and Sources: Lieutenant General Streich and General Erwin Rommel had a mutual distaste for one another, which led to Rommel's relieving Streich of his command for his failure to take Tobruk in May 1941. Ravenstein was captured by the New Zealanders on November 28, 1941, during the Crusader battles. Georg von Bismarck was promoted to major general on March 1, 1942. He was killed near Alma Haifa Ridge on September 1, 1942. Liebenstein was simultaneously commander of the 164th Light Afrika Division. Hildebrandt and Huelsen were promoted to major general on March 1 and May 1, 1943, respectively. Huelsen was captured on May 12, 1943, when Tunisia fell. Feuchtinger was promoted to major general on August 1, 1943, and to lieutenant general on August 1, 1944. He was arrested for being away without leave on Christmas Eve, 1944. Marcks was promoted to lieutenant general on April 20, 1945. He was captured in the Halbe Pocket and remained in Soviet prisons until 1955.

Blumenson 1960: 324; Bradley et al., Vol. 1: 417–18; Vol. 2: 99–101; Vol. 3: 457–58; Vol. 5: 427–28; Chant, Volume 17: 2277; Cole 1950: 553; Carlo D'Este, *Decision in Normandy* (1983): 140, 475n (hereafter cited as "D'Este, Normandy"); Hartmann: 66–67; Keilig: 35–36, 141, 217, 267, 269, 337; Mehner, Vol. 4: 383; Vol. 5: 330; Vol. 6: 546; Vol. 7: 354, 359; Mitcham 2001: 157–63; Scheibert: 419; Schmitz et al., Vol. 3: 185; Tessin, Vol. 2: 294–95; Thomas, Vol. 2: 59; OB 45: 298. Also see Carell 1970.

22ND PANZER DIVISION

Composition: 204th Panzer Regiment, 129th Panzer Grenadier Regiment, 140th Panzer Grenadier Regiment, 140th Panzer Artillery Regiment, 24th Motorcycle Battalion, 140th Tank Destroyer Battalion, 140th Panzer Engineer Battalion, 140th Panzer Signal Battalion, 289th Army Anti-Aircraft Battalion (added, 1942), 140th Panzer Divisional Supply Troops

Home Station: Schwetzingen, later Neustadt and Heidelberg, Wehrkreis XII

The 22nd Panzer Division was activated in France on September 25, 1941. Initially, it consisted of the 204th Panzer Regiment, the 22nd Rifle Brigade (129th and 140th Rifle Regiments and the 24th Motorcycle Battalion), the 140th Panzer Artillery Regiment, and assorted divisional units. The division's formations were equipped largely with captured foreign material or obsolete German equipment. The 204th Panzer Regiment, for example, included mainly French tanks, Czech-made Skoda 38(t)s, and obsolete PzKw IIs and IVs. Some PzKw IIIs were added later. The flak battalion, with its self-propelled 88mm guns, was much better equipped than the rest of the division. Sent to the Crimea on the Eastern Front in February 1942, this green division was mauled in the Battle of Parpach on March 20. Two months later, however, it broke through the Soviet 10th Army on the Kerch peninsula and sealed the fate of ten Red Army divisions. It fought at Rostov in July, and in November 1942, it attempted unsuccessfully to prevent the encirclement of the 6th Army. In December 1942, it retreated to the Don, and then on to the Chir. In December, the 22nd Panzer had ninety-six tanks left; by March 1943, this number had dropped to thirty-one and most of these were not up to standards mechanically; in fact, Field Marshal von Manstein called the division "a complete wreck." It was probably on his recommendation that the 22nd Panzer was ordered to disband on March 4, 1943. This order was carried out by April 7. Much of the division was absorbed by the 27th Panzer Division; the rest was transferred to the 6th and 23rd Panzer Divisions.

Commanders of the 22nd Panzer Division were Major General Wilhelm von Apell (September 23, 1941), Colonel Rudolf Kuett (October 1, 1942), Colonel Hellmuth von der Chevallerie (October 7, 1942), and Colonel/Major General Eberhard Rodt (November 8, 1942).

Notes and Sources: Rodt was promoted to major general on March 1, 1943.

Bradley et al., Vol. 1: 81-82; Vol. 2: 423–24; Carell 1966: 482, 486, 535, 620–21, 650; Keilig: 12, 192; Kursietis: 105; Manstein: 322, 389; Mehner, Vol. 5: 330; Vol. 6: 546; Scheibert: 63; Rolf Stoves, *Die 22./25./27. Panzer-Divisionen und die 233. Reserve Panzer-Division* (1985): ff. 1; Tessin, Vol. 6: 179–80; OB 42: 62; OB 45: 207, 299.

23RD PANZER DIVISION

Composition (1943): 23rd (formerly 201st) Panzer Regiment, 126th Panzer Grenadier Regiment, 128th Panzer Grenadier Regiment, 128th Panzer Artillery Regiment, 128th Panzer Reconnaissance Battalion, 128th Tank Destroyer Battalion, 51st Panzer Engineer Battalion, 128th Panzer Signal Battalion, 278th Army Anti-Aircraft Battalion, 128th Field Replacement Battalion, 128th Panzer Divisional Supply Troops

Home Station: Ludwigsburg, later Reutlingen, Wehrkreis V

The 23rd Panzer Division was activated near Paris on September 21, 1941. It absorbed Colonel Wolfgang Elster's 101st Panzer Brigade (203rd and 204th *Beute* Panzer Regiment.s) of the 1st Army. (A *Beute-Panzer-Regiment* was one outfitted almost solely with captured foreign weapons and equipment—in this case French equipment.) The new division consisted mainly of Wuerttemburgers and included the 23rd Rifle Brigade (126th and 128th Rifle Regiment.s and the 23rd Motorcycle Battalion), the 128th Panzer Artillery Regiment and the usual compliment divisional troops. The following spring (after being reequipped with German tanks) it was sent to the Russian Front. It fought in the fierce battles for Kharkov (May 1942) and in the drives across the Don and Terek Rivers, toward the Caucasus oilfields. In the fall of 1942, it was sent north, to the Volga, and narrowly escaped encirclement near Stalingrad that November. It took part in the 4th Panzer Army's attempt to relieve the city but was unsuccessful.

By January 1943, it was down to twenty tanks—about 15 percent of its original strength. It nevertheless took part in the retreat to the Don (December 12, 1942–February 11, 1943), in the fighting in the Donetz (February 14–March 4, 1943), and in the retreat to the Mius River (March 5–31, 1943). By now, it had proven itself as an excellent combat division. During its first year in Russia, the 23rd Panzer Division had lost more than 90 percent of its armor, but destroyed at least six times as many Soviet tanks. Placed in the new 6th Army's reserve at Odessa in the spring of 1943, it was hastily and only partially rebuilt, because it was needed back at the front. The 23rd Panzer was involved in the Mius withdrawal that summer and was heavily engaged in the battles of the Dnieper Bend in autumn. In February 1944 it was cited for its conduct in the fighting west of the river, where it was encircled in March. Breaking out with heavy losses, the 23rd Panzer was at battle group strength thereafter. It was nevertheless used as a fire brigade at such widely separated points as Krivoy Rog, the Crimea, the Nikopol Bridgehead, the Bug River, northern Bessarabia and the Carpathian Mountains.

It fought in Poland in the fall of 1944 and was transferred to Hungary after the disaster in Romania. It led 8th Army's counterattack on Nyiregyhaza (October 23–29, 1944) and took the town, destroying or causing the abandonment of about 600 Soviet tanks—a major German victory for the fifth year of the war. The 23rd Panzer also took part in the counterattack west of Debrecen and was again cited for distinguished conduct in the battles around Puszta. A large part of the division was trapped in the medieval town of Szekesfehervar (Stuhlweissenburg), when the 6th Army's front in Hungary collapsed, and was destroyed there in March 1945. The remnants of the 23rd Panzer Division fought in the Battle of Lake Balaton and were still fighting in the Steiermark sector of Austria when the war ended. The division managed to disengage from the Red Army, however, and surrendered to the British 5th Northampton Regiment at Mauterndorf on May 10, 1945. Its strength at that time as 2,000 men—about one-sixth of what it was in 1942. During its combat career, the 23rd Panzer Division lost 7,476 men killed, approximately 20,921 wounded, and 2,883 captured or missing. It destroyed 2,672 Soviet tanks and assault guns during the same period. By any measurement, it was an excellent division.

Commanders of the 23rd Panzer included Major General/Lieutenant General Baron Hans von Boineburg-Lengsfeld (November 1, 1941), Major General Erwin Mack (July 20, 1942), Colonel Fritz von Buch (August 1942), Colonel Erich Brueckner (September 1942), Boineburg-Lengsfeld again (September

1942), Colonel Josef Rossmann (December 1942), Colonel/Major General/Lieutenant General Nikolaus von Vormann (December 26, 1942), Colonel/Major General Ewald Kraeber (October 25, 1943), Colonel Heinz-Joachim Werner-Ehrenfeucht (November 1, 1943), Kraeber (returned November 18, 1943), and Colonel/Major General/Lieutenant General Josef von Radowitz (June 6, 1944–end).

Notes and Sources: Baron von Boineburg-Lengsfeld was relieved of his command for a security violation, for which he was indeed guilty. His successor, General Mack, was killed in action in the Caucasus sector on August 26, 1942. Boineburg was given a second chance to command the division in late August 1942. He made the most of it and even earned a promotion to lieutenant general (December 1, 1942). Shortly thereafter, he was accidently run over by one of his own tanks, ending his career as a field commander and almost his life. Vormann was promoted to major general on January 1, 1943, and to lieutenant general on July 1, 1943. Kraeber was promoted to major general on January 1, 1944. Radowitz became a major general on September 1, 1944, and a lieutenant general on March 1, 1945.

Bradley et al., Vol. 2: 127; Carell 1966: 491, 512, 550; Chant, Volume 15: 2057; Clark: 266; Edwards, *Panzer*: 76–77; Hartmann: 68; Keilig: 44, 214, 266, 358, 368; *Kriegstagebuch des OKW*, Volume III: 258; Manstein: 330; Mehner, Vol. 4: 383; Vol. 5: 330; Vol. 6: 546; Mitcham, 2001: 168–73; Ernst Rebentisch, *Zum Kaukasus und zu den Tauern: Die Geschichte der 23. Panzer-Division, 1941–1945* (1963): ff. 1; Seaton: 494; Tessin, Vol. 6: 195–96; RA: 72; OB 42: 62–63; OB 45: 299.

24TH PANZER DIVISION

Composition (1945): 24th Panzer Regiment, 21st Panzer Grenadier Regiment, 26th Panzer Grenadier Regiment, 89th Panzer Artillery Regiment, 24th Panzer Reconnaissance Battalion, 40th Tank Destroyer Battalion, 40th Panzer Engineer Battalion, 86th Panzer Signal Battalion, 283rd Army Anti-Aircraft Battalion, 89th Field Replacement Battalion, 40th Panzer Divisional Supply Troops

Home Station: Frankfurt-on-the-Oder, Wehrkreis III

Originally this was the 1st Cavalry Division of the German Army—the only cavalry division it had when the war broke out.

The division was created in late 1939, from the 1st Cavalry Brigade, which had fought in Poland. The 1st Cavalry Division took part in the Western campaign of 1940, during which it overran most of the Netherlands. The division also did very well in Russia in 1941, fighting at the Dnieper crossings and at Smolensk, and protecting the southern flank of Guderian's 2nd Panzer Army from Russian attacks out of the Pripyet marshes. It was transferred back to eastern France in the winter of 1941 and converted to a panzer unit. The 1st Cavalry Division's colors were retired in on November 28, 1941, an event that was considered historic. Meanwhile, the 24th Panzer returned to Russia in June 1942, was attached to the 6th Army for the summer offensive, and was encircled in the Stalingrad Pocket in November. It was destroyed there in early 1943.

A new 24th Panzer was organized in Normandy in March-April 1943, under Headquarters, 15th Army. It abosrbed the 891st Panzer Grenadier Regiment from Wehrkreis IX and the 127th Panzer Signal Battalion from the 27th Panzer Division. Sent to northern Italy in August, it was transferred to the Russian Front as winter approached. It fought in the Battle of Kiev in November, where it suffered heavy casualties. By December, its II/24th Panzer Regiment had suffered so many casualties that it had to be dissolved. In February 1944, the 24th participated in the Cherkassy relief operation, for which it was officially cited. The following month it again sustained heavy losses in the withdrawal from the lower Dnieper bend. By July 1944, the remains of the division were fighting in southern Poland at battle group strength. Transferred to the Hungarian sector, the 24th Panzer Division took part in the counterattack west of Debrecen and took heavy casualties in the unsuccessful defense of Kecskemet. Sent north again, the 24th Panzer Division fought the Russians in Slovakia, Poland, and East Prussia. By January 1945, the only extant combat units left to the division were two tank companies (equipped with Tigers), the 21st Panzer Grenadier Regiment, and the 40th Tank Destroyer Battalion. The 9th Grenadier Regiment (three battalions) of the 23rd Infantry Division was attached to the division in March and remained with it until the end of the war. The division was evacuated by sea to northern Germany in April 1945, and surrendered to the British in Schleswig-Holstein in May 1945.

Commanders of the 1st Cavalry/24th Panzer Division included Colonel/Major General/Lieutenant General Kurt Feldt (October 25, 1939), Major General Bruno Ritter von Hauenschild (April 15, 1942), Major General/Lieutenant General Arno von Lenski (September 12, 1942), Major General/Lieutenant General Reichsfreiherr (Reichsbaron) Maximillian von Edelsheim (March 1, 1943), and Colonel/Major General Gustav-Adolf von Noslilz-Wallwitz (August 1, 1944), and Colonel Rudolf von Knebel-Doeberitz (March 27, 1945).

Notes and Sources: Feldt was promoted to major general on February 1, 1940, and to lieutenant general on February 1, 1942. Lenski was promoted to lieutenant general on January 1, 1943. He surrendered the survivors of the 24th Panzer Division to the Russians at Stalingrad on February 2, 1943, along with parts of the 389th Infantry Division. Edelsheim became a lieutenant general on March 1, 1944. Nostitz-Wallwitz was promoted to major general on November 9, 1944. He was killed in action on March 25, 1945. Knebel-Doeberitz normally commanded the division's artillery regiment.

Bradley et al., Vol. 3: 277–78; Vol. 5: 181–82; Carell 1966: 83, 521, 585; Hartmann: 69–70; Richard Hauschild, *Der springende Reiter—1. Kavallerie-Division—24th Panzer-Division im Bild* (1984); Kennedy: 10B, 69, Map 7; Kursietis: 107; Manstein: 139, 143, 487, 525; Mellenthin 1956: 225; Seaton: 336; Ferdinand von Senger und Etterlin, *Die 24. Panzer-Division vormal 1. Kavallerie-Division, 1939–1945* (1962); Scheibert: 193; Tessin, Vol. 2: 35–36; Vol. 4: 211–12; OB 42: 63; OB 45: 300.

25TH PANZER DIVISION

Composition (1943): 9th Panzer Regiment, 146th Panzer Grenadier Regiment, 147th Panzer Grenadier Regiment, 91st Panzer Artillery Regiment, 87th Motorcycle Battalion, 87th Tank Destroyer Battalion, 87th Panzer Engineer Battalion, 87th Panzer Signal Battalion, 279th Army Anti-Aircraft Battalion, 87th Field Replacement Battalion, 87th Panzer Divisional Supply Troops

Home Station: Wuppertal, Wehrkreis VI

The Rhinelander-Westphalian 25th Panzer was formed in Norway on February 25, 1942, from the understrength Rifle Verbaend Oslo, for a possible invasion of Sweden. A full panzer division was not considered necessary to accomplish this task, so the 25th Panzer was well below strength until August 1943, when it was transferred to northern France via Oslo and Copenhagen. Soon it was on its way to Russia, where it fought on the central and southern sectors for two and a half years, with only one major respite. It suffered heavy losses—largely due to inexperience—in the Kiev battles of October and November 1943 It nevertheless played a significant role in sealing off a major Soviet breakthrough east of Fastov (southwest of Kiev), and in counterattacks against the Kiev salient, and in the battles of Vinnitsa, Proskurov, Chortkov and Stanislav.

By January 1944, the 25th Panzer Division had suffered such serious losses that the 147th Panzer Grenadier Regiment had been absorbed by its sister regiment; its remaining tank battalion and its tank destroyer battalion had been virtually wiped out; and its artillery regiment had the strength of a weak battalion. It also took severe casualties in the withdrawal across the northern Ukraine in March 1944, when it and the rest of the 1st Panzer Army was encircled in the "Hube Pocket" (also called the Kamenetz-Podolsk Pocket). Sent to Denmark to reform in April, the 25th Panzer returned to the Eastern Front in September and helped defend the Vistula River line in Poland. It fought in Pomerania and was also engaged in the defense of Warsaw in January 1945. It retreated across Pomerania, fought on the Oder and at Muencheberg in March. In April 1945, it was sent to Vienna, along with the Fuhrer Grenadier Division. The move cost Army Group Vistula half its armor on the eve of the Battle of Berlin, and its armor was weak already. The 25th Panzer, for example, was a mere battle group by this time. Its 146th Grenadier Regiment had only 1,000 men, its panzer regiment and tank destroyer battalion had only forty-five tanks and assault guns, and its artillery regiment had only sixteen guns. The 25th, however, did not fight in the Battle of Vienna, but was sent north, to defend the Austrian oilfields. At the end of the war, it was on the lower Danube in Austria. It surrendered to the Americans but, along with the Fuehrer Grenadier Division and the 3rd SS Panzer Division "Totenkopf," was turned over to the Russians.

The 25th Panzer's divisional commanders included Lieutenant General Johann Haarde (February 25, 1942), Lieutenant General Adolf von Schell (January 1, 1943), Major General/Lieutenant General Hans Troeger (November 20, 1943), Major General Oswin Grolig (January 15, 1944), and Colonel/Major General Dipl. Ing. Oskar Audoersch (August 19, 1944–end).

Notes and Sources: Troeger was promoted to lieutenant general on April 1, 1944. Audoersch was promoted to major general on November 9, 1944.

Bradley et al., Vol. 1: 119; Vol. 4: 432–33; Vol. 5: 6–7; Chant, Volume 17: 2277; Hartmann: 70–71; Keilig: 115, 120, 296; Kursietis: 107; Manstein: 488; Mellenthin 1977: 207–8; Tessin, Vol. 4: 226–27; Vol. 14: 193; RA: 100; OB 43: 208; OB 45: 301; Ziemke 1966: 469.

26TH PANZER DIVISION

Composition (1943): 202nd (later 26th) Panzer Regiment, 9th Panzer Grenadier Regiment, 67th Panzer Grenadier Regiment, 93rd Panzer Artillery Regiment, 26th Panzer Reconnaissance Battalion, 26th Motorcycle Battalion, 51st Tank Destroyer Battalion, 93rd Panzer Engineer Battalion, 93rd Panzer Signal Battalion, 304th Army Anti-Aircraft Battalion, 93rd Panzer Divisional Supply Troops

Home Station: Potsdam, Wehrkreis III

A "first-wave" unit from the Brandenburg/Berlin area, this division originally bore the title 23rd Infantry Division and was formed by the expansion of cadres of the historic 9th Infantry ("Potsdam") Regiment in 1934–35, adopting much of the tradition of the old Imperial Guards. During World War II, it lived up to its ancestor unit's reputation as a fine combat unit. It was officially activated on October 15, 1935. The 23rd Infantry was lightly engaged in Poland (in the northeast or

Pomeranian sector), fought in France in 1940, spent the winter in East Prussia, and invaded Russia in 1941. It crossed the Dnieper with the 2nd Panzer Army on the central sector and fought at Bialystok, Minsk and Smolensk. It took part in the Siege of Mogilev on the Dnieper from July 20–26, where it lost more than 1,000 men, and in the defensive battle of Vjasma (September–October). The 23rd Infantry pushed on to the gates of Moscow, suffering heavy casualties along the way. By January 1942, it had barely 1,000 infantrymen left, and its nine infantry battalions were consolidated into three because of casualties. The divisional artillery was down to one 50mm antitank gun and three howitzers. It was surrounded south of Fedorovka by the Soviet winter offensive of 1941–42.

Relieved, the 23rd Infantry remained on the central sector around Gshatsk until summer 1942, when it was sent to Amiens, France, to reform as the 26th Panzer Division, which it became on September 14, 1942. The new unit trained in France for about a year before being sent to Italy in August 1943. It remained on this front for the rest of the war, fighting in the Anzio counterattacks, the battles of the Gustav Line, on the Arno, and in the retreat up the peninsula to the Gothic Line. Meanwhile, it absorbed the 1027th Reinforced Grenadier Regiment in June and the remnants of the 20th Luftwaffe Field Division in November. In November the division was cited for distinguished action between the Apennines and the Adriatic. It defended a sector of the Adriatic in early 1945 and fought its last battle south of the Po River in April. Stopped by one of Hitler's senseless orders, the 26th Panzer (and the bulk of the LXXVI Panzer Corps) were unable to retreat behind the Po. Caught between the river and the Apennines, it was destroyed by the Allied armies. Only a few men managed to swim across the Po and escape. The division lost all of its tanks and vehicles and virtually ceased to exist. The remnants of the 26th Panzer Division surrendered near Bozen, Italy, on May 2, 1945.

Commanders of the 23rd Infantry/26th Panzer Division included Lieutenant General Ernst Busch (October 15, 1935), Major General Count Erich von Brockdorff-Ahlefeld (March 1,

The crew of a Panzer Mark II (PzKw II). This photograph seems to have been taken at the Panzer Troops School at Wuensdorf on August 5, 1938. The PzKw II was markedly inferior to later model German tanks and had been relegated to the status of a reconnaissance vehicle by 1942. HITM ARCHIVE

1938), Major General Heinz Hellmich (June 1, 1940), Colonel/Major General Kurt Badinski (January 17, 1942), Colonel/Major General/Lieutenant General Baron Smilo von Lüttwitz (July 14, 1942), Colonel Hans Hecker (January 22, 1944), Lüttwitz (returned February 20, 1944), Colonel/Major General Eduard Crasemann (July 6, 1944), Major General Dr. Hans Boelsen (July 19, 1944), Crasemann (August 26, 1944), Colonel Alfred Kuhnert (January 29, 1945), and Major General/Lieutenant General Viktor Linnarz (March 1, 1945).

Notes and Sources: Smilo von Lüttwitz became a major general on September 1, 1942, and a lieutenant general on October 1, 1943. Crasemann was promoted to major general on October 1, 1944. Linnarz became a lieutenant general on April 1, 1945.

Blumenson 1969: 289, 419; Bradley et al., Vol. 1: 153–54, 474–75; Vol. 2: 85–86; Vol. 5: 221–22; Carell 1966: 80, 85–86, 181, 184; Fisher: 19, 82, 302, 498; Garland and Smyth: 75; Keilig: 52, 62, 193, 212; Kennedy: 74; Mehner, Vol. 5: 330; Georg Staiger, *26. Panzer-Division: Ihr Werden und Einsatz, 1942–1945* (1958); Tessin, Vol. 4: 192–93; RA: 46; OB 43: 208; OB 45: 147, 301. Also see Seaton: 232.

27TH PANZER DIVISION

Composition: 127th Panzer Battalion, 140th Panzer Grenadier Regiment, 127th Panzer Artillery Regiment, 127th Tank Destroyer Battalion, 127th Panzer Engineer Battalion, 127th Panzer Signal Battalion, 127th Divisional Supply Troops

Home Station: Heidelberg, Wehrkreis XII

The 27th Panzer Division was apparently formed in two echelons—part of the divisional base (including the artillery regiment) was formed in France in the summer and autumn of 1942 and then was sent to Voronezh, Russia, in the rear area of the 2nd Army. Here it was joined by Brigade Michalik—which mainly consisted of the 140th Panzer Grenadier Regiment (formerly of the 22nd Panzer Division)—to form the 27th Panzer Division, which was activated on October 1, 1942. The new division's total strength was slightly less than 3,000 men. It was nevertheless broken up into as many as seven battle groups and was scattered over the entire southern sector of the Eastern Front. The 127th Panzer Engineer Battalion was trapped and destroyed at Stalingrad and never joined the rest of the unit. Other elements of the new division fought on the Don, in the retreat from Stalingrad, and in the battles south of Kharkov. Still other parts were attached to the Hungarian 2nd Army and the Italian 8th Army. By January 1, 1943, the division had lost half of its grenadiers and only had eleven tanks left (excluding twenty which had been appropriated by Headquarters, 2nd Army.) By February 8, the division's estimated strength was 1,590. The 27th Panzer Division was disbanded on or about March 3, 1943, after the Soviet winter offensive of 1942–43 had been stopped. Most of its equipment and survivors were absorbed by the 7th Panzer Division, although the men of the 127th Panzer and 127th Panzer Signal Battalions were sent to France and assigned to the 24th Panzer Division.

The commanders of the 27th Panzer Division were Colonel Helmut Michalik (October 1, 1942), Colonel/Major General Hans Troeger (November 30, 1942), and Colonel Joachim von Kronhelm (January 26, 1943).

Notes and Sources: Troeger was promoted to major general on January 1, 1943.

Kriegstagebuch des OKW, Volume II: 1387, 1394; Mehner, Vol. 5: 330; Vol. 6: 546; Stoves, *Die 22. Panzer-Division*: 195–262, 301; Tessin, Vol. 4: 253; Vol. 6: 319; Vol. 10: 93; OB 43: 209; OB 45: 302.

116TH PANZER (FORMERLY 16TH PANZER GRENADIER) DIVISION

Composition (1943): 16th Panzer Regiment, 60th Panzer Grenadier Regiment, 156th Panzer Grenadier Regiment, 146th Panzer Artillery Regiment, 59th Motorcycle Battalion, 116th (formerly 341st) Panzer Reconnaissance Battalion, 146th Tank Destroyer Battalion, 146th Motorized Engineer Battalion, 228th Motorized Signal Battalion, 281st Army Anti-Aircraft Battalion, 66th Panzer Divisional Supply Troops

Home Station: Wuppertal, Wehrkreis VI

This division was created on August 6, 1940, when the 16th Infantry Division was divided. Most of the old division (including the divisional headquarters) was used to form the 16th Panzer Division, which was destroyed at Stalingrad. The rest was used to form what successively became the 16th Motorized Division, the 16th Panzer Grenadier Division, and the 116th Panzer Division. The new 16th Motorized Division received the 60th Infantry Regiment from the 16th Infantry and its other units from the 4th Infantry Division and VI Military District. Its headquarters was the former HQ, 228th Infantry Division. By the fall of 1940, it included the 60th and 156th Motorized Regiments, the 146th Artillery Regiment and various divisional troops. It was sent to western France in November 1940, to complete its unit training.

It was hurriedly sent to Hungary in March 1941, and took part in the invasion of Yugoslavia the following month. It fought in the battles in the Ukraine in 1941, helping to break the Stalin Line in July, in the Battle of Kiev, and in the drive on Moscow. It spent the winter of 1941–42 fighting in the vicinity of Kursk. The following June, it added the 116th Panzer Battalion (formerly I/1st Panzer Regiment) to its table of organization. The division was transferred back to the southern sector in 1942, fighting in the Battle of Voronezh and in the drive to the Caucasus before being shifted north, to cover the large gap between the 1st and 4th Panzer armies in the vast wilderness south of Stalingrad. The recon battalion penetrated to within twenty miles of Astrakhan, the furthest eastward advance of any German unit during the entire war. The 16th Panzer Grenadier fought against the Russians in the winter of 1942–43, before being transferred to the newly reconstituted 6th Army in the spring of 1943. It did not take part in the Battle of Kursk but did fight in the retreat to the Mius, suffering heavy casualties in the fighting around Zaporozhe. It also fought in the battles of Taganrog, Krivoy Rog, Novo, Uman and others. The following spring it bore very heavy losses in the withdrawal from the lower Dnieper, after which the remnants of the 16th Panzer Grenadier were then transported to France, where they were merged with the much larger 179th Reserve Panzer Division to form the 116th Panzer Division. The new division was on the north bank of the Seine on D-Day (in the Pas de Calais zone) but was not committed to action until late July. It fought in the counterattack at Mortain in August but was unable to halt the American breakout or the encirclement of the 5th Panzer and 7th Armies. The 116th was surrounded at Falaise and broke out with heavy losses.

The Greyhound Division—as the 116th Panzer was nicknamed—was down to 600 men, twelve tanks, and no artillery by August 21, 1944. In mid-September it was in action at Aachen when its divisional commander, Lieutenant General Count Gerhard von Schwerin-Krosigk, was relieved of his command by Hitler for ordering an unauthorized retreat from the city. Hitler's decision led to bloody street fighting in Aachen, but seems to have been the tactically correct one this time, for it significantly delayed the American advance into western Germany. Meanwhile, the 116th Panzer was withdrawn to the Dusseldorf area to reform in September and October 1944 and was reinforced to a strength of 11,500 men, but still had a total of only forty-one tanks. The division was sent to Cologne, fought at Aachen in October and in the Huertgen Forest in November, where it inflicted heavy casualties upon the Americans. It took part in Hitler's Ardennes offensive in December 1944, and suffered heavy losses. Withdrawn to Kleve in January 1945, the 116th Panzer was in action in the Netherlands in February, trying unsuccessfully to halt the British and Canadian advance on Germany. The division was almost trapped in the Wesel Pocket (on the western bank of the Rhine) on March 5, but managed to escape, blowing up the bridge behind it. Shifted south in the spring, most of the 116th Panzer was encircled and destroyed in the Battle of the Ruhr Pocket. One battle group, however, had been sent to the 11th Army in central Germany and thus escaped the debacle. It fought on the Elbe and surrendered to the Americans at the end of the war.

Commanders of the 16th Infantry/16th Motorized/16th Panzer Grenadier/116th Panzer Division included Colonel/ Major General/ Lieutenant General Gerhard Glokke (April 1, 1934), Major General/Lieutenant General Gotthard Heinrici (October 1, 1937), Major General Heinrich Krampf (February 6, 1940), Major General Hans Valentin Hube (May 17, 1940), Lieutenant General Friedrich Wilhelm von Chappuis (August 8, 1940), Major General/Lieutenant General Sigfrid Henrici (March 16, 1941), Lieutenant General Johannes Streich (August 13, 1941), Henrici (resumed command, November 12, 1941), Major General/Lieutenant General Count Gerhard von Schwerin (November 13, 1942), Colonel Wilhelm Crisolli (May 20, 1943), Schwerin (returned June 27, 1943), Colonel Günther von Manteuffel (February 10, 1944), Colonel Heinrich Voigtsberger (March 15, 1944), Colonel Dr. Ernst Pean (March 20, 1944), Schwerin (returned April, 1944), Voigtsberger (September 1, 1944), and Colonel/Major General Siegfried von Waldenburg (September 14, 1944–end).

Notes and Sources: The 16th Motorized Division was officially redesignated the 16th Panzer Grenadier Division on June 23, 1943. Sigfrid Henrici was promoted to lieutenant general on June 1, 1941. Gerhard von Schwerin was promoted to lieutenant general on June 1, 1943. He was relieved of his command in September 1944, for attempting to evacuate Aachen against Hitler's orders. (For once, Hitler was right both to order the position held and to sack a general.)

Blumenson 1960: 296, 505, 539–49, 577, 579; Bradley et al., Vol. 2: 420–21; Vol. 5: 327–29; Carell 1966: 119, 521, 550–56; Carell 1971: 134; Chant, Volume 14: 1859–61; Volume 16: 2133; Cole 1965: 195; Harrison: Map VI; Hartmann: 71–72; Keilig: 133, 136, 216, 232, 335, 361; Kennedy: 74, Map 7; MacDonald 1963: 82, 282, 284; MacDonald 1973: 140, 357, 370; Mehner, Vol. 3: 381; Vol. 6: 543; Vol. 7: 353; Fritz Memminger, *Die Kriegsgeschichte der Windhund-Division—16. Infanterie-Division (mot.), 16. Panzergrenadier-Division, 116. Panzer-Division* (1962), 3 volumes; Schmitz et al., Vol. 3: 207–15, 225-35; Speidel: 42; Tessin, Vol. 4: 30–32; RA: 100; OB 42: 64; OB 43: 191–92, 205; OB 45: 302.

(130TH) PANZER LEHR DIVISION

Composition: 130th Panzer Lehr Regiment, 901st Panzer Lehr Grenadier Regiment, 902nd Panzer Lehr Grenadier Regiment, 130th Panzer Lehr Artillery Regiment, 130th Panzer Lehr Reconnaissance Battalion, 130th Tank Destroyer Battalion, 130th Panzer Lehr Engineer Battalion, 130th Panzer Signal Battalion, 311th Army Panzer Anti-Aircraft Battalion

Home Station: Wehrkreis III

The Panzer Lehr was formed on January 10, 1944, in the Nancy-Verdun area of France, from the Demonstration (*Lehr*) units of the training school at Krampnitz, the Potsdam War School, the training units in the Bergen Maneuver Area, Wehrkreis XI, and elements of the recently disbanded 137th Infantry Division. Its staff was from the School for Mobile Troops at Krampnitz. It was especially designed to repel the Western Allies' invasion of 1944. The new division was hurriedly sent to Hungary in early 1944, when it appeared that country might attempt to defect from the Axis. While there, the division incorporated the 901st Infantry Lehr Regiment (which had been operating as an independent formation in the Balkans) into its ranks.

In the spring of 1944, after the political situation in Hungary had more or less stabilized, Panzer Lehr returned to France. It was camped in the Orleans area in May 1944, and in the LeMans area in early June. When the Allied invasion came, the Panzer Lehr Division was one of the strongest divisions in the German Army, with 109 tanks, forty assault guns, and 612 half-tracked vehicles—double the normal panzer division's component of half-tracks. The division was rushed to Normandy and thrown into the Battle of Caen, where it helped halt Montgomery's advance, but at a terrible cost. On June 25 it had only sixty-six tanks left, and by July 25 its combined tank/assault gun total stood at fifty. Sent to oppose the American advance from St. Lo, it was struck by 1,600 U.S. heavy and medium bombers on July 25. Two days later, the divisional commander reported Panzer Lehr as "finally annihilated."

In early August, part of its remnants were temporarily absorbed by the 2nd SS Panzer Division, under which it fought at Falaise. In September, when it was assigned to the 1st Army as an independent formation, the division's strength was one panzer grenadier battalion, six 105mm howitzers, one engineer company, five tanks, a reconnaissance platoon and a 200-man special battalion formed from stragglers. It fought in the early Siegfried Line battles with LXXXI Corps, before being rebuilt by the 6th Panzer Army at Paderborn, Wehrkreis VI. It received seventy-two new tanks, twenty-one assault guns and hundreds of replacement soldiers, mostly of indifferent quality. It was quickly returned to the 1st Army, then fighting in the Saar sector, in November 1944 and helped prevent Army Group G from collapsing under Patton's heavy attacks. Once again sent north in December, it was committed to the Battle of the Bulge, where Panzer Lehr besieged Bastogne as part of the XXXXVII Panzer Corps but failed to take the town. By January 1, 1945, it had lost 2,465 men killed and another 1,475 were wounded or ill. After the defeat of the Ardennes offensive, Panzer Lehr fought in the Battle of the Maas Line in the Netherlands (March 1945) but could not prevent the British and Canadians from breaking through the position. The division attempted to eradicate the American bridgehead at Remagen in early March but failed. In this battle the Lehr had only 300 men and fifteen tanks left. The burned-out division retreated into the Ruhr Pocket in April 1945, and at the end of this battle surrendered to the U.S. 99th Infantry Division on April 15.

Commanders of the Panzer Lehr Division were Major General Oswin Grolig (assumed command December 27, 1943), Lieutenant General Fritz Bayerlein (February 5, 1944), Colonel Rudolph Gerhardt (August 23, 1944), Colonel Baron Paul von Hauser (September, 1944), Bayerlein (returned to command, September 8, 1944), Kauffmann (January 8, 1945), Colonel/ Major General Horst Niemack (February, 1945), and Hauser again (April 3–15, 1945).

Notes and Sources: Niemack was promoted to major general on April 1, 1945. He was seriously wounded on April 3.

An instructor talks to the men of a tank unit. The vehicle in the foreground is probably a Panzer Mark II Model B (PzKw IIb) without a main battle gun. This photograph was probably taken at the Panzer Troops School at Wuensdorf. HITM ARCHIVE

Blumenson 1960: 273, 422; Bradley et al., Vol. 1: 241–42; Cole 1950: 464–65, 469; Cole 1965: 37. 473; Harrison: 234, 334; Hartmann: 72–73; Keilig: 23, 243; MacDonald 1963: Map III, 42; MacDonald 1973: 140, 221, 346, 370; Helmut Ritgen, *Die Geschichte der Panzer-Lehr Division im Westen, 1944–1945* (1979): ff. 1; Scheibert: 174; Stauffenberg MS and personal communications; Tessin, Vol. 14: 273–74; OB 45: 302–3. For the story of the destruction of Panzer Lehr in the Normandy campaign, see Carell 1973.

155TH RESERVE PANZER (FORMERLY REPLACEMENT) DIVISION

Composition (1943): 7th Reserve Panzer Battalion, 5th Reserve Panzer Grenadier Regiment, 25th Reserve Motorized Grenadier Regiment, 260th Reserve Motorized Artillery Battalion, 7th Reserve Tank Destroyer Battalion, 5th Reserve Panzer Reconnaissance Battalion, 19th Reserve Panzer Engineer Battalion, 1055th Reserve Panzer Signal Company, Panzer Divisional Supply Troops

Home Station: Ulm, later Stuttgart and Ludwigsberg, Wehrkreis V

This division was activated on August 26, 1939, as *Kommandeur der Ersatztruppen V* (V Replacement Troop Command). It later became Division Nr. 155 (November 9, 1939) and still later became the 155th Motorized Replacement Division (1942). It was transferred to Prague on November 9, 1939, but returned to Ulm in September 1940. The divisional headquarters was moved to Stuttgart on August 23, 1941. At that time, it controlled the 25th, 35th and 215th Infantry Replacement Regiments, the 25th Artillery Replacement Regiment, the 18th Cavalry Replacement Battalion, the 5th Tank Destroyer Replacement Battalion and the 35th Engineer Replacement Battalion, among others. On May 12, 1942, the divisional headquarters was moved yet again, this time to Ludwigsburg, and the division was completely reorganized. This time it controlled more mobile units, including the 7th Panzer Replacement Battalion, the 5th Panzer Grenadier Replacement Regiment, the 25th Motorized Replacement Regiment, and the 260th Motorized Artillery Replacement Regiment. On April 5, 1943, it was redesignated 155th Panzer Replacement Division and was sent to Remnes in northwestern France with the motorized and panzer training units of the V Military District. On August 1, 1943, it became the 155th Reserve Panzer Division. By March 1944, the division had only sixty tanks (PzKw IIIs and IVs). Admiral Ruge, Rommel's naval advisor, noted that the loss of trained personnel, which the 155th supplied to other armored units, had severely retarded the division's combat readiness. In early May 1944, the 155th Reserve Panzer was absorbed by the 9th Panzer Division.

The commanders of the 155th included Major General Otto Tscherning (August 26, 1939), Major General/Lieutenant General Franz Landgraf (May 1, 1942), Major General Max Fremerey (October 1, 1942), and Major General Kurt von Jesser (August 24, 1943).

Notes and Sources: Landgraf was promoted to lieutenant general on September 1, 1942.

Bradley et al., Vol. 4: 71–72; Keilig: 95, 158, 196; 350; Mehner, Vol. 4: 384; Vol. 5: 329; Vol. 6: 544; Vol. 7: 357; Mitcham 2001: 206–8; Friedrich Ruge, *Rommel in Normandy* (1979): 96; Tessin, Vol. 7: 92–94; RA: 6, 88; OB 43: 148; OB 45: 184.

178TH PANZER REPLACEMENT DIVISION

Composition (May 1943): 15th Panzer Replacement and Training Battalion, 85th Panzer Grenadier Replacement and Training Regiment, 128th Motorized Replacement and Training Regiment, 55th Panzer Reconnaissance Replacement and Training Battalion, 8th Tank Destroyer Replacement Battalion, Panzer Replacement and Training Divisional Supply Troops

Home Station: Liegnitz, Wehrkreis VIII

This division was created on December 15, 1940, as Division Nr. 178. It initially controlled the motorized elements that previously belonged to the 148th and 158th Replacement Divisions in Lorraine and Alsace. The 178th never left Silesia. It was redesignated 178th Motorized Replacement Division on April 20, 1942. In autumn 1942 it retained both its training and replacement functions, despite the fact that almost all of the other replacement divisions in the Home Army gave up their training formations. The 178th was redesignated a panzer replacement division staff on April 5, 1943. It was deactivated on February 6, 1945, and its men were absorbed by Panzer (Field Training) Division Tatra. The 128th Motorized Grenadier Training Regiment, however, remained in Silesia directly under HQ, Wehrkreis VIII, and was destroyed when the Soviets overran the province in 1945.

Commanders of the 178th included Lieutenant General Curt Bernard (December 12, 1940), Lieutenant General Friedrich-Wilhelm von Loeper (May 1, 1942), Lieutenant General Karl-Friedrich von der Meden (October 1, 1944), Major General Hans-Ulrich Back (October 9, 1944), and Meden again (January 1, 1945).

Sources: Bradley et al., Vol. 1: 343–44; Keilig: 16, 30, 45, 208; Mehner, Vol. 4: 384; Tessin, Vol. 7: 194–95; RA: 132–33; OB 43: 152; OB 45: 194.

179TH RESERVE PANZER DIVISION

Composition: 1st Reserve Panzer Battalion, 81st Reserve Panzer Grenadier Regiment, 29th Reserve Motorized Grenadier Regiment, 29th Reserve Panzer Artillery Battalion, 1st Reserve Panzer Reconnaissance Battalion, 1st Reserve Tank Destroyer Battalion, 1st Reserve Panzer Engineer Battalion, 81st Reserve Panzer Signal Battalion, Reserve Panzer Divisional Supply Troops

Home Station: Weimar, Wehrkreis IX

This unit was originally created on January 5, 1940, as the 179th Replacement Division, to control replacement and training units in the IX Military District (Hessen and Thuringia). It was reorganized as the 179th Motorized Replacement Division on February 27, 1942, as the 179th Panzer Replacement Division on April 5, 1943, and as the 179th Reserve Panzer Division on July 30, 1943, when it was and sent to the Laval area of western France. It was used to supply the demands of the regular panzer divisions for trained replacements which, in the fifth year of the war, was tremendous. By late January 1944, the division could only deploy one panzer company, one combat-ready foot battalion, and one coastal defense battalion. It lacked anti-tank weapons, communications equipment, and even transport for its artillery. On May 1, 1944, it was combined with the 16th Panzer Grenadier Division to form the 116th Panzer Division.

The commanders of the 179th included Major General Herbert Stimmel (January 5, 1940), Lieutenant General Max Hartlieb gennant Walsporn (June 20, 1940), and Lieutenant General Walter Boltenstern (January 20, 1942).

Notes and Sources: Who commanded the division between April 11 and June 20, 1940, is not known.

Bradley et al., Vol. 2: 131–32; Hartmann: 71; Keilig: 45, 335; Mehner, Vol. 4: 384; Vol. 7: 357; Ruge: 62; RA: 146; OB 43: 33; OB 45: 194.

232ND PANZER DIVISION

Composition: 101st Panzer Grenadier Regiment, 102nd Panzer Grenadier Regiment

On February 21, 1945, this division was formed in Slovakia, from Panzer Field Training Division Tatra. The 101st Panzer Grenadier Regiment was the former 82nd Panzer Grenadier Replacement and Training Regiment, and the 102nd Panzer Grenadier Regiment was the former 85th Panzer Grenadier Replacement and Training Regiment. Hurriedly sent to Army Group South on the Eastern Front, the 232nd fought in the Battle of the Raab Bridgehead, where it was overwhelmed at the end of March 1945. Only small remnants of the division escaped.

Its only reported commander was Major General Hans-Ulrich Back.

Notes and Sources: General Back only escaped the disaster at Raab because he was severely wounded on March 29.

Bradley et al., Vol. 1: 142–46; Keilig: 16; Mehner, Vol. 12: 459; Tessin, Vol. 8: 148; Windrow: 13.

233RD RESERVE PANZER DIVISION

Composition: 5th Reserve Panzer Battalion, 83rd Reserve Panzer Grenadier Regiment, 3rd Reserve Motorized Grenadier Regiment, 59th Reserve Artillery Battalion, 3rd Reserve Panzer Reconnaissance Battalion, 3rd Reserve Tank Destroyer Battalion, 3rd Reserve Panzer Engineer Battalion, 1233rd Reserve Panzer Signal Company, 1233rd Divisional Supply Troops

Home Station: Frankfurt-on-the-Oder, Wehrkreis III

Established as a special purposes motorized division on May 15, 1942, its mission was to control motorized replacement and training units in the III Military District. It was reorganized as a reserve panzer grenadier division on July 7, 1942. On August 10, 1943, it became the 233rd Reserve Panzer Division. It was sent to central Jutland shortly thereafter. It remained in Denmark, headquartered at Horsens, training panzer crews and motorized troops, until the end of the war. Although it officially became a panzer division on February 22, 1945, it never saw combat. It had only thirty-four tanks in any case.

Commanders of the 233rd Reserve Panzer included Lieutenant General Curt Jahn (May 15, 1942), Lieutenant General Heinrich Wosch (March 1, 1943), Major General Kurt Cuno (August 8, 1943), and Lieutenant General Max Fremerey (June 7, 1944–end).

Notes and Sources: Bradley et al., Vol. 2: 485–86; Keilig: 63, 95, 195, 377; Mehner, Vol. 4: 384; Vol. 7: 358; Stoves, *Die 22. Panzer Division*: 263–71; Tessin, Vol. 7: 151–54; RA: 6; OB 43: 26,161; OB 45: 211.

273RD RESERVE PANZER DIVISION

Composition: 25th and 35th Reserve Panzer Battalions, 92nd Reserve Panzer Grenadier Regiment, 73rd Reserve Motorized Grenadier Regiment, 167th Reserve Artillery Battalion, 7th Reserve Panzer Reconnaissance Battalion, 7th and 10th Reserve Tank Destroyer Battalions, 19th Reserve Panzer Engineer Battalion, Reserve Panzer Divisional Supply Troops

Home Station: Würzburg, Wehrkreis XIII

The 273rd was formed on November 1, 1943, to control motorized and panzer training units and to train mobile troops from Wehrkreis XIII, VII and others. It was the only German reserve division not derived from a replacement division staff. Sent to France shortly after it was formed, the 273rd was assigned to the 1st Army and held a sector between Bordeaux and the Spanish frontier. It existed only about seven months, being absorbed by the 11th Panzer Division in May 1944.

Its commander was Lieutenant General Helmuth von der Chevallerie (November 11, 1943–May 9, 1944).

Sources: Bradley et al., Vol 2: 422–24; Hartmann: 64; Mitcham 2001: 219–20; Tessin, Vol. 8: 312–13; RA: 6, 118; OB 45: 223.

PANZER DIVISION "CLAUSEWITZ"

Composition: Panzer Regiment Clausewitz, II/1st Panzer Regiment Feldhernnhalle, 1st Panzer Grenadier Regiment Clausewitz, 2nd Panzer Grenadier Regiment Clausewitz, Tank Destroyer Battalion Clausewitz, Clausewitz Divisional Supply Troops

This ad hoc division was raised mainly from boys in the Hitler Youth on April 6, 1945. The troops and subordinate units were drawn from several sources, while the staff came from Panzer Division Holstein. It also included the remnants of the 106th Panzer Brigade "Feldhernnhalle," which had been destroyed in the Ruhr Pocket. In the last days of the war, it attempted to rescue Berlin, which had been surrounded by the Soviets. It penetrated to within twenty miles of the Führerbunker but was unable to relieve the city. Retreating to the west, it attacked the U.S. 1st Army in an attempt to prevent the encirclement of German forces in the Harz Mountains. It raised considerable havoc in the Allied rear but was ultimately encircled and finally destroyed by the U.S. 5th Armored Division near Brunswick (Braunschweig) on April 21, 1945. The young men and boys of this division still believed in Hitler and Nazism and had high morale despite their hopeless situation. They added the last touch of elan to the Nazi war effort.

The division was commanded by Lieutenant General Martin Unrein.

Sources: Chant, Volume 17: 2357–61; Keilig: 352; Mehner, Vol. 12: 459; Mitcham 2001: 221–22; Tessin, Vol. 15: 45–46; Ziemke 1966: 491.

PANZER DIVISION "FELDHERRNHALLE" (1)

See 60th Panzer Grenadier Division in the next chapter.

PANZER DIVISION "FELDHERRNHALLE" (2)

Composition: Panzer Regiment Feldherrnhalle 2, Panzer Grenadier Regiment Feldherrnhalle 3, Panzer Artillery Regiment Feldherrnhalle 2, 13th Panzer Reconnaissance Battlion, Tank Destroyer Battalion Feldherrnhalle 2, Motorized Engineer Battalion Feldherrnhalle 2, Motorized Signal Battalion Feldherrnhalle 3, Army Anti-Aircraft Battalion Feldherrnhalle 2, Divisional Supply Troops Feldherrnhalle 2

Home Station: Wehrkreis XX

This unit was formed in March 1945, from Replacement and Training Brigade "Feldherrnhale," the remnants of the 13th Panzer Division, the 110th Panzer Brigade and elements of the I Cavalry Corps. Very much understrength, the new division formed part of Panzer Korps "Feldherrnhalle" of the 8th Army in Slovakia, where it fought its only battles on the upper Danube. It tried to capitulate to the Americans at the end of the war, but they insisted in surrender to the Soviets. Major General Dr. Franz Bäke, the division's only commander, withdrew a short distance and disbanded the unit. It broke into small groups. Some managed to infiltrate through American lines and to surrender to the U.S. Army; others fell into Russian hands.

Notes and Sources: Bäke was promoted to major general on April 1, 1945.

Bradley et al., Vol. 1: 158–59; *Kriegstagebuch des OKW,* Volume I: 1146; Frank Kurowski, *Panzer Aces,* David Johnston, trans. (1992): 66; Mehner, Vol. 12: 443; Tessin, Vol. 14: 83.

A tank commander and a member of his crew. The commander is wearing a radio headset. The German tank radio enabled the panzer divisions to win many victories over otherwise superior Russian tanks, which did not have them and were unable to communicate. HITM ARCHIVE

PANZER DIVISION "GROSSDEUTSCHLAND"

See Panzer Grenadier Division "Grossdeutschland" in the next chapter.

(1ST) PARACHUTE PANZER DIVISION "HERMANN GOERING"

Composition: Hermann Goering Panzer Regiment, 1st Hermann Goering Panzer Grenadier Regiment, 2nd Hermann Goering Panzer Grenadier Regiment, 1st Hermann Goering Panzer Artillery Regiment, 1st Hermann Goering Anti-Aircraft Regiment, 1st Hermann Goering Panzer Reconnaissance Battalion, 1st Hermann Goering Tank Destroyer Battalion, 1st Hermann Goering Panzer Engineer Battalion, 1st Hermann Goering Panzer Signal Battalion, 1st Hermann Goering Divisional Supply Troops

Home Station: Thorn, Wehrkreis XX

This unit, which was actually part of the Luftwaffe, was an all-volunteer force into which foreigners and Volksdeutsche were not accepted. Its designation as a parachute division was honorary only. It was formed in occupied France as a Anti-Aircraft regiment, expanded to a brigade in July 1942, and was enlarged to divisional size in Belgium in November 1942. The regiment had already distinguished itself in Poland, France and in Operation "Barbarossa"—in an anti-tank role in the last campaign. Elements of the division were hurriedly sent to Tunisia in early 1943, and were destroyed when Army Group Afrika collapsed in May. Meanwhile, the rest of the division was assembled in Italy for shipment to Africa but was committed to the defense of Sicily instead.

The Hermann Goering Division was reconstituted while in Italy and fought in all the major battles on the Italian Front until May 1944, when it was placed in OKW Reserve at Leghorn, northern Italy, en route to France. At that moment the Allies started their Gustav Line offensive against Cassino and broke out of the Anzio beachhead. The Hermann Goering rushed into the counterattack, temporarily slowing the Allied advance on Rome, and enabled a large segment of the 14th Army to escape. (It had already crushed a battalion of elite American Rangers north of Anzio.) After the fall of Rome, the division was sent to the Russian Front and in August halted the Russian summer offensive north of Warsaw (along with the 5th SS and 19th Panzer Divisions) by destroying the Soviet III Armored Corps. The parachute panzer division remained on the central sector of the Eastern Front during the Vistula battles, in East Prussia (where it suffered heavy casualties), and in the retreat into eastern Germany. It surrendered to the Russians in the Dresden-Grossenhain area on May 8, 1945.

Commanders of the first Hermann Goering Division included Luftwaffe Major General/Lieutenant General Paul Conrath (October 17, 1942), Luftwaffe Major General Wilhelm Schmalz (April 16, 1944), Major General Hans-Horst von Necker (November 1, 1944), and Colonel/Major General Max Lenke (January 31, 1945).

Notes and Sources: Conrath was promoted to lieutenant general on September 1, 1943. Lemke was promoted to major general on April 20, 1945.

Blumenson 1969: Map II, 419–21; Edwards: 142; Fisher: 39, 169–71; Garland and Smyth: 51, 81; Stoves, *Gepanzerten*: 260; OB 45: 304–5; Ziemke 1966: 340.

PANZER DIVISION "HOLSTEIN"

Composition: 44th Panzer Battalion, 139th Panzer Grenadier Regiment, 142nd Panzer Grenadier Regiment, 144th Panzer Artillery Regiment, 44th Panzer Reconnaissance Battalion, 144th Tank Destroyer Battalion, 144th Panzer Engineer Battalion, Holstein Panzer Signal Company, 144th Army Anti-Aircraft Battalion, Holstein Panzer Divisional Supply Troops

Home Station: Frankfurt/Oder, Wehrkreis III

This division was formed in the Aarhus area of Denmark (on the Jutland peninsula) on February 10, 1945, mainly using Alarm units and elements of the 233rd Reserve Panzer Division. It had only forty-five tanks and was well below divisional strength in terms of manpower. It was rushed to the Eastern Front, where it took part in Hitler's ill-conceived Stargard offensive in February. It also fought at Kolberg, where it escaped encirclement only at the last minute. Then it defended the west bank of the Oder north of Stettin. By now it had only eighteen tanks and twenty to twenty-five of its original eighty armored personnel carriers. It was absorbed by the 18th Panzer Grenadier Division on April 6, 1945. The divisional staff was sent to Lauenburg and was used to build Panzer Division Clausewitz.

The commander of Panzer Division Holstein was Colonel Joachim Hesse. Colonel Ernst Wellmann was acting as divisional commander when it was absorbed by the 18th Panzer Grenadier.

Sources: *Kriegstagebuch des OKW*, Volume IV: 1898; Mehner, Vol. 12: 458; Seemen: 268; Stoves, *Gepanzerten*: 263; Tessin, Vol. 14: 113–14; Thomas, Vol. 2: 433.

PANZER DIVISION JÜTERBOG

Composition: Panzer Battalion Jueterbog, Panzer Grenadier Regiment Jüterbog 1, Panzer Artillery Regiment Jüterbog, Panzer Reconnaissance Company Jüterbog, Panzer Engineer Company Jüterbog, Panzer Signal Company Jüterbog, Panzer Anti-Aircraft Battalion Jüterbog, Panzer Divisional Supply Troops Jüterbog

Home Station: Jüterbog, Wehrkreis III

Another 1945 "division" which barely reached regimental strength, this unit was formed on February 20, 1945, at the Jüterbog Troop Maneuver Area, the main German Army artillery facility, south of Berlin. The headquarters was the former Staff, 10th Panzer Brigade. The tank battalion was formed from the former Panzer Lehr (Demonstration) Battalion Kummersdorf at Jüterbog, while most of the other units came from Alarm (emergency) units in Berlin. It is not clear whether the division's flak battalion ever formed. Plans were made to created a 2nd Jüterbog Panzer Grenadier Regiment, and one battalion arrived from Munich for that purpose, but this regiment never materialized, because Panzer Division Jüterbog was dubbed a Kampfgruppe on February 26 and was attached to the 16th Panzer Division in Silesia. Shortly thereafter, in March 1945, the 16th Panzer absorbed the new division outright.

Notes and Sources: The Jüterbog Panzer Artillery Regiment had only its staff and one battalion. Panzer Grenadier Regiment Jüterbog 1 had only two understrength battalions.

Lexikon; Mitcham 2001: 237–38; Stoves, *Gepanzerten*: 263–64; Tessin, Vol. 14: 126–27.

PANZER DIVISION KURMARK

Composition: (151) Panzer Regiment Kurmark, (152) Panzer Grenadier Regiment Kurmark, Panzer Fusilier Regiment Kurmark, (151) Panzer Artillery Regiment Kurmark, Panzer Reconnaissance Battalion Kurmark, Tank Destroyer Battalion Kurmark, Panzer Engineer Battalion Kurmark, (151) Panzer Signal Company Kurmark, Army Anti-Aircraft Artillery Battalion Kurmark, Panzer Divisional Supply Troops Kurmark

Home Station: Frankfurt/Oder, Wehrkreis III

The history of Panzer Division Kurmark, author James Lucas wrote, was "short, hard and disastrous." It was formed as a panzer grenadier division on January 31, 1945, at Frankfurt/Oder, from emergency units and the understrength Grossdeutschland Motorized Replacement Brigade. Its panzer grenadier regiment had only two weak battalions, and they were mounted on bicycles. Its artillery battalion had only two battalions, and its anti-tank battalion was equipped with *Panzerschreck* rocket launchers and single-shot, disposable *Panzerfausten.* Every unit in the division was well below strenght. The Fusilier regiment was formed from the officer cadets of Fahnenjunker School I in Dresden, so the division had some excellent human material. On the other hand, some of the men in other units had been pulled off leave trains. The elite Grossdeutschland NCOs, however, soon instilled their spirit into the division, and morale was remarkably high.

Kurmark was hurriedly sent to 9th Army on the Eastern Front (then very close to Frankfurt) and fought in the Battle of

Sternberg, where it broke through encircling Soviet forces and rescued the garrison. Kurmark itself, however, was quickly surrounded by Red Army forces, equipped with the latest Stalin heavy tanks. It fought its way out but lost all of its soft-skin vehicles and heavy weapons in the process. Kurmark was sent to the rear and rebuilt. On April 16, 1945, the Red Army launched its final offensive, aimed at Berlin. More than a million men, backed by 22,000 guns, attacked the weak 9th Army. On April 17, the units on either side of Kurmark collapsed and the division was quickly encircled. Elements of the division managed to break out, but almost the entire 9th Army was encircled at Halbe on April 21. The Kurmark Division, however, managed to break out of even this encirclement and escape to the Colpin woods, southwest of Frankfurt an der Oder. Here most of the division's survivors were rounded up by the Red Army. Elements of the determined division, however, managed to escape to the west, crossed the Elbe River, joined the 12th Army on May 5, and surrendered to the Americans on May 8, 1945.

Colonel Willi Langkeit, who was promoted to major general on April 20, was the division's only commander.

Sources: Angolia, *Field*, Volume 2: 291; Keilig: 197; *Kriegstagebuch des OKW*, Vol. IV: 1898; Seemen: 34, 174; Tessin, Vol. 14: 132–33, 138. For a detailed account of General Langkeit's career, see James Lucas, *Hitler's Enforcers* (1996): 54–70.

PANZER DIVISION MÜNCHEBERG

Composition: Panzer Battalion Kummersdorf, Panzer Grenadier Regiment Müncheberg 1, Panzer Grenadier Regiment Müncheberg 2, Panzer Artillery Regiment Müncheberg, Panzer Reconnaissance Company Müncheberg, 682nd Tank Destroyer Battalion, Tank Destroyer Company Müncheberg, Motorized Engineer Company Müncheberg, Signal Company Müncheberg, 301st Army Anti-Aircraft Battalion, Panzer Divisional Supply Troops Müncheberg

Home Station: Müncheberg, Wehrkreis III

Activated on March 8, 1945, in the Müncheberg sector (between Frankfurt/Oder and Berlin), this unit was a panzer division in name only. It never neared divisional strength, had only a handful of tanks, and barely had enough vehicles to carry its wounded. Its artillery regiment had only one battalion of four or five light batteries. It was nevertheless committed to a sector of the Oder, where it fought very well. Later it took part in the Battle of Seelow Heights, where the Red Army finally broke through, but only after suffering appalling losses. The division retreated to Müncheberg, where it was involved in street fight, and then to the Hardenberg Position, and finally into Berlin itself. It lost its last tank near the Brandenburg Gate. It finally broke up on May 4, 1945. Its survivors tried to reach the West but few of them made it; most of the survivors ended up in Soviet prisons.

Notes and Sources: Major General of Reserves Werner Mummert was the division's only commander. He was wounded on May 1 but continued in command until the division broke up. He died in a Soviet prison.

Chant 1979, Vol. 17: 2376; Keilig: 235; Ryan, 1966; Tessin, Vol. 14: 161–62; Jürgen Thorwald, *Defeat in the East* (1951, 1980): 206–43.

PANZER DIVISION "NORWAY"

Composition: Panzer Battalion "Norway," Panzer Grenadier Regiment "Norway," Artillery Battalion "Norway", Tank Destroyer Battalion "Norway", Engineer Battalion "Norway", Signal Battalion "Norway," Panzer Divisional Supply Troops "Norway"

Home Station: Bielefeld, Wehrkreis VI

This unit was officially activated in Norway on October 1, 1943, to deter Swedish adherence to the Allies. It was about regimental strength and had forty-seven PzKw III tanks that had been left behind when the 25th Panzer Division was transferred to Russia. All its tanks had unsatisfactory transmissions. The division never saw combat. It was cannibalized on July 1, 1944, when almost all of its units were sent to the 25th Panzer Division, and it was left with a single grenadier battalion. The Staff was downgraded to a brigade staff on July 13. Later, a small panzer battalion was added to it, and it sent to Narvik (northern Norway) in

January 1945, to counter a possible Soviet invasion, which never came. It surrendered to the British in May 1945.

Its commanders were Lieutenant Colonel Prince Max zu Waldeck (1943), Colonel/Major General Reinhold Gothsche (October 1–November 1, 1943), and Colonel Max Roth (November 1, 1943–1944). Colonel Maetschke reportedly commanded Panzer Brigade Norway in 1945.

Notes and Sources: Prince Max commanded the division reception staff before the division was formally activated. Gothsche was promoted to major general the day he assumed command of the division.

Bradley et al., Vol. 4: 368–70; Keilig: 111; *Kriegstagebuch des OKW*, Volume IV: 1878; Schiebert: 107; Seemen: 307; Stoves, *Gepanzerten*: 332; Tessin, Vol. 14: 176–77; Ziemke 1959; 267.

PANZER DIVISION SILESIA

Composition: Panzer Battalion Silesia, 100th Panzer Grenadier Regiment Silesia, Panzer Artillery Battalion Silesia, Panzer Reconnaissance Company Silesia, Tank Destroyer Company Silesia, Panzer Engineer Company Silesia, Panzer Signal Company Silesia, Panzer Divisional Supply Troops Silesia

Home Station: Döberitz, Wehrkreis III

This unit (which was also known as Panzer Division Doeberitz) was organized on February 20, 1945, around a handful of extant units of the Silesian 178th Reserve Panzer Division, as well as emergency units and kampfgruppen from Wehrkreis III and IV. Its headquarters was formed from parts of Staff, Wehrkreis IV. Its commander was Colonel Ernst Wellmann. In March 1945, the division was reinforced with the 303rd Panzer Battalion, which was equipped with assault guns. Its Panzer Grenadier Regiment Silesia 2 was in the process of forming later that month when the division was absorbed by Panzer Division Holstein. This unit was, in turn, absorbed by the 18th Panzer Grenadier Division on March 26. It was largely destroyed on the Oder Front the following month. Panzer Division Silesia never exceeded regimental strength.

Sources: Keilig: 220; Kursietis: 237, Lexikon; Mehner, Vol. 14: 456; Seeman: 39, 354; Stoves, *Gepanzerten*: 274; Tessin, Vol. 14: 228–29.

PANZER (LATER PANZER FIELD TRAINING) DIVISION TATRA

Composition: Panzer Battalion Tatra 1; one company, 4th Panzer Replacement and Training Battalion; 82nd Panzer Grenadier Replacement and Training Regiment; 85th Panzer Grenadier Replacement and Training Regiment; one company, Artillery Battalion Tatra; 8th Tank Destroyer Battalion; one company, 89th Panzer Engineer Lehr Replacement and Training Regiment; 1 and 2 Companies, 482nd Grenadier Training Battalion; Field Replacement Battalion Tatra, Divisional Supply Troops Tatra

This division was formed in Slovakia in August 1944, when it looked as if that country might try to defect from the Axis. Its staff included cadres from the veteran 1st Panzer Division. Its other units came from all over the map. Its panzer battalion included twenty-eight obsolete PzKw IIIs and IVs and three Tiger tanks. Despite the improvished nature of its organization, the Tatra Panzer Division performed well and played a major role in suppressing the Slovak Military Mutiny of 1944 and in recapturing Bratislava (Pressburg) from the rebels and their Soviet advisors. Following the completion of this mission, the division was redesignated Panzer Field Training Division Tatra and became a training unit. It absorbed XVII Panzer Command (including its panzer grenadiers) from Wehrkreis XVII in December 1944, as well as the tank units of Wehrkreis VIII. It was itself absorbed by the 232nd Reserve Panzer Division in March 1945.

Its commanders were Lieutenant General Friedrich-Wilhelm von Loeper (August 1944) and Major General Hans-Ulrich Back (January 1, 1945).

Sources: Keilig: 16, 208; Stoves, *Gepanzerten*: 275; Tessin, Vol. 6: 265, 322; Vol. 14: 239.

A German motorized infantry unit passes a column of panzers. The last tank (far right) is a PzKw II. HITM ARCHIVE

CHAPTER 2

The Motorized and Panzer Grenadier Divisions

2nd MOTORIZED INFANTRY DIVISION

See 12th Panzer Division in the previous chapter.

3rd PANZER GRENADIER DIVISION

Composition (September 1943): 103rd Panzer Battalion, 8th Panzer Grenadier Regiment, 29th Panzer Grenadier Regiment, 3rd Motorized Artillery Regiment, 103rd Panzer Reconnaissance Battalion, 3rd Motorized Engineer Battalion, 3rd Motorized Signal Battalion, 3rd Army Anti-Aircraft Battalion, 3rd Panzer Grenadier Divisional Supply Troops

Home Station: Frankfurt-on-the Oder, Wehrkreis III

Originally the 3rd Infantry Division of the peacetime army, this unit was formed in Hitler's initial military expansion by the enlargement of the 8th Infantry Regiment of the old Reichswehr. It included the 8th, 29th, and 50th Infantry Regiments. The 3rd fought in northern Poland in 1939 and in France in 1940. It was reorganized in the fall of 1940, was fully motorized, and had to give up its 50th Infantry Regiment to the 111th Infantry Division. It now included the 8th and 29th Motorized Infantry Regiments, the 3rd Motorized Artillery Regiment, the 53rd Motorcycle Battalion and the 53rd Reconnaissance Battalion. It crossed into Russia in 1941 as part of Army Group North, took part in the initial drive on Leningrad, and fought at Demyansk. Shifted south late in the year, it was involved in the final thrusts on Moscow and opposed the Russian winter offensive of 1941–42. In March 1942, it was reorganized again. The 53rd Motorcycle and Reconnaissance Battalions were combined, and the 312th Army Anti-Aircraft Battalion was added to its table of organization. That next summer it was sent to Army Group South, took part in the Battle of Vyasma, the advance across the Don, the push to the Volga, and the Stalingrad fighting. It was encircled in the Stalingrad Pocket in November. It surrendered to the Russians in the southern part of the Stalingrad Pocket on January 31, 1943.

A second 3rd Motorized Division was formed in southwestern France in the spring of 1943, by absorbing most of the 386th Motorized Division, a mediocre formation, into a newly formed divisional table of organization. The reborn 3rd Motorized Grenadier, however, included many veterans of the old division (mostly returning wounded) and performed well in combat. Its 103rd Panzer Battalion had forty-two StuG assault guns and six command tanks. On June 23, 1943, it was redesignated a panzer grenadier division, along with all of the German motorized divisions except the 14th and 36th. Sent to Italy in June, it opposed the Allied landings at Salerno in September, fought in the Battles of Cassino and the Bernhard Line, opposed the Allied beachhead at Anzio in January 1944, and took part in the retreat to Rome in May and June 1944. Withdrawn to Florence in late June, it was transferred to the Western Front in August and was initially engaged southeast of Paris. The 3rd Panzer Grenadier Division took part in the withdrawal from France, the evacuation of Nancy, and was resisting near Metz, covering the Saar industrial area, in September 1944. Two months later it had been rebuilt to a strength of 12,000 men, thirty-one 75mm anti-tank guns, and thirty-eight artillery pieces, making it a considerable combat force for the fifth year of the war. Sent to Aachen in November, it both suffered and inflicted severe casualties in the battle for that city. Withdrawn briefly to the interior of Germany for rest and reorganization, it was back in action in the Ardennes in December 1944, and fought in the Eifel battles of January 1945. Defending in the vicinity of Cologne in March 1945, it unsuccessfully tried to wipe out the U.S. Army's bridgehead at Remagen. It was finally trapped and destroyed in the Ruhr Pocket in April 1945. It surrendered to the Americans on April 16.

Commanders of the 3rd Motorized Division included: Colonel/Major General Curt Haase (April 1, 1934), Major General/Lieutenant General Walter Petzel (March 7, 1936), Major General/Lieutenant General Walther Lichel (November 10, 1938), Lieutenant General Paul Bader (October 1, 1940), Lieutenant General Curt Jahn (May 25, 1941), Major General/Lieutenant General Helmuth Schloemer (April 1, 1942), and Colonel Baron Jobst von Hanstein (January 15, 1943–end). Commanders of the 3rd Panzer Grenadier Division included Lieutenant General Fritz-Hubert Graeser (March 1, 1943), Colonel/Major General Hans Hecker (March 1944), Lieutenant General Hans-Guenther von Rost (June 1, 1944), Hecker (returned June 25, 1944), and Major General/Lieutenant General Walter Denkert (October 3, 1944).

Notes and Sources: The 3rd Field Replacement Battalion was used to form the III/307th Infantry Regiment of the 163rd Infantry Division. Curt Haase was promoted to major general on April 1, 1935. Petzel, Lichel and Schloemer were promoted to the rank of lieutenant general on January 1, 1938, February 1, 1940, and December 1, 1942, respectively. Hecker became a major general on June 1, 1944. Denkert was promoted to lieutenant general on April 20, 1945.

Cole 1950: 60, 193; Cole 1965: 83; Gerhard Dieckhoff, *3. Infanterie-Division, 3. Infanterie-Division (mot.), 3. Panzergrenadier-Division* (1960); Fisher: Map III; Garland and Smyth: 203; Hartmann: 54; Keilig: 302; Kursietis: 81; MacDonald 1963: 284, 290, 410; MacDonald 1973: 70, 190, 353, 370; Nafziger 1999: 38; Scheibert: 139; Tessin, Vol. 2: 166–68; RA: 46; OB 44: 263; OB 45: 305.

10TH PANZER GRENADIER DIVISION

Composition (Fall 1943): 10th Panzer Battalion, 20th Panzer Grenadier Regiment, 41st Panzer Grenadier Regiment, 10th Motorized Artillery Regiment; 40th Panzer Reconnaissance Battalion, 10th Tank Destroyer Battalion, 10th Motorized Engineer Battalion, 10th Motorized Signal Battalion, 10th Field

Replacement Battalion, 10th Divisional Supply Troops. The 275th Army Anti-Aircraft Battalion was added later.

Home Station: Regensburg, Wehrkreis XIII

The 10th was originally formed in October 1934, as an infantry division by the expansion of the 20th Infantry Regiment of the old Reichswehr. Its men came from northern Bavaria and the western Sudetenland, and it initially included the 20th, 41st, and 85th Infantry Regiments. It was codenamed "Kommandant of Regensburg" until October 15, 1935, when it officially became the 10th Infantry Division. It fought in southern Poland in September 1939 and in France in 1940. On November 15, 1940, the 10th was reformed as a motorized division and gave up its 85th Infantry Regiment to the 5th Mountain Division. It took part in the Balkans campaign of 1941 and invaded Russia with Army Group Center on June 22. The division crossed the Bug and fought at Bobruisk, Smolensk, the Dnieper crossings, Gomel, Kiev, Bryansk, and Tula, and in the Battle of Moscow and other important battles in 1941, suffering heavy casual ties in the process.

After the Soviet winter offensive of 1941–42 was halted, the 10th Motorized remained on the central sector during the defensive actions of 1942 (mainly at Moshaisk, Juchnow and Spass Demjansk), and took part in the unsuccessful Kursk offensive of July 1943. Meanwhile, it was officially redesignated the 10th Panzer Grenadier Division on June 13, 1943, and received the 7th Panzer Battalion in October. Sent to the southern sector, the 10th suffered heavy losses in the Battle of Kiev in the fall of 1943. It also fought at Krementschug and in the retreat to the Dnieper. By January 1944, it had only 3,700 men and was defending ten miles of frontage. It retreated through the Ukraine and suffered such heavy losses in the Bessarabia (Romania) debacle in August 1944, that it had to be withdrawn for rest and reorganization. Later that year, it returned to the Eastern Front; now, however, it was only at battle group strength and had only three panzer grenadier and one motorized artillery battalion remaining. In late 1944 and

A German StuG assault gun unit being transported via flat cars. HITM ARCHIVE

early 1945, it fought at Krakau, Radom, in the retreat from the Vistula, at Goerlitz, and in Silesia. By now, however, the tanks of the 7th Panzer Battalion had been lost and had been replaced by assault guns; the 41st Panzer Grenadier Regiment had apparently been disbanded; and the 10th Panzer Artillery Regiment had only one battalion left. The division, however, continued to resist. It was forced to retreat into Moravia in April, and the remnants of the 10th Panzer Grenadier Division surrendered to the Soviets at Deutsch-Brod on May 10, 1945.

Commanders of the 10th included Major General/Lieutenant General Alfred Waeger (October 1934), Lieutenant General Conrad von Cochenhausen (March 1, 1938), Lieutenant General Friedrich Wilhelm von Loeper (October 5, 1940), Colonel Hans Traut (April 15, 1942), Major General/Lieutenant General August Schmidt (April 25, 1942), Colonel Hans Mikosch (October 2, 1943), Schmidt (returned December 23, 1943), Colonel Walter Ackemann (March 1, 1944), Schmidt (April 1944), Colonel/Major General Walter Herold (September 30, 1944), Colonel Alexander Vial (November 28, 1944), and Colonel/Major General Karl-Richard Kossmann (January 1945)

Notes and Sources: Waeger was promoted to lieutenant general around 1938. He died before the war began. Schmidt was promoted to lieutenant general on January 1, 1943. He was captured in Romania. Walter Herold was promoted to major general on November 9, 1944, and was killed in action nineteen days later. Colonel Vial was captured by the Russians in January 1945. Kossmann was promoted to major general on April 20, 1945. He was released from Soviet prison in January 1956.

Carell 1966: 80, 557; Hartmann: 55; Keilig: 182–83, 304; Kennedy: 74; Kursietis: 91; Lexikon; August Schmidt, *Geschichte der 10. Division, 10. Infanterie-Division (mot.), 10. Panzergrenadier-Division, 1935–1945* (1963); Seaton: 415, 483; RA: 204; OB 42: 64; OB 43: 191; OB 44: 264; OB 45: 306.

14TH MOTORIZED INFANTRY DIVISION

Composition: 11th Motorized Regiment, 53rd Motorized Regiment, 14th Motorized Artillery Regiment, 114th (later 14th) Panzer Reconnaissance Battalion, 14th Tank Destroyer

Battalion, 14th Motorized Engineer Battalion, 14th Motorized Signal Battalion, 14th Divisional Supply Troops

Home Station: Leipzig, Wehrkreis IV

Created in October 1934, as an infantry division in Hitler's enlarged peacetime army, this Saxon unit was codenamed *Kommandant von Leipzig* until October 15, 1935. It took part in the invasions of Poland and France "without winning special distinction," according to U.S. military intelligence report. Nevertheless, it was converted into a motorized infantry division in the fall of 1940, losing its third infantry regiment (the 101st) in the process. (This regiment became the 101st Rifle Regiment of the 18th Panzer Division. Its I Battalion remained with the 14th Division as the 54th Motorcycle Battalion. Meanwhile, the horse-drawn elements of the 14th Artillery Regiment were given to the 122nd Infantry Division.) Sent to Russia in 1941, the 14th Motorized Division was on the Eastern Front from the first day of the invasion until the fall of Berlin. It was part of Army Group Center (later North) from beginning to end. In 1941, the 14th was prominent in the Battle of Vitebsk, the battles of encirclement at Vyazma-Bryansk, and the drive on Moscow. In late October 1941, it helped establish the Kalinin bridgehead on the upper Volga, between Moscow and Leningrad. The division spent 1942 in the Rzhev sector and played a part in the withdrawal from the Rzhev salient in 1943, and was then sent to Nevel, on the northern flank of the 4th Army.

In July 1943, it was withdrawn, demotorized, and converted into a three-regiment infantry division, adding a new 101st Grenadier Regiment in the process; however, all of its grenadier regiments were reduced to two battalions. The unit was redesignated 14th Infantry Division on June 30 and was returned to the Eastern Front, where it fought at Bryansk (September 1943) and Vitebsk (October 1943–June 1944). It was the only division in the reserve of the 4th Army when Army Group Center was smashed in July 1944; as such, it escaped total destruction but was reduced to battle group strength. The remnants of the 14th Division fought on the Narew in northern Poland

(August 1944–January 1945) and East Prussia (February–May 1945) until the end. It surrendered to the Soviets near Stuthof on the Frischen Nehrung, East Prussia, in May 1945.

The commanders of the 14th Infantry/Motorized/Panzer Grenadier/Infantry included Lieutenant General Franz Kress von Kressenstein (October 15, 1935), Major General/Lieutenant General Peter Weyer (October 6, 1936), Major General Dr. Lothar Rendulic (June 15, 1940), Major General Friedrich Fuerst (October 6, 1940), Major General Heinrich Wosch (June 1, 1941), Major General Walter Krause (October 1, 1942), Colonel Rudolf Holste (January 1, 1943), Colonel/Major General/Lieutenant General Hermann Floerke (May 15, 1943), Lieutenant General Erich Schneider (December 28, 1944), Major General of Reserves Werner Schulze (March 20, 1945), Colonel Gerhard Kircher (April 1945), and Colonel Johann Heldmann (April 1945–end).

Notes and Sources: The 14th Field Replacement Battalion was transferred to the 164th Infantry Division in January 1940, and became the II/382nd Infantry Regiment. Weyer was promoted to lieutenant general on August 1, 1937. Floerke was promoted to major general on June 1, 1943, and to lieutenant general on December 1, 1943.

Carell 1966: 141, 154–55; Carell 1971: 309, 570; Keilig: 92, 369–70; Lexikon; RA: 72; OB 42: 64; OB 44: 264; OB 45: 143.

15TH PANZER GRENADIER DIVISION

Composition (1944): 215th (later 115th) Panzer Battalion, 104th Panzer Grenadier Regiment, 115th Panzer Grenadier Regiment, 33rd Motorized Artillery Regiment, 999th Schnelle (Mobile) Battalion, 33rd Motorized Engineer Battalion, 999th Motorized Signal Battalion, 315th Army Anti-Aircraft Battalion, 33rd Panzer Grenadier Divisional Supply Troops

Home Station: Landau, Wehrkreis XII

This unit was formed in Sicily as Command Colonel Baade in May 1943, from the remnants of the 15th Panzer Division, which escaped destruction in Tunisia; several "march" battalions, which were en route to North Africa when the front in Tunisia collapsed; and the 129th Panzer Grenadier Regiment of the defunct 22nd Panzer Division from the Russian Front. The 129th was later absorbed by the 115th Panzer Grenadier Regiment, which was formed from Afrika Korps veterans and troops already in Sicily. The division was renamed Division "Sizilien" on May 14, 1943, and was designated 15th Panzer Grenadier on July 1. Although not completely trained or equipped, the 15th Panzer Grenadier Division fought in Sicily with considerable skill and was highly praised by General von Senger (commander of the XIV Panzer Corps) for its conduct at Salerno in September 1943. From October until March 1944, the 15th Panzer Grenadier fought in the Cassino area of southern Italy, before being placed in reserve. It took part in the retreat from Rome and the withdrawal to the Gothic Line.

Sent to southern France in September 1944, it was split up and scattered in 1st Army's makeshift effort to slow the Allied advance. The next month it was finally pulled out of the line—after over a year of more or less continuous action—and rebuilt under the direction of the XXXXVII Panzer Corps. By the first of November it had a strength of 13,000 men, but only seven tanks, even thought it had absorbed the remnants of the 113th Panzer Brigade. It did, however, have about thirty assault guns. In November, it fought in the Battle of the Peel Marshes and in the Siegfried Line battles around Aachen and Geilenkirchen. In December, the division took part in the Siege of Bastogne. After this defeat it retreated to the Kleve (Cleve) area and was involved in the Battle of the Maas Line in the Netherlands in February 1945. Unable to prevent the British-Canadian breakthrough, the survivors of the 15th Panzer Grenadier retreated across the lower Rhine, the Ems and Weser, and were retreating across north-central Germany when the war ended. It surrendered to the British near Lamstedt on May 5, 1945.

Commanders of the division included Colonel Ernst Gunther Baade (May 1943), Colonel (General Staff) Heckel (June 1943), Major General/Lieutenant General Eberhard Rodt

(June 9, 1943), Colonel Karl-Theodor Simon (September 5, 1944), Colonel Hans-Joachim Deckert (October 9, 1944), and Colonel Wolfgang Maucke (January 28, 1945).

Notes and Sources: In January 1940, the 15th Field Replacement Battalion was transferred to the 169th Infantry Division and became the III/392nd Infantry Regiment. Rodt was promoted to lieutenant general on March 1, 1944. Colonel Simon was an acting commander. In 1945, he was back at his permanent assignment: commander of the division's 33rd Motorized Artillery Regiment. Colonel Maucke was formerly commander of the division's 115th Panzer Grenadier Regiment, and was apparently deputizing for Rodt.

Blumenson 1969: 323–24, Map II; Cole 1950: 48–49, 96, 475; Cole 1965: 473–74; Fisher: 18; Garland and Smyth: 51; Keilig: 280; MacDonald 1963: 243, 567; MacDonald 1973: 140; Nafziger 1999: 54; Tessin, Vol. 4: 14–16; RA: 188; OB 45: 306–7.

16th PANZER GRENADIER DIVISION

See 116th Panzer Division in the previous chapter.

18th PANZER GRENADIER DIVISION

Composition (late 1943): 118th Panzer Battalion, 30th Panzer Grenadier Regiment, 51st Panzer Grenadier Regiment, 18th Motorized Artillery Regiment, 118th Panzer Reconnaissance Battalion, 118th Tank Destroyer Battalion, 118th Motorized Engineer Battalion, 118th Motorized Signal Battalion, 18th Divisional Supply Troops

Home Station: Liegnitz, Wehrkreis VIII

This unit began its career in October 1934, under the codename "Infantry Command III." On October 15, 1935, it became the original 18th Infantry Division and should not to be confused with the 18th Volksgrenadier Division, which was formed in 1944. It initially included the 30th, 51st, and 54th Infantry Regiments. The 18th Infantry was part of the German spearhead in Poland in 1939, and fought at Kutno and Warsaw. Sent to the lower Rhine in late 1939, it fought in Belgium and the drive on Dunkirk during the Western campaign of

1940, where it lost 558 men killed, 1,993 wounded, and thirty-nine missing. It returned to Germany in October. That fall, this Silesian division gave up the 54th Infantry Regiment and was motorized. Officially designated the 18th Motorized Division on November 1, 1940, it was committed to the Russian Front in 1941. As part of Hoth's 3rd Panzer Group, it fought in the Bialystok and Minsk encirclements, in the drive on Leningrad, and at Volchov, among others. It was badly mauled in the Soviet winter offensive of 1941–42, losing 9,000 men and dropping to a strength of 741 combat effectives by December 22. Soon after it was put into reserve behind the northern sector of the front.

In March 1942, however, it was back in the line and took part in the rescue of II Corps at Demyansk. Remaining on the northern sector in the defensive battles of 1942 and 1943, where it held a sector of the front near Tichvin, the 18th Panzer Grenadier also fought around Demyansk and Lake Ilmen and at Staraya Russa. On June 23, 1943, it added the 118th Panzer Battalion (which was equipped with assault guns), and it was redesignated 18th Panzer Grenadier Division. That autumn, it was sent to Army Group Center, where it fought in the unsuccessful defense of Smolensk that fall. In the spring of 1944 it was officially cited for distinguished action in the central Dnieper fighting. The 18th Panzer Grenadier was virtually destroyed in the Russian summer offensive of 1944. Encircled in the Bobruisk Pocket, divisional commander Lieutenant General Karl Zutavern committed suicide, rather than surrender to the Russians. The tiny remnants of the burned-out division that escaped the destruction of the 4th Army were sent to Silesia, where they were temporarily absorbed by the 105th Panzer Brigade. The division was rebuilt as a *Kampfgruppe* in November and early December 1944, and absorbed both the 105th and 103rd Panzer Brigades. It had four panzer grenadier battalions, a panzer battalion and three artillery battalions, but no tank destroyer or engineer battalions. Its tank battalion was equipped with obsolete PzKw IVs. It returned to the Eastern Front in East Prussia in December and was decimated there in the winter fighting of 1944–45. Evacuated by sea to northern Germany, it fought in the battles of Seelow Heights and Berlin, where it was finally destroyed. Most of its survivors fell into Communist hands.

Commanders of the division included Lieutenant General Erich von Manstein (February 4, 1938), Major General/Lieutenant General Friedrich-Karl Cranz (August 26, 1939), Major General/Lieutenant General Friedrich Herrlein (March 28, 1941), Colonel/Major General/Lieutenant General Werner von Erdmannsdorff (December 15, 1941), Major General/Lieutenant General Karl Zutavern (October 5, 1943), Lieutenant General Curt Jahn (April 14, 1944) and Zutavern (May 24, 1944). The commanders of the rebuilt 18th Panzer Grenadier Division were Major General Dr. Hans Boelsen (September 10, 1944), and Colonel/Major General Erwin Rauch (January 1, 1945–end).

Notes and Sources: Manstein was promoted to lieutenant general on April 1, 1938. Cranz was promoted to lieutenant general on July 1, 1940. He was killed "through an error in judgement" on March 24, 1941. Herrlein was promoted to lieutenant general on September 1, 1942. Erdmannsdorff was promoted to major general on March 1, 1942 and to lieutenant general on January 1, 1943. Zutavern was promoted to lieutenant general on April 1, 1944. Rauch was promoted to major general on April 20, 1945. He surrendered the division and remained in Soviet prisons until 1955.

Carell: 1966: 67, 80, 286, 373–74, 427–34; Carell 1971: 300, 597; Chant, Volume 18: 2381; Cole 1965: 143; Joachim Engelmann, *Die 18. Infanterie- und Panzergrenadier-Division, 1934–1945* (1984); Keilig: 83; Kennedy: 74. Map 7; Kursietis: 100–101; Lexikon; Manstein: 21, 269; MacDonald 1963: 599; Mellenthin 1977: 24; Nafziger 1999: 274–76; Seaton: 575; Stoves, *Gepanzerten*: 125–27; Tessin, Vol. 4: 88–90; RA: 116; OB 42: 64–65; OB 43: 192; OB 45: 308.

20TH PANZER GRENADIER DIVISION

Composition (1944): 8th Panzer Battalion, 76th Panzer Grenadier Regiment, 90th Panzer Grenadier Regiment, 20th Motorized Artillery Regiment, 120th Panzer Reconnaissance Battalion, 20th Tank Destroyer Battalion, 20th Motorized Engi-

The crew of a German armored vehicle watches an airplane, circa 1940. During the early blitzkrieg campaigns, German panzers often pushed forward so rapidly that they crossed into areas without the knowledge of the Luftwaffe. The swastika flag was displayed not to indicate sympathy for the Nazi cause, but rather to show Luftwaffe pilots that the vehicle was, in fact, German and should not be bombed. HITM ARCHIVE

neer Battalion, 20th Motorized Signal Battalion, 284th Army Anti-Aircraft Battalion, 20th Field Replacement Battalion

Home Station: Hamburg. Wehrkreis X

Created in October 1934, under the codename Army Service Depot Hamburg, it became the 20th Infantry Division on October 15, 1935. It initially included the 69th, 76th, and 90th Infantry Regiments. Most of its troops were recruited from the Hamburg area. In 1937–38, it was motorized and received the designation "motorized infantry division." It was earmarked for the attack on Prague in 1938, but did not see combat there because of the Munich agreement between Hitler and British Prime Minister Neville Chamberlain. On September 1, 1939, it experienced its first action when it struck into the Danzig corridor of Poland. It fought well in Poland and took part in the conquests of Holland, Belgium and France, where it traveled great distances but saw relatively little shooting.

On the Eastern Front in 1941, it fought with Army Group Center at Bialystok, Minsk, Smolensk, and the Dnieper crossings, before being sent to the northern sector, where it fought its way across the Dvina River and spearheaded the 16th Army's drive on Oreshek, on the road to Leningrad. The 20th remained on the northern sector until December 1942, fighting in the Volkhov sector (February–July 1942), at Staraja Russa (July–August), and at Volkhov again (September–October). In December 1942, it was sent to Army Group Center, where it held a sector near Welish (December 1942–June 1943) and fought in the defensive battles of Orel (August) and Bryansk (September). Meanwhile, it was redesignated a panzer grenadier division on July 23, 1943. Transferred south that autumn, the 20th suffered heavy losses in the Battle of Kiev and the subsequent retreat to the Dniper in November 1943. It nevertheless remained in the line and fought at Winniza (January 1944), in the Hube Pocket (March–April 1944), in the defensive victory at Brody (i.e., in the first battle of Brody) (May 1944), in the retreat across southern Poland to the Vistula (June–August 1944), and in the efforts to eliminate and then contain the Baranov Bridgehead (August–January 1945). After the Soviets broke out of the Baranov sector, the 20th Panzer Grenadier Division was forced into Silesia in February 1945. In was transferred to the north in March (i.e., the Oder sector), where the remnants of the division defended Seelow Heights in the Third Reich's last stand (April 16–19, 1945) and were crushed there after a gallant defense. The remnants of the division surrendered to the Americans at Tangermünde on the Elbe River.

Commanders of the division included Major General/Lieutenant General Maximilian Schwandner (October 1934), Lieutenant General Mauritz von Wiktorin zu Hainburg (November 10, 1938), Major General Hans Zorn (November 10, 1940), Lieutenant General Erich Jaschke (January 12, 1942), Colonel/ Major General/Lieutenant General Georg Jauer (January 30, 1943), and Colonel/Major General Georg Scholze (January 1, 1945).

Notes and Sources: Schwandner was promoted to lieutenant general on May 1, 1935. Jauer was promoted to major general on April 1, 1943, and to lieutenant general on October 1, 1943. Scholze was promoted to April 20, 1945. He committed suicide on April 24, after his division was annihilated. His wife had been killed a few days before in an Allied bombing attack.

Benoist-Mechin: 290; Carell 1966: 76, 80, 265, 421; Hartmann: 55–56; Keilig: 317–18, 382; Kennedy: 74, Map 7; Lexikon; Mehner, Vol. 4: 381; Vol. 6: 543; Vol. 7: 354; Plocher 1943: 104; Salisbury: 308–9; Stoves, *Gepanzerten*: 143; Tessin, Vol. 4: 133–35; OB 42: 65; OB 43: 192; OB 45: 308–9.

25TH PANZER GRENADIER DIVISION

Composition: 5th Panzer Battalion, 35th Panzer Grenadier Regiment, 119th Panzer Grenadier Regiment, 25th Motorized Artillery Regiment, 25th Panzer Reconnaissance Battalion, 25th Tank Destroyer Battalion, 25th Motorized Engineer Battalion, 25th Motorized Signal Battalion, 292nd Army Anti-Aircraft Battalion, 25th Field Replacement Battalion, 25th Divisional Supply Troops

Home Station: Ludwigsburg, later Stuttgart, Wehrkreis V

The 25th was formed on April 1, 1936, as an infantry division by the expansion of the 13th Infantry Regiment of the old Reichswehr. It initially included the 13th, 35th, and 119th Infantry Regiments. The 25th Infantry sent to the Saar in 1939, and fought in France and Belgium in 1940. That October, it was reorganized as a motorized unit, and its 13th Regiment was transferred to the 6th Mountain Division. It was officially designated a motorized division on November 15. It was sent to the Russian Front in June 1941, and served on the central sector for the next three years. It fought in the 2nd Panzer Group's battles at Zhitomir, Uman, Kiev, Bryansk, and Tula (south of Moscow). It spent January 1942 to June 1943 in the Bryansk/Orel sector, took heavy casualties at Kursk in July, and fought at Smolensk in October 1943. Meanwhile, on June 23, 1943, it was redesignated the 25th Panzer Grenadier Division. From November 1943 to June 1944, it held part of 4th Army's sector near Orscha. In the summer of 1944, the 25th Panzer Grenadier suffered heavy losses in the encirclement east of Minsk. The parts of the division which escaped were assigned to the 107th Panzer Brigade.

A new 25th Panzer Grenadier Division was established at the Grafenwoehr Maneuver Area (Wehrkreis XIII) in October 1943. The new unit (which absorbed the 107th Panzer Brigade) was a *Kampfgruppe* and controlled the understrength 35th Panzer Grenadier Regiment, the 25th Artillery Battalion, the 25th Tank Destroyer Battalion, the 25th Engineer Company, the 25th Signal Company and an armored car platoon. In December, it added the 119th Panzer Grenadier Regiment, the 5th Panzer Battalion, the 125th Panzer Reconnaissance Battalion, the 292nd Army Anti-Aircraft Battalion and the 25th Field Replacement Battalion. Its signal and engineer units were also upgraded to battalions. The rebuilt division was sent to the Western Front after the German collapse in France. That fall it was engaged at Puettlingen, north of Saarbrücken, and in the Vosges. Elements of the rebuilt division unsuccessfully opposed the United States advance on Metz in November. The 25th Panzer Grenadier was holding the Bilche sector in December 1944, during the Battie of the Bulge. After the defeat of the

Ardennes offensive, it was sent to the East, where it defended a sector on the Oder north of Berlin during the last Russian offensive; most of its survivors, however, managed to escape to surrender to the English and Americans.

The commanders of this division included Major General/ Lieutenant General Christian Hansen (October 12, 1936), Lieutenant General Erich Clossner (October 15, 1939), Major General Siegfried Heinrici (January 15, 1942), Colonel/Major General/Lieutenant General Anton Grasser (January 25, 1942), Major General Dr. Fritz Benicke (November 5, 1943), Colonel/ Major General/Lieutenant General Paul Schuermann (March 4, 1944), and Colonel/Major General Arnold Burmeister (February 10, 1945).

Notes and Sources: Hansen was promoted to lieutenant general on March 1, 1938. Grassner was promoted to major general on April 1, 1942, and to lieutenant general on January 1, 1943. Schuermann was promoted to major general on June 20, 1944 and to lieutenant general on September 1, 1944. Burmeister was promoted to major general on April 20, 1945.

Carell 1966: 196; Chant, Volume 13: 1777; Volume 18: 2381; Cole 1950: 390, 471; Keilig: 27–28, 57, 75, 113, 314; Tessin, Vol. 4: 223–25; OB 42: 65; OB 43: 193; OB 45: 309; Ziemke 1966: 487.

29TH PANZER GRENADIER DIVISION

Composition (1944): 29th Panzer Battalion, 15th Panzer Grenadier Regiment, 71st Panzer Grenadier Regiment, 29th Motorized Artillery Regiment, 129th Panzer Reconnaissance Battalion, 29th Tank Destroyer Battalion, 29th Motorized Engineer Battalion, 29th Motorized Signal Battalion, 313th Army Anti-Aircraft Battalion, 29th Field Replacement Battalion, 29th Panzer Grenadier Divisional Supply Troops

Home Station: Erfurt, Wehrkreis IX

Formed on October 1, 1936, by the expansion of the 15th Infantry Regiment of the old Reichswehr, it initially included the 15th, 71st, and 86th Infantry Regiments. Its personnel were mainly from Thuringia, with draftees from other parts of Germany. It became a motorized unit in 1937–38, and gave up the 86th Motorized Infantry Regiment to the 10th Panzer Division in the summer of 1939. The division fought hard in Poland and distinguished itself in the German drive to the English Channel in 1940. It fought in Luxembourg, Belgium and France, including the Battle of Dunkirk, and ended the campaign near Belfort, behind the Maginot Line. It was on occupation duty in eastern France from July 1940 to February 1941, when it returned to Germany. The "Falcon Division," as it was nicknamed, performed in an outstanding manner in all of its battles. Crossing into Russia in 1941, it fought in the Bialystok and Minsk encirclements, in the Dnieper crossings, at Smolensk, Bryansk, Tula (in the Moscow sector), and against the Soviet winter offensive of 1941–42. In 1942, it fought in the 2nd Battle of Kharkov, in the Don crossings, in the drive on the Volga and at Stalingrad, where it was itself surrounded in November 1942, and was destroyed in the southern Stalingrad pocket on January 31, 1943. Even as late as January 12, 1943, when it was in its death throes, the 29th, together with the 3rd Motorized Infantry Division, repulsed ten to twelve Soviet divisions and knocked out 100 tanks, all in a single day.

A second 29th—this one a panzer grenadier division—was formed in southwestern France on June 23, 1943. The new unit absorbed the bulk of the 345th Reserve Panzer Grenadier Division. It fought in Sicily in July 1943 and took part in all the major campaigns in Italy, including Salerno, Anzio, the Gothic Line and the Po River campaign in 1945. On April 24 of that year it (and the rest of the LXXVI Panzer Corps) was caught by the British 8th Army between the Po and the Apennine Mountains and was destroyed. Only a few survivors of the division managed to reach the Po River and swim across it to safety. Even these were rounded up in the next few days, but the division itself ceased to exist as of April 28, when the divisional headquarters was captured. The remnants of the division surrendered to the Americans on May 2.

Commanders of the 29th Motorized Division included Lieutenant General Gustav von Wietersheim (October 5, 1936),

A pair of German light machine-gun crews on a halt. HITM ARCHIVE

Major General/Lieutenant General Joachim Lemelsen (March 1, 1938), Major General Baron Willibald von Langermann und Erlenkamp (May 7, 1940), Major General Walter von Boltenstern (September 7, 1940), Major General Max Fremerey (September 20, 1941), and Colonel/Major General Hans Georg von Leyser (September 25, 1942–end). The commanders of the 29th Panzer Grenadier Division included Colonel/Major General/Lieutenant General Walter Fries (March 1, 1943), Colonel Hans Hecker (February 1944), Colonel Dr. Hans Boelsen (March 5, 1944), Fries (returned March 20, 1944), and Major General/Lieutenant General Dr. Fritz Polack (August 24, 1944).

Notes and Sources: Lemelsen was promoted to lieutenant general on April 1, 1939. Leyser was promoted to major general on November 1, 1942. He surrendered the remnants of the original 29th Division to the Soviets when Stalingrad fell. Fries was promoted to major general on June 1, 1943, and to lieutenant general on January 1, 1944. Dr. Polack became a lieutenant general on March 15, 1945. He was captured on April 28, 1945.

Benoist-Mechin: 133; Blumenson 1969: 289, 419–21; Carell 1966: 41–42, 67, 80, 512–13, 629; Chapman: 347–48; Fisher: 302, 498; Garland and Smyth: 74, 284; Keilig: 45, 95, 260, 370; Kennedy: 74, Map 7; Kursietis: 109–10; Joachim Lemelsen, *29. Division* (1955); Lexikon; Manstein: 355–56; RA: 144; Nafziger 1999: 284–85; OB 42: 65; OB 43: 193; OB 45: 309–10.

36TH PANZER GRENADIER (LATER INFANTRY AND VOLKSGRENADIER) DIVISION

Composition (1942): 87th Motorized Infantry Regiment, 118th Motorized Infantry Regiment, 36th Motorized Artillery Regiment, 36th Panzer Reconnaissance Battalion, 36th Tank Destroyer Battalion, 36th Motorized Engineer Battalion, 36th Motorized Signal Battalion, 36th Divisional Supply Troops

Home Station: Wiesbaden, Wehrkreis XII

Formed in Kaiserslautern on October 1, 1936, as the 36th Infantry Division of the peacetime army, the troops of this unit were mainly Bavarians from the Palatinate. Initially, it included the 70th, 87th, and 118th Infantry Regiments. Remaining on the Western frontier in 1939, the 36th fought well in the French campaign of 1940. That autumn, it returned to Germany and was converted to a motorized infantry division, effective November 1, 1940, and gave up the 70th Infantry Regiment to the 111th Infantry Division in the process. It fought its way through the Baltic States in 1941, and was especially heavily engaged at Kalinin, where it helped establish a bridgehead on the upper Volga in late October. Later it stormed the last Leningrad fortifications on Duderhof Hill, before being halted by the order of Adolf Hitler, who thought Leningrad would fall without costly street fighting. The division then fought at Kalinin in the Moscow sector and suffered heavy casualties against the Russian winter offensive of 1941–42. It fought in the defensive battles around Rzhev and Baranova in the summer of 1942, and again took heavy losses.

The division was officially declared demotorized on May 1, 1943, and became the 36th Infantry Division once again, although it did retain more motorized vehicles than the average infantry division. In July 1943 it fought in the bitterly contested Battle of Kursk. Reduced to battle group strength, it took part in the retreats of 1943–44, on the central sector. In May 1944, it was finally reformed into a two-regiment infantry division. In June 1944, it was smashed near Bobruisk by the massive Soviet summer offensive. Many of its men, including divisional commander Major General Conrady, were taken prisoner. The surviving remnants of the 36th were returned to Germany and reformed at the Baumholder Maneuver Area as a three-regiment Volksgrenadier division (Division Group 268 being added). Some of its units were still partially motorized, however, and were sent to the Western Front in September to oppose Patton's advance through France. The division was badly mauled in the battles in eastern France, Luxembourg and the Saar in 1944, but was still reckoned a good combat division. In January 1945, it took part in Himmler's abortive attempt to retake Strasbourg. The 36th Volksgrenadier fought in the retreat through the Saar, southern Germany and into Franconia, where it was when the war ended.

Commanders of the 36th Infantry/Motorized Infantry Division included Major General/Lieutenant General Georg Lindemann (October 6, 1936), Major General/Lieutenant General Otto Ottenbacher (October 1, 1940), Major General/Lieutenant General Hans Gollnik (October 15, 1941), Colonel Gotthard Froelich (August 10, 1943), Major General Rudolf Stegmann (September 20, 1943), Colonel Horst Kadgien (January 1, 1944), Major General Egon von Neindorff (January 17, 1944), and Colonel/Major General Alexander Conrady (January 19, 1944). The 36th Grenadier/Volksgrenadier Division was commanded by Colonel/Major General August Welln (August 1, 1944), and Major General Helmuth Kleikamp (March 1945).

Notes and Sources: The division was officially redesignated 36th Grenadier Division on August 3, 1944, and the 36th Volksgrenadier Division on October 9. Lindemann, Ottenbacher and Gollich were promoted to lieutenant general on April 1, 1938, March 1, 1941, and January 1, 1943, respectively. Stegmann became a major general on August 1, 1943. Conrady reached the rank of major general on May 1, 1944. He was captured on July 1, 1944, and spent the next eleven years in Soviet prisons. The division commander's position was vacant from July 1 to 31, 1944. Welln was promoted to major general on August 1, 1944.

Carell 1966: 154-59, 230, 267; Carell 1971: 230, 309, 578, 597; Chant, Volume 17: 2277; Cole 1950: 50, 365, 482, 526; Keilig: 61, 97, 171; Kursietis: 113; Lexikon; MacDonald 1963; 64; Tessin, Vol. 5: 53–55; RA: 188; OB 42: 65–66; OB 43: 194; OB 45: 151–52.

60TH MOTORIZED INFANTRY DIVISION (LATER PANZER GRENADLER DIVISION "FELDHERRNHALLE")

Composition (1944): 160th Panzer Battalion, 120th Panzer Grenadier Regiment "Feldherrnhalle," 27lst Fusilier Regiment "Feldherrnhalle," 160th Motorized Artillery Regiment, l60th Panzer Reconnaissance Battalion, 160th Tank Destroyer Battalion, 160th Motorized Engineer Battalion, 160th Motorized Signal Battalion, 160th Divisional Supply Troops

Home Station: Danzig, Wehrkreis XX

This division had a unique beginning: it was formed by the German-controlled Senate of the Free State of Danzig as a provincial police home defense force. Formed on July 1, 1939, as the German-Polish diplomatic crisis worsened and war seemed more and more inevitable, it was augmented with S.A. (Brownshirt or Stormtrooper) auxiliaries, members of the Danzig *Heimwehr* (Home Army) and disguised soldiers smuggled in from Germany proper. These included Major General Friedrich-Georg Eberhardt, the unit's commander. By the time war broke out on September 1, 1939, Group Eberhardt had two infantry regiments, a battalion of artillery, plus support troops. It quickly seized most of the city and the surrounding areas, including the Westerplatte and the Hela peninsula, and surrounded the Polish forces it did not immediately destroy. On October 15, 1939, after the Polish surrender, Group Eberhardt was expanded into the 60th Infantry Division. Its 92nd Infantry Regiment was provided by the 2nd Motorized Division and the 243rd and 244th Infantry Regiments were the former 1st and 2nd Danziger Infantry Regiments, respectively. Its artillery battalion was gradually expanded into an artillery regiment. Its divisional troop units were either added or expanded. It also added the 282nd Army Anti-Aircraft Battalion on April 1, 1940.

It fought in France in 1940, after which it was sent to the Gross-Born Troop Maneuver Area and was reorganized as a motorized division in the fall of 1940, losing the 243rd Infantry Regiment in the process. Simultaneously, its 244th Infantry Regiment was redesignated 120th Motorized Infantry Regiment. It was sent to Romania in January 1941 and, after helping overrun Yugoslavia, it fought on the southern zone of the Russian Front in 1941 and 1942, during the advance through the Ukraine and the Donets Basin. It fought in the Battles of

Zhitomir, Uman, the Dnieper crossings, Kiev, Rostov (1941 and 1942), and Kharkov (1942). It took part in the battles on the Don, the drive to the Volga, and in the Stalingrad street fighting. It was surrounded with the rest of the 6th Army on November 23, 1942, and surrendered in the northern Stalingrad pocket on February 1, 1943.

A second 60th Motorized Division was created in southern France on February 17, 1943. Officially activated on March 15, 1943, it was built around the 271st Infantry Regiment "Feldherrnhalle," which had previously served with the 93rd Infantry Division in Russia, and several other cadre units from a variety of sources. The division received the honorary title "Feldherrnhalle" because it contained a high number of Brownshirt volunteers. It was redesignated Panzer Grenadier Division "Feldherrnhalle" (FHH) on May 27. Its units were all renamed and the division now consisted of the Grenadier Regiment FHH, the Fusilier Regiment FHH, the Panzer Battalion FHH, the Artillery Regiment FHH, the Panzer Reconnaissance Battalion FHH, and so on. In August 1943, it was sent to southern France during the period of vacillation of the post-Mussolini Italian government, while the Italian 4th Army evacuated the area and returned home.

Ultimately the new mobile division was posted to the Greco-Turkish frontier region, and then was sent to the Eastern Front in the fall of 1943. It fought against the massive Soviet summer offensive of 1944 that annihilated Army Group Center. The division was smashed near Minsk and was almost trapped east of the Dnieper. Divisional commander Major General Friedrich-Carl von Steinkeller was among those captured. The remnants of the FHH were withdrawn to the Estergom Troop Maneuver Area in Hungary and a second FHH Panzer Grenadier Division began to form on July 19, 1944. Later it was sent to Debreczen in the Warthegau, a district of Poland annexed by the Third Reich in 1939. Here the new FHH Panzer Grenadier Division was officially activated on September 1, 1944. Built around the 109th Panzer Brigade (which it absorbed), the new division had a strength of 8,000 men, twenty-five tanks, and a battalion of superb Hummel 150mm self-propelled howitzers by November 1. Redesignated Panzer Division Feldherrnhalle on November 27, 1944, it was sent to Hungary and was soon involved in the Siege of Budapest. The FHH, along with the rest of the IX SS Mountain Corps, was surrounded in the city on December 26, 1944. The garrison broke out on February 11, 1945, but was cut to pieces before it could reach German lines. Only 800 of its 30,000 men escaped.

A third FHH Division, which included the remnant of the second, was formed in Slovakia in March 1945. It also absorbed the remnants of the 182nd and 711th Infantry Divisions, making it a reasonable sized unit. It fought in Slovakia and Moravia and ended the war in the huge Deutsch-Brod Pocket east of Prague. It surrendered to the Red Army on May 8 and 9, 1945. A handful of the division's men escaped to the west and surrendered to the U.S. 7th Army northeast of Linz.

Commanders of the 60th Infantry/Motorized Division included Eberhardt (October 15, 1939), Colonel/Major General/Lieutenant General Otto Kohlermann (May 15, 1942) and Colonel Hans Adolf von Arenstorff (November 1942–February 1, 1943). The commanders of the 60th Panzer Grenadier Division "FHH" and the Panzer Division FHH were Kohlermann (February 17, 1943), Colonel Albert Henze (February 13, 1944), Colonel/Major General Friedrich-Carl von Steinkeller (April 3, 1944), and Colonel/Major General Günther Pape (September 1, 1944).

Notes and Sources: Kohlermann was promoted to major general on July 1, 1942 and to lieutenant general exactly one year later. Arenstorff was captured in Stalingrad. Steinkeller was captured near Mogilev on July 8, 1944. He was promoted to major general while in captivity. He died in a Soviet prison in 1952.

Bradley et al, Vol. 5: 332-34; Carell 1966: 490, 590; Carell 1971: 575–76, 597; Chant, Volume 15: 2054, 2057; Volume 17: 2376; Garland and Smyth: 294; Harrison: 148; Hartmann: 57–58; Keilig: 12, 76, 136–37, 179, 251; Mehner, Vol. 12: 443, 458; Mellenthin 1956: 225; Seaton: 500; Tessin, Vol. 5: 233–34; Vol. 12: 75–76; Vol. 14: 75–76; Thomas, Vol. 2: 142; RA: 244; OB 42: 66; OB 43: 194; OB 45: 310–11.

90TH PANZER GRENADIER (FORMERLY LIGHT) DIVISION

Composition (1944): 190th Panzer Battalion, 200th Motorized Grenadier Regiment, 361st Motorized Grenadier Regiment, 190th Motorized Artillery Regiment, 190th Panzer Reconnaissance Battalion, 190th Tank Destroyer Battalion, 190th Motorized Engineer Battalion, 190th Motorized Signal Battalion, 190th Field Replacement Battalion, 190th Divisional Supply Troops

Home Station: Frankfurt/Oder, later Kuestrin, Wehrkreis III

This division began forming in Libya on June 26, 1941, as the Afrika Division z.b.V. ("for special purposes"), but it was redesignated 90th Light Division on November 26. It initially included the 155th, 200th, and 361st Motorized Infantry (later Panzer Grenadier) Regiments, which were not fully motorized until the spring of 1942. The 190th Motorized Artillery Regiment, the 580th Panzer Reconnaissance Battalion, and the 900th Motorized Engineer Battalion were also part of its table of organization. The 90th Light took part in the Siege of Tobruk (1941), where it helped stabilize Italian infantry units and fought well against both the Tobruk garrison and elements of the British 8th Army, which finally succeeded in relieving Tobruk after three weeks of bitter fighting during Operation Crusader (November–December 1941). The division was involved in the retreat from Cyrenaica, the recapture of Benghazi (January 1942), the three-week Battle of the Gazala Line (May–June 1942), the storming of Tobruk (June 1942), the drive into Egypt, the Battle of Mersa Matruh (June 26–27, 1942), and the battles of El Alamein. By June 27 it had only 1,600 men left; nevertheless, except for a brief moment of panic in the First Battle of El Alamein, it fought extremely well throughout the Desert War and was as feared and respected as the Afrika Korps, of which it only briefly a part. After Panzer Army Afrika was crushed in the Second Battle of El Alamein (October 23–November 4, 1942), the 90th Light formed Rommel's rearguard and retreated through Egypt, Libya, and

Tunisia, where it was finally surrendered on May 12, 1943, when the German front in North Africa finally collapsed.

The second 90th—this one designated panzer grenadier—was formed in June 1943 from miscellaneous units in Sardinia and was briefly known as "Division Sardinia." It became the 90th Panzer Grenadier Division on September 16, 1943. That fall it was withdrawn to Corsica and then to northern Italy. That winter it was sent to the front and was engaged near Cassino. From then on it fought in all the major campaigns of the Italian Front, including the Anzio counterattack, the retreat from Rome, the battles of the Caesar and Gothic lines, and the Battle of the Po River. Finally burned out by almost constant combat, the 90th Panzer Grenadier was virtually destroyed near Bologna in April 1945. The remnants surrendered to the Americans near Lake Garda at the end of the war.

The commanders of the 90th Light Division included Major General Max Suemmermann (September 1, 1941), Major General Richard Veith (December 30, 1941), Major General Ulrich Kleeman (April 10, 1942), Colonel Carl-Hans von Lungershausen (July 13, 1942), Kleeman (returned August 10, 1942), Luftwaffe Major General Bernhard Ramcke (September 8, 1942), Colonel Heuthaus (September 1942), and Major General Count Theodor von Sponeck (November 1, 1942). The 90th Panzer Grenadier Division was commanded by Major General/Lieutenant General von Lungershausen (May 23, 1943), Lieutenant General Ernst Baade (December 20, 1943), Lieutenant General Count Gerhard von Schwerin (December 9, 1944), and Major General Baron Heinrich von Behr (December 27, 1944).

Notes and Sources: The 361st Motorized Infantry Regiment of the 90th Light Division contained a high portion of veterans of the French Foreign Legion. Major General Suemmermann was killed in the Cyrenaican retreat on December 15, 1941, near Gazala. Between his death and the arrival of General Veith on December 30, 1941, the division was probably commanded by Colonel Johann Micki as senior regimental commander. Kleeman was wounded near Alma Halfa Ridge in September 1942. Count von Sponeck, who performed brilliantly in the retreat from Egypt and Libya (1942–43), was captured when Tunisia fell in May 1943. Lungershausen was promoted to lieutenant general on September 1, 1943. Baade was promoted to lieutenant general on August 1, 1944. He was seriously wounded on December 9, 1944.

Fisher: 167, 471, 476; Keilig: 15–16; Richard D. Law and Craig W. H. Luther, *Rommel* (1980): 180; Ronald Lewin, *Rommel as a Military Commander* (1970): 12; Tessin, Vol. 6: 111–13; RA: 46; OB 45: 311. Also see Carell 1960, Irving 1977, and Mellenthin 1956.

345TH MOTORIZED DIVISION

Composition: 345th Reserve Panzer Battalion, 148th Reserve Motorized Grenadier Regiment, 152nd Reserve Panzer Grenadier Regiment, 345th Artillery Regiment, 345th Motorcycle Battalion , 345th Engineer Battalion, 345th Signal Battalion, 345th Divisional Supply Troops

Home Station: Wehrkreis IX

The 345th was formed in the Wildflecken Troop Maneuver Area on November 24, 1942. It was sent to southern France the following month. On March 1, 1943, it was absorbed by the 29th Panzer Grenadier Division, which was created to replace a division destroyed at Stalingrad. The 345th Motorized's only commander was Lieutenant General Karl Boettcher.

Notes and Sources: The 345th Artillery Regiment had only two battalions.

Blumenson 1969: 289; Keilig: 42–43; Lexikon; Tessin, Vol. 9: 237; RA: 144; OB 45: 311.

386TH MOTORIZED DIVISION

Composition: 386th Reserve Panzer Battalion, 149th Motorized Regiment, 153rd Motorized Regiment, 386th Artillery Regiment, 386th Motorcycle Battalion, 386th Engineer Battalion, 386th Signal Battalion, 386th Divisional Supply Troops

Home Station: Frankfurt/Oder, Wehrkreis III

This division was formed on November 25, 1942, and was absorbed by the 3rd Panzer Grenadier Division on March 1, 1943, to replace a division destroyed at Stalingrad. It was sta-

Heinz Guderian, "father of the blitzkrieg." He commanded the 2nd Panzer Division in 1935, later led the 2nd Panzer Army on the Eastern Front, and was chief of the General Staff in 1944–45.

tioned in southern France at the time. The 386th Motorized was considered a mediocre unit.

Notes and Sources: The commander of the 386th Motorized was Major General Kurt Jesser.

Blumenson 1969: 289; Keilig: 158; Lexikon; Tessin, Vol. 10: 42–43; RA: 46; OB 45:

BRANDENBURG DIVISION (LATER PANZER GRENADIER DIVISION "BRANDENBURG")

Composition (1943): 1st Brandenburg Panzer Grenadier Regiment, 2nd Brandenburg Panzer Grenadier Regiment, 3rd Brandenburg Panzer Grenadier Regiment, 4th Brandenburg Panzer Grenadier Regiment, 5th Brandenburg Panzer Grenadier Regiment, 5th Brandenburg Artillery Regiment, Brandenburg Reconnaissance Battalion, a parachute company and other special units, including some with foreign language skills; Brandenburg Divisional Supply Troops

Home Station: Berlin, Wehrkreis III

This division began its career on October 25, 1939, as the 800th Construction Training Company. It was made up of commando units that performed well in Poland and was directly under the *Abwehr*—the German Armed Forces Military Intelligence Department. On January 10, 1940, it was redesignated the *Bau-Lehr-Battalion z.b.V. 800* (800th Construction Training Battalion for Special Employment). It was steadily expanded to a regiment and finally a division. Elements of the "Brandenburgers" fought in practically every major campaign from 1940 to 1943, including the Balkans, Italy, North Africa, Russia, and France (1940), where it particularly distinguished itself. In the Western campaign of 1940, 75 percent of the then battalion won Iron Crosses—probably the highest percentage ever achieved by any German unit during the entire war.

Elements of the division also earned special distinction by disguising themselves as wounded Russians and seizing the critical Dvina River bridge at Daugavpils, behind Soviet lines, on June 26, 1941. They then turned back repeated Soviet counterattacks until they were relieved by the LVI Panzer Corps. In autumn 1942, the special units were upgraded to divisional status. However, as the Abwehr's influence at Fuehrer Headquarters declined, the Brandenburgers came increasingly under the control of OKW, which used it as a regular line unit. By early 1943, only the 5th Brandenburg Regiment "Kurfurst" was employed in commando-style missions. Posted to the Balkans in late 1943, the special functions of the division and affiliated units were taken over by the new SS Raiding Detachments (*Jagdverbände*) in the fall of 1944. In October of that year, it was reformed in Vienna as a panzer grenadier division and transferred to the Eastern Front. As of December 13, 1944, it included the Brandenburg Panzer Regiment (with one Panther battalion and one battalion of modern Panzer Mark IVs), the 1st and 2nd Brandenburg Jaeger Regiments, the Brandenburg Artillery Regiment (three battalions), Brandenburg Tank Destroyer Battalion, Brandenburg Engineer Battalion, Brandenburg Signal Battalion, and Brandenburg Divisional Supply Troops. It fought in Hungary, the Protectorate and Sieslia, and ended the war at battle group strength with the 4th Panzer Army, resisting the last Russian advance in the vicinity of Dresden. Most of the division surrendered to the Soviets, but at least one battle group (under a Dr. Brodt) crossed the Moldau and surrendered to the Americans.

The division's commanders included Colonel Paul Hähling von Lanzenauer (November 28, 1942), Colonel Erwin Lahousen (early 1943), Lieutenant General Alexander von Pfuhlstein (April 1, 1943), Lieutenant General Fritz Kuehlwein (April 13, 1944), and Colonel/Major General Hermann Schulte-Heuthaus (October 16, 1944).

Notes and Sources: Hähling von Lanzenauer fell ill in early 1943 and had to be relieved. He died of natural causes on February 8. General von Pfuhlstein was involved in the July 20, 1944, plot to assassinate Hitler. His guilt, however, could not be conclusively proven, so he was demoted to the rank of private. He had previously served ten days' confinement because an SS lawyer (with the rank of SS general) had cast dispersions on the courage of the Brandenburgers, so Pfuhlstein beat him with his fists. Pfuhlstein survived the war.

Heinz Hoehne, *Canaris,* (1979): 377, 415, 467, 497; Hoffmann: 275–76; Keilig: 122, 256; *Kriegstagebuch des OKW,* Volume III: 1160, Volume IV: 1896; Seaton: 103; Tessin, Vol. 13: 27–29; OB 45: 103. Also see Carell 1960, for the story of the Brandenburg units in North Africa.

PANZER GRENADIER DIVISION "FELDHERRNHALLE"

See 60th Panzer Grenadier Division earlier in this chapter.

PANZER GRENADIER DIVISION "GROSSDEUTSCHLAND"

Composition: Grossdeutschland Panzer Regiment, Grossdeutschland Panzer Grenadier Regiment, Grossdeutschland Fusilier Regiment, Grossdeutschland Artillery Regiment, Grossdeutschland Panzer Reconnaissance Battalion, Grossdeutschland Tank Destroyer Battalion, Grossdeutschland Panzer Engineer Battalion, Grossdeutschland Panzer Signal Battalion, Grossdeutschland Panzer Army Anti-Aircraft Battalion, Grossdeutschland Assault Gun Battalion, Grossdeutschland Divisional Supply Troops

Home Station: Berlin, Wehrkreis III

This division was formed as a motorized infantry division on March 3, 1942, from the elite Infantry Regiment "Grossdeutschland," which had served in France, the Balkans, and Russia. Its soldiers were specially selected volunteers from all over Germany. Its unofficial title was, in fact, "the Bodyguard of the German People." "Grossdeutschland" (which means Greater Germany and was abbreviated "GD") fought exceptionally well throughout the war. It was organized and equipped as a panzer division and is often referred to as one; however, it never officially received this designation. Initially assembled in the Wandern Troop Maneuver Area near Berlin, it was sent to the southern sector in June 1942, where it fought at Kursk, Voronezh (July 1942), and Rzhev. In late November 1942, it was practically encircled in the Lutschessa Valley (east of Rzhev) and suffered more than 10,000 casualties (more than half of its strength) before it could extricate itself.

The division was nevertheless back in the line by January 1943. It was shifted back to the south after Stalingrad fell, and fought at Kharkov and the subsequent Manstein counteroffensive in March 1943. It was heavily and continuously in combat during the Russian winter offensive of 1942–43 and the battles of 1943, including Orel, Bryansk, Kursk, the Kharkov battles, in the Donetz basin withdrawal, and in the retreat to Dnieper (September 1943). By this time, the division had only one operational tank left. (It had 200 tanks when it arrived in Russia.) It was withdrawn to Krementschug to rebuilt in September. Sent back to the front, the veteran division fought at Kirovograd (January 5–18, 1944), on the lower Dnieper (January 19–March 6), north of Nikolayev and in the retreat to the Bug (March 7–27), northern Bessarabia and in the Carpathian foothills (March 27–April 25), in the defensive battles of the Upper Moldau (April 26–end of May), and in the counterattacks north of Jassy (June 2–6). Placed in reserve in June, it was sent to what was then the most critical sector of the Eastern Front—Gumbinnen, East Prussia. Army Group North was isolated from the rest of the Reich by the Soviet summer offensive of 1944, and Grossdeutschland was ordered to spearhead the offensive to reestablish contact. This it was able to do by August 25. Hitler, however, did not take advantage of the opportunity to withdraw the 16th and 18th Armies. The Reds launched another offensive on October 5 and soon isolated Army Group North again—this time permanently. Grossdeutschland was pushed back into the Memel bridgehead, where it was evacuated to East Prussia by the German Navy at the end of 1944.

Grossdeutschland reformed at Willenberg, East Prussia, and continued to offer fierce resistance until the end of the war, fighting at Koenigsberg (now Kaliningrad), the Frisches Haff, Samland (including Pillau), and in the defense of Frische Nehrung (April 12–30, 1945). It had suffered 17,000 casualties since January 1945, and only 4,000 men survived. They were evacuated to Schleswig-Holstein by the German Navy and surrendered to the British in May 1945.

A StuG assault gun. These self-propelled anti-tank guns were mounted on Panzer Mark III chassis, were cheap and easy to manufacture, and were much more effective than most historians have realized, having destroyed 20,000 tanks on the Eastern Front by January 1944.

Commanders of the Grossdeutschland Regiment/Division included Colonel/Major General Wilhelm-Hunold von Stockhausen (assumed command June 1, 1939), Colonel/Major General/Lieutenant General Walter Hoernlein (August 8, 1941), Lieutenant General Baron Hasso von Manteuffel (February 1, 1944), and Colonel/Major General Karl Lorenz (September 1, 1944). Acting commanders included Lieutenant General Hermann Balck (as of December 1, 1942 and April 3-June 30, 1943). Three independent units that were extensions of the Grossdeutschland Division were the Fahrer Escort Battalion, the Fuehrer Grenadier Battalion, and the Brandenburg Panzer Grenadier Division.

Notes and Sources: Stockhausen was promoted to major general on April 1, 1941. Hoernlein was promoted to major general on April 1, 1942, and to lieutenant general on January 1, 1943. Lorenz became a major general on November 1, 1944.

Carell 1966: 521, 542; Carell 1971: 17, 199; Chapman: 347–48; Hartmann: 52–53; Keilig: 146, 210, 335; Mellenthin 1977: 206; Mehner, Vol. 5: 335; Bruce Quarrie, *Panzer-Grenadier-Division "Grossdeutschland"* (1977): ff. 3; Horst Scheibert, *Die Panzergrenadier-Division Grossdeutschland* (2nd ed., 1980); Helmut Spaeter, *Panzerkorps Grossdeutschland Bilddokumentation* (1984): ff. 1; Stoves, *Gepanzerten*: 254; Tessin, Vol. 14: 94–101; Thomas, Vol. 2: 38; RA: 46; OB 43: 195; OB 45: 303–4. For a classic account of the war on the Eastern Front from the viewpoint of an enlisted man in the G. D. Division, see Guy Sajer, *The Forgotten Soldier* (1965).

(2ND) PARACHUTE PANZER GRENADIER DIVISION "HERMANN GOERING"

Probable Composition: 3rd Hermann Goering Panzer Grenadier Regiment, 4th Hermann Goering Panzer Grenadier Regiment, 2nd Hermann Goering Motorized Artillery Regiment, 2nd Hermann Goering Reconnaissance Battalion, 2nd Hermann Goering Assault Gun Battalion, 2nd Hermann Goering Engineer Battalion, 2nd Hermann Goering Signal Battalion, 2nd Hermann Goering Field Replacement Battalion, 2nd Hermann Goering Divisional Supply Troops

This unit, which never reached full strength, was created as the sister unit of the (1st) Parachute Panzer Division "Hermann Goering." In both cases the term "parachute" was honorary. The "H.G." Panzer Grenadier Division was formed in the Radom zone of Poland on September 24, 1944. Its 3rd Panzer Grenadier Regiment was the former 16th Parachute Regiment, and the 4th Panzer Grenadier Regiment was the former Hermann Goering Guard Regiment. The new division assigned to the new Parachute Panzer Corps "Hermann Goering," held a sector on the Vistula (October 1944–January 1945) and was smashed in heavy fighting East Prussia (February and March 1945). It surrendered to the Soviets at the end of the war.

Its commanders were Luftwaffe Colonel/Major General Erich Walther (September 24, 1944), Colonel Wilhelm Soeth (November 1944), Colonel Georg Seegers (February 1945), Colonel Helmut Hufenbach (March 1945), and Walther again (March 1945).

Notes and Sources: Walther was promoted to major general on January 30, 1945. He starved to death in a Soviet prison cell on December 26, 1947.

Kriegstagebuch des OKW, Volume I: 1147; Volume IV: 1897; Lexikon; Tessin, Vol. 14: 118; RA: 252; OB 45: 639.

PANZER GRENADIER DIVISION "KURMARK"

See Panzer Division "Kurmark" in the previous chapter.

CHAPTER 3

The SS Divisions

SS DIVISION VERFÜGUNGSTRUPPE (SS-VT)

Composition: SS-Standarte Deutschland, SS-Standarte Germania, SS-Standarte Der Führer, 1st SS-Artillery Standarte, 2nd SS-Reconnaissance Battalion, SS-Engineer Troop, SS-Signal Troop, SS-Replacement Troop. The SS-VT Panzer Tank Destroyer Battalion and the SS-VT Fla Battalion were added later.

Home Station: Various SS posts

This division was the "grandfather" of many of the Waffen-SS divisions. It was formed after the Polish campaign, in which most of its units had participated. Its units were from all over Germany. The Deutschland *Standarte* (regiment) came from Munich, the Germania from Hamburg and Der Führer from Vienna. It was officially activated on April 1, 1940. SS-VT fought well in the Netherlands and France in 1940, and was on occupation during in France until February 25, 1941, when it was disbanded. Its units were used to form the 2nd SS Division "Das Reich," which later distinguished itself in combat as the 2nd SS Panzer Division "Das Reich"and other units.

Its commander was SS Lieutenant General Paul Hausser.

Sources: Mark C. Yerger, *SS-Oberst-Gruppenführer und Generaloberst der Waffen-SS Paul Hausser* (1986); Tessin, Vol. 14: 248–49.

1st SS PANZER DIVISION "LEIBSTANDARTE ADOLF HITLER"

Composition (1945): 1st SS Panzer Regiment, 1st SS Panzer Grenadier Regiment, 2nd SS Panzer Grenadier Regiment, 1st SS Panzer Artillery Regiment, 1st SS Panzer Reconnaissance

Battalion, 1st SS Tank Destroyer Battalion, 1st SS Assault Gun Battalion, 1st SS Panzer Engineer Battalion, 1st SS Panzer Signal Battalion, 1st SS Anti-Aircraft Battalion, 1st SS Rocket Launcher Battalion (added September 1944), 1st SS Divisional Supply Troops

Home Station: Berlin-Lichterfelde

Formed from SS volunteers in March 1933 as a bodyguard unit for Adolf Hitler, the LAH (as it was called) grew from 133 men to more than 20,000 at its peak. It guarded Hitler at all important functions in the 1930s, and took part in the occupation of Austria (1938), the Sudetenland (1938) and Czechoslovakia (1939). It served as an independent motorized regiment in Poland and France before being expanded to a full motorized infantry division in early 1941. It took part in the Balkans campaign of 1941 and crossed into southern Russia with Army Group South in July 1941. It advanced along the Black Sea coast in August, took part in the opening phases of the Crimean campaign, and was devastated in the Battle of Rostov during the Soviet winter offensive of 1941–42. After seeing some action in the summer of 1942, the Leibstandarte was pulled out of the line and sent to northern France in August, where it rested, refitted, was reinforced, and was redesignated an SS panzer grenadier unit. While the 1st SS was refitting, the Allies landed in French North Africa, so the Leibstandarte took part in the occupation of Vichy France in response.

Returned to the Eastern Front in the spring of 1943, the division took part in the Kursk offensive and suffered heavy casualties in the Battle of Kharkov (1943) before being transferred to northern Italy. While there it was upgraded to an SS panzer division and helped disarm the Italian Army after the Fascist regime collapsed, but it did not see any fighting, except against partisans. (It did, however, commit at least one major atrocity.) Returning to southern Russia in the autumn, the 1st SS was involved in heavy combat west of Kiev, at Tarnopol, and in the Dnieper battles. It unsuccessfully tried to prevent the encirclement of the 1st Panzer Army in 1944. The division was itself surrounded at Skala in the spring of that year and suffered ruinous losses in the ensuing breakout.

Transferred to northern Belgium to be rebuilt again, the Leibstandarte was reinforced to a strength of 21,386 men. It fought in the Caen sector during the Battle of Normandy, was involved in the unsuccessful German counterattack at Mortain, and was surrounded at Falaise. Before it broke out of this pocket, the 1st SS Panzer was reduced to an armored strength of only thirty tanks. Withdrawn to northwestern Germany, the veteran SS division was rebuilt once more before being placed in reserve behind the Aachen front. It fought in the Ardennes counteroffensive, where it committed a number of atrocities, most notably the murder of seventy-two American prisoners of war at Malmedy. It lost almost all of its tanks when its Kampfgruppe Peiper (the 1st SS Panzer Regiment and several attached units under the command of SS Colonel Joachim Peiper) was surrounded at La Gleize. Peiper broke out, but only 800 of his original 5,000 men escaped. The division was subsequent withdrawn and sent to Hungary, where it fought in the unsuccessful Lake Balaton counterattack. Hitler, displeased with the failure of one of the Leibstandarte's attacks, ordered it to remove the Adolf Hitler cuffband from the uniforms of its troops. The division responded by sending him a pile of their medals—in a latrine bucket. The survivors of the division retreated into Austria in 1945, and fought in the Battle of Vienna. It ended the war on the southern sector of the Eastern Front, although most of the men of the division managed to surrender to the Americans.

Commanders of the Leibstandarte included SS Lieutenant General Otto "Sepp" Dietrich (March 1933), SS Major General Theodor Wisch (July 4, 1943), SS Major General Wilhelm Mohnke (August 20, 1944), and SS Major General Otto Kumm (February 6, 1945).

Notes and Sources: Both Wisch and Mohnke were forced to give up command of the 1st SS due to wounds. Both of Wisch's legs were amputated after he was wounded near Falaise, France on August 20, 1944. Mohnke was wounded in an American air attack. Otto Kumm was the last SS general of World War II to die. He passed away on March 23, 2004, at the age of ninety-four.

Blumenson 1960: 190, 505, 570; Carell 1966: 294–95, 297, 542, 623; Carell 1971: 17, 510–11; Chant, Volume 14: 1858–61; Volume 17: 2372; Cole 1965: 260; Harrison: 240, Map VI: John Keegan, *Waffen SS: The Asphalt Soldiers* (1970): 76, 82 (hereafter cited as "Keegan"); Kennedy: Map 7; Manstein: 209–10, 482; Charles W. Snydor, Jr., *Soldiers of Destruction: The SS Death's Head Division, 1939–1945* (1977): 275–76 (hereafter cited as "Snydor"). Speidel: 42; OB 43: 216; OB 44: 325; OB 45: 336–37; Ziemke 1966: 225.

2ND SS PANZER DIVISION "DAS REICH"

Composition (late 1943): 2nd SS Panzer Regiment, 3rd SS Panzer Grenadier Regiment "Deutschland," 4th SS Panzer Grenadier Regiment "Der Fuhrer," 2nd SS Panzer Artillery Regiment, 2nd SS Panzer Reconniassance Battalion, 2nd SS Tank Destroyer Battalion, 2nd SS Engineer Battalion, 2nd SS Panzer Signal Battalion, 2nd SS Anti-Aircraft Battalion, 2nd SS Rocket Launcher Battalion, 2nd SS Field Replacement Battalion, 2nd SS Divisional Supply Troops

Home Station: "Deutschland" Regiment: Munich; "Der Führer" Regiment: Vienna.

The 2nd SS Division was formed on December 21, 1940, from two regiments of the old SS Verfugungstruppe Division and the SS Motorcycle Regiment "Langemarck," which was made up of Germans and Germanic volunteers. Divisional troops were added quickly. Initially designated SS Division (mot.) "Das Reich," it first saw action in the Balkans campaign, and later in 1941 it took part in the invasion of the Soviet Union, fighting in the battles of the Dnieper crossings, Smolensk, Kiev, Vyasma, and the Battle of Moscow. It also played a major role in saving the 9th Army in the Rzhev Pocket during the winter of 1941–42. It lost almost 10,000 men in the bitter winter fighting: 60 percent of its combat strength. Sent to France in the summer of 1942 to rest and refit, Das Reich was converted to a panzer grenadier division and, beginning on November 9, 1942, took part in the occupation of Vichy France.

Returned to the Russian Front soon after, it fought at Kharkov in March 1943, at Kursk in July, and at Kiev in November, where it suffered heavy casualties. Meanwhile, it was officially upgraded to SS panzer division status on October 22, 1943. Transferred to the Toulouse area of southwestern France in February 1944, it was ordered to Normandy when the Allies landed. On route to the front in June, it committed a famous atrocity at Tulle, where its men hanged ninety-five Frenchmen, and at Oradour, where it killed 642 people, including 245 women and 207 children, in an unauthorized reprisal for the murder of SS Major Helmut Kampfe, commander of the division's reconnaissance battalion. (The man who was directly responsible for the atrocity, SS Lieutenant Colonel August Dieckmann, was later killed in action in Normandy.)

In the Normandy campaign it was used as a "fire brigade," being divided into several combat groups and fighting on various sectors of the front. In this battle its commander, SS Lieutenant General Heinz Lammerding, was wounded and his replacement, SS Colonel Christian Tychesen, was killed. After taking part in the counterattack at Mortain, the division was surrounded with the bulk of Army Group B at Falaise. The 2nd SS Panzer broke out, but by August 21 had a strength of only 450 men, fifteen tanks, and six guns. By September it was down to its last three tanks. After a brief rebuilding period in Paderborn in western Germany (October–November), the greatly reduced Das Reich Division was in reserve near Aachen, took part in the Ardennes offensive, and was subsequently sent to Hungary, where it took part in the 6th SS Panzer Army's Lake Balaton offensive, Hitler's last major attack in the war. The division was still in action on the Eastern Front at the end of the war, but managed to surrender to the Americans west of Pilsen and north of Linz on May 8, 1945.

Commanders of the 2nd SS Panzer Division and its predecessors included SS Lieutenant General/General of Waffen SS Paul Hausser (October 19, 1939), SS Oberführer/SS Major General Wilhelm Bittrich (October 14, 1941), SS Major General Matthias Kleinheisterkamp (January 1, 1942), SS Lieutenant General Georg Keppler (April 19, 1942), SS Oberführer Herbert Ernst Vahl (February 10, 1943), SS Oberführer Kurt

A Jagdpanzer self-propelled tank destroyer.

Brasack (March 18, 1943), SS Lieutenant General Walter Krueger (April 3, 1943), SS Oberführer/SS Major General Heinz Lammerding (January 1944), SS Colonel Christian Tychsen (July 26, 1944), SS Colonel Otto Baum (July 28, 1944), Lammerding (returned October 23, 1944), SS Colonel Karl Kreutz (January 20, 1945), SS Lieutenant General Werner Ostendorff (February 10, 1945), SS Colonel Rudolf Lehmann (March 9, 1945), and Kreutz (April 13, 1945).

Notes and Sources: The SS Rifle Regiment "Langemark" was dissolved in the summer of 1943. Hausser was seriously wounded (and lost an eye) on October 14, 1941. Bittrich was promoted to SS major general on October 19, 1941. Lammerding officially assumed command of Das Reich on January 1, 1944. The command, however, was divided at the time. Lammerding led a *Kampfgruppe* of 5,000 men in Russia until March 8, 1944, when he left for France. SS Colonel Otto Weidinger assumed command of the kampfgruppe in Russia. SS Colonel Sylvester Stadler commanded the units rebuilding in France until Lammerding arrived. Lammerding was promoted to SS major general on April 20, 1944. Tychsen was killed in action by members of the U.S. 2nd Armored Division on July 28, 1944. Ostendorff was seriously wounded by an incendiary shell on March 9, 1945. He succumbed to his wounds on May 1. Lehmann was seriously wounded in the Battle of Vienna in April 1945.

Blumenson 1960: 275, 422, 554, 577; Blumenson 1969: 42; Carell 1966: 80, 90, 623; Carell 1971: 17, 525; Chant, Volume 14: 1859–61; Volume 17: 2372; Cole 1965: 583; Keegan: 76, 82, 91; Manstein: 488; MacDonald 1973: 27; George Stein, *Waffen SS* (1966): 176–68 (hereafter cited as "Stein"); Tessin, Vol. 2: 144–45; Vol. 14: 144–45; OB 43: 216–17; OB 44: 325; OB 45: 337; Otto Weidinger, *Division Das Reich: Der Weg der 2. SS-Panzer-Division "Das Reich"* (1967-1982), Volumes 1–5; Otto Weidinger, *Division Das Reich in Bild* (1981); Mark C. Yerger, *Waffen-SS Commanders: The Army, Corps and Divisional Leaders of a Legend*, Volume I, *Augsberger to Kreutz* (1997): 294; Volume II, *Krüger to Zimmermann*, (1999): 75, 136, 138. For the story of the division's atrocities in France in June 1944, see Max Hasting's excellent book, *Das Reich* (1981).

3RD SS PANZER DIVISION "TOTENKOPF"

Composition (1943): 3rd SS Panzer Regiment, 5th SS Panzer Grenadier Regiment "Thule," 6th SS Panzer Grenadier Regiment "Theodor Eicke," 3rd SS Panzer Artillery Regiment,

3rd SS Panzer Reconnaissance Battalion, 3rd SS Tank Destroyer Battalion, 3rd SS Assault Gun Battalion, 3rd SS Panzer Engineer Battalion, 3rd SS Panzer Signal Battalion, 3rd SS Anti-Aircraft Battalion, 3rd SS Rocket Launcher Battalion, 3rd SS Field Replacement Battalion, 3rd SS Divisional Supply Troops

Home Station: Berlin (Oranienburg)

The "Totenkopf," or Death's Head, Division was created as an SS motorized division on October 16, 1939. Probably the most brutal German division to serve in World War II, most of its men had previously served as concentration camp guards at Dachau, Sachsenhausen, or Buchenwald. It originally included the 1st, 2nd, and 3rd SS Totenkopf Infantry Regiments and the usual divisional troops. Its men fought well in France and Flanders in 1940, although elements of the division did show signs of panic when struck by the British armored counterattack at Arras in May. Totenkopf was not well-led initially, but this situation improved as the SS officers gained practical experience. The division murdered a number of Allied prisoners during the Flanders campaign and committed at least one atrocity against the British.

After the French capitulation, the 3rd SS was assigned to occupation duties in the Bay of Biscay area near Bordeaux, until being sent to Poland to prepare for the invasion of Russia in the spring of 1941. Totenkopf fought on the northern sector of the Eastern Front from June 1941 to October 1942. It suffered such heavy losses in the initial advance on Leningrad that its 2nd SS Totenkopf Motorized Infantry Regiment (as it was then called) had to be dissolved in July 1941. Later surrounded in the Battle of the Demyansk Pocket in the winter of 1941–42, it distinguished itself in the heavy fighting, although it suffered tremendous losses. Of the 17,265 men who crossed into Russia with "Totenkopf," 12,625 were casualties by March 20, 1942. Of these, only 5,029 had been replaced. Nevertheless, fighting with fanatical bravery, it remained in the line, playing a decisive role in keeping the sole supply route to II Corps at Demyansk open against repeated Russian attacks.

By September 1942, its infantry and artillery regiments, reconnaissance, engineer, and anti-tank battalions had all suffered an average of 80 percent casualties, and the division was at less than regimental strength. Finally, in October 1942, it was sent to France, where it was rebuilt as an SS panzer division. After taking part in the occupation of Vichy France in November 1942, it briefly served on guard duty on the Mediterranean coast and was upgraded to a panzer grenadier division on November 9, 1942, before being returned to Russia in February 1943. Upon its return to the Eastern Front, its commander and founder, General of SS Theodor Eicke, was killed when his reconnaissance plane was shot down by the Russians on February 26. The 3rd SS spent the rest of its career on the Eastern Front, serving as a fire brigade and fighting as Kharkov, Kursk (where it lost 50 percent of its tanks and vehicles), and the Dnieper campaign, where it again suffered heavy casualties. It fought at Krivoy Rog (November 1943–June 1944), in the Cherkassy sector (February–March 1944), and helped slow the Russian spring offensive of 1944 west of Kirovograd. It was transferred to Army Group Center in July 1944, after the 4th and 9th Armies collapsed.

Despite its reduced numbers, Totenkopf participated in the defense of Modlin and Warsaw and once again took heavy losses and inflicted heavy casualties on the Soviets. Transferred to Hungary in December 1944, it took part in the unsuccessful counterattack west of Budapest and in the Battle of Vienna. It ended the war in Austria, having suffered more than 54,000 casualties during the conflict—a truly incredible statistic. On May 8, 1945, the 3rd SS surrendered to the U.S. Army south of Linz. A week later, the Americans turned them over to the Russians. Many of the former members of the division disappeared while in Soviet captivity.

Commanders of the division included General of Waffen-SS Theodor Eicke (October 16, 1939), SS Colonel Matthias Kleinheisterkamp (July 7, 1941), SS Major General Georg Keppler (July 15, 1941), Eicke (returned September 19, 1941), SS Major General Max Simon (February 26, 1943), SS Oberführer/

Major General Hermann Priess (early April 1943), SS Colonel Karl Ullrich (June 20, 1944), and SS Oberführer/Major General Helmuth Becker (June 21, 1944).

Notes and Sources: Totenkopf was officially upgraded to panzer division status on April 10, 1944. Eicke, the former commandant of the Dachau concentration camp (1933–34) and Inspector of Concentration Camps and SS Guard Formations (1934–39), was seriously wounded when his car hit a mine on July 6, 1941. Priess was promoted to SS major general on July 15, 1943. He became ill in the summer of 1944, and had to be relieved. Hellmuth Becker was promoted to SS major general on October 1, 1944. He was executed by the Russians without trial in 1953.

Carell 1966: 237–46, 623; Carell 1971: 17, 218; Cole 1950: 48; *http://www.feldgrau.com* (created and maintained by Jason Pipes and hereafter cited as "Pipes:); Keegan: 64–65, 76, 82, 91; Kursietis: 257; Snydor: 35, 165–66, 168, 222, 243–45, 250, 290, 311; Karl Ullrich, *Wie ein Fels im Meer: Kriegsgeschichte der 3. SS-Panzer-Division "Totenkopf"* (1984 and 1987), Vol.s 1–2; OB 43: 217; OB 44: 326; OB 45: 338; Robert Wistrich, *Who's Who in Nazi Germany* (1982): 63–65; Yerger 1997: 50, 154, 292; Yerger 1999: 164, 244; Ziemke 1966: 284.

4TH SS PANZER GRENADIER DIVISION "POLIZEI"

Composition (1945): 4th SS Panzer Battalion, 7th SS Panzer Grenadier Regiment, 8th SS Panzer Grenadier Regiment, 4th SS Panzer Artillery Regiment, 4th SS Panzer Reconnaissance Battalion, 4th SS Tank Destroyer Battalion, 4th SS Assault Gun Battalion, 4th SS Panzer Engineer Battalion, 4th SS Signal Battalion, 4th SS Anti-Aircraft Battalion, 4th SS Field Replacement Battalion, 4th SS Divisional Supply Troops

Home Station: See below

The SS Police Division was formed from members of the German Order Police in October 1939. It was not transferred to the Waffen-SS until February 10, 1942, and was not designated a panzer grenadier unit until June 1943. It became the 4th SS Panzer Grenadier Division on October 22, 1943. Initially it consisted of the 1st, 2nd, and 3rd Police Infantry Regiments. After finishing training in February 1940, the division fought in the French campaign and took part in the invasion of Russia in

June 1941. It never distinguished itself in combat to the degree its brother German Waffen-SS divisions did, although it performed creditably. It fought in all the major battles of Army Group North from June 1941 to May 1943, including Nevel, Luga, Lake Ilmen, Volkhov, and Lake Ladoga, where it suffered heavy casualties. The 4th SS performed security duties in the Protectorate (formerly Czechoslovakia) and Poland in the spring of 1943, before being transferred to Greece that summer. By September 1944, the unit was in Serbia, fighting Tito's partisans, before returning to action against the Russians in Hungary in October. The 4th SS fought in Pomerania and West Prussia, and as part of Army Group Vistula, was cut off in the Hela Peninsula by the Soviet advance on Berlin. It surrendered to the Russians on May 8, 1945, although some members of the division were attached to Army Group Steiner and managed to surrender to the Americans at the end of the war.

The commanders of the Police Division included Lieutenant General of Police Konrad Hitschler (October 1, 1939), SS Major General/SS Lieutenant General Karl von Pfeffer-Wildenbruck (October 10, 1939), SS Lieutenant General Arthur Mülverstedt (November 10, 1940), SS Major General Walter Krüger (August 8, 1941), SS Major General/Lieutenant General Alfred Wünnenberg (December 15, 1941), Colonel of Police Alfred Borchert (May 15, 1942), Wünnenberg (July 18, 1942), SS Oberführer/Major General Fritz Schmedes (January 6, 1943), Wünnenberg (February 1943), Schmedes (June 10, 1943), SS Lieutenant Colonel Otto Bing (June 20, 1943), Schmedes (August 1943), SS Colonel/Oberführer/Major General Karl Schümers (June 18, 1944), SS Major General Herbert Vahl (July 5, 1944), Schümers again (July 18, 1944), SS Colonel Helmut Doerner (August 18, 1944), SS Colonel Walter Harzer (November 27, 1944), SS Colonel Fritz Goehler (March 1, 1945), and Harzer (March 1945–end).

Notes and Sources: Pfeffer-Wildenbruck was promoted to SS Lieutenant General on April 20, 1940. Mülverstedt was killed in action on August 8, 1941. Wünnenberg was promoted to SS lieutenant general on July 1, 1942. Bock was promoted to SS colonel on November

9, 1943. Vahl was killed in an accident in Greece, July 22, 1944. Schmedes was killed on August 18, 1944, when hit command car hit a land mine. He had been promoted to SS major general on November 9, 1943.

Carell 1966: 250, 421; Carell 1971: 279; Keegan: 66; Lexikon; Seaton: 491; Tessin, Vol. 2: 275–76; Vol. 14: 287–88; OB 43: 218; OB 45: 338–39; Yerger 1999: 196–97, 226–27, 309; Ziemke 1966: 477.

5TH SS PANZER DIVISION "VIKING"

Composition: 5th SS Panzer Regiment, 9th SS Panzer Grenadier Regiment "Germania," 10th SS Panzer Grenadier Regiment "Westland," 5th SS Panzer Artillery Regiment, 5th SS Panzer Reconnaissance Battalion, 5th SS Tank Destroyer Battalion, 5th SS Assault Gun Battalion, 5th SS Panzer Engineer Battalion, 5th SS Panzer Signal Battalion, 5th SS Anti-Aircraft Battalion, 5th SS Rocket Launcher (Projector) Battalion, 5th SS Field Replacement Battalion, 5th SS Field Replacement Battalion

Home Station: Hamburg and Klagenfurt

The 5th SS Division was formed on November 20, 1940, from the "Germania" Motorized Regiment of the SS Verfügungstruppe Division and two regiments of Scandinavian, Dutch and Flemish volunteers—the Nordland and Westland Motorized Regiments. Subsequent replacements were drawn from Volksdeutsche from the Balkans and from German volunteers, giving the unit a real international character (as well as a real language problem) by the end of the war. Nevertheless, it fought well in all of its engagements.

As the "Germania" *Standarte* (Regiment), it took part in the French campaign, where it distinguished itself. Remustered as a panzer grenadier division in December 1940, "Viking" served on the southern sector of the Russian Front in 1941–42, fighting in the frontier battles, at Tarnopol, Kiev, Rostov (1941), on the Mius River (in the winter of 1941–42), and in the recapturing of Rostov. It eventually ended up in the Caucasus (fall 1942). It was redesignated 5th SS Panzer

Grenadier Division "Viking" on Novmeber 9, 1942. It retreated to the Don (1942–43) and fought in the Battle of Kursk in July 1943, and suffered heavy losses at Iszum, Kharkov, and in the retreat to the Dnieper. Briefly withdrawn from the line, the 5th SS was converted to a panzer division on October 23, 1943. With several other divisions, it was encircled at Cherkassy in February 1944, escaping only after suffering heavy casualties. It nevertheless fought in the Battle of Kovel the following month. Sent to Poland in April, it again sustained heavy losses in the battles around Warsaw that autumn. Transferred to Hungary, it took part in the unsuccessful attempt to relieve Budapest in December and suffered severe losses in the Battle of Vienna in April 1945. The bulk of the Viking Division surrendered to the Americans at Radstadt, Czechoslovakia, in May 1945.

Its commanders included SS Major General/SS Lieutenant General Felix Steiner (December 1, 1940), SS Major General/ Lieutenant General Herbert Gille (May 1, 1943), SS Colonel Joachim Muhlenkamp (August 12, 1944), and SS Oberführer Karl Ullrich (October 9, 1944).

Notes and Sources: SS Colonel Dr. Edmund Deisenhofer was named commander of the division on July 20, 1943, but never actually assumed command. Steiner was promoted to SS lieutenant general on January 1, 1942. Gille was promoted to SS lieutenant general on November 9, 1944.

Carell 1966: 533, 546, 552; Carell 1971: 89; Keegan: 68, 91; Tessin, Vol. 2: 321–22; Vol. 14: 259–60; Peter Strassner, *Europäische Freiwillige: Die Geschichte der 5. SS-Panzer-Division "Wiking"* (1968); OB 43: 217; OB 44: 327, OB 45: 339; Yerger 1997: 188–89; Yerger 1999: 263–65; Ziemke 1966: 340. For an excellent personal history of a young SS man, as well as the story of the battles of the Viking Division, see Peter Neumann, *The Black March* (1960).

6TH SS MOUNTAIN DIVISION "NORD"

Composition: 11th SS Mountain Infantry Regiment "Reinhard Heydrich," 12th SS Mountain Infantry Regiment "Michael Gesimar," 6th SS Mobile Battalion "Nord," SS Ski Jaeger Battalion "Norge," 6th SS Mountain Artillery Regiment,

6th SS Assault Gun Battalion, 6th SS Mountain Reconnaissance Battalion, 6th SS Tank Destroyer Battalion, 6th SS Mountain Engineer Battalion, 6th SS Mountain Signal Battalion, 6th SS Anti-Aircraft Battalion. The 506th SS Panzer Grenadier Battalion was attached to the division in February 1945.

Home Station: Austria

Raised in Austria as an SS regiment in 1940, "North" was first upgraded to a brigade and then became the SS Mountain Division "North" in September 1942. It included many Volksdeutsche mountaineers. It was sent to Finland in 1941, from whence it struck into Russia with the Army of Norway in the unsuccessful drive on Murmansk. It behaved badly at first, a fact partially attributable to the dark, depressing Finnish forests, but became more reliable as the war progressed. The 6th SS remained in northern Russia and was more or less continuously engaged until autumn 1944. It took part in the retreat from Lapland to Norway and in mid-November 1944, embarked from Oslo, bound for Denmark. By December it was fighting on the Western Front, in the Saar sector around Landau. Most of the 6th SS was cut off on the wrong (western) side of the Rhine River by the rapid Allied advance of March 1945. The division—now 6,000 strong—put up a spirited resistance, and it took U.S. forces several days to run it to earth. The divisional commander, SS Lieutenant General Karl Heinrich Brenner, was captured on April 2, ending organized resistance by the 6th SS. SS Colonel Franz Schreiber took command of the remnants of the 6th SS Mountain Division (which had escaped to the east bank) and led them until the end of the war. They surrendered to the Americans in May 1945.

Divisional commanders included SS Major General Richard Herrmann (June 12, 1940), SS Major General Karl Demelhuber (May 15, 1941), SS Colonel Bernard Voss (November 2, 1941), Demelhuber (resumed command November 1941), SS Major General Matthias Kleinheisterkamp (April 1, 1942), SS Colonel Hans Schneider (April 20, 1942), Kleinheisterkamp (returned June 14, 1942), SS Lieutenant General Lother Debes

An American Sherman tank (right) passes an abandoned Panzer Mark IV in the Ardennes, December 1944 or January 1945.

(October 15, 1943), General of Waffen-SS Friedrich-Wilhelm Krüger (May 20, 1944), SS Colonel Gustav Lombard (August 23, 1944), Brenner (August 26, 1944), and Schreiber (April 3, 1945).

Notes and Sources: Carell 1966: 454; Keegan: 156; Kursietis: 259; MacDonald 1973: 250, 349–50; Pipes; Tessin, Vol. 3: 44–45; OB 43: 217-18; OB 44: 327; OB 45: 340; Yerger 1997: 101–2, 306; Yerger 1999: 15; Ziemke 1966: 159–60, 222–23, 292–93, 312.

7TH SS VOLUNTEER MOUNTAIN DIVISION "PRINZ EUGEN"

Composition: 13th SS Volunteer Mountain Infantry Regiment "Artur Phelps," 14th SS Volunteer Mountain Infantry Regiment "Skanderberg," 7th SS Volunteer Mountain Artillery Regiment, 7th SS Mountain Reconnaissance Battalion (Motorized), 7th SS Motorcycle Battalion, 7th SS Cavalry Battalion, 7th SS Tank Destroyer Battalion, 7th SS Mountain Engineer Battalion, 7th SS Mountain Signal Battalion, 7th SS Anti-Aircraft Battalion, 7th SS Field Replacement Battalion, 7th SS Divisional Supply Troops

Home Station: Serbia

The 7th SS Mountain Division (which was initially designated the SS Volunteer Mountain Division "Prince Eugen") was formed in northern Serbia in October 1942. Its troops were *Volksdeutsche* (ethnic Germans) from Hungary, Romania, and Yugoslavia. Eventually, it grew to a stength of 15,000 men. In the spring of 1943, the 7th SS was transferred to Bosnia and the Dalmatian coast, where it operated against partisans. In October 1944 it was shifted to the Belgrade area to cover the eastern flank of the German withdrawal through Yugoslavia, where it suffered heavy losses. These casualties were made good near the end of the year when some of the more reliable elements of the disbanded 21st SS Mountain Division "Skanderberg" or "Albanian #1" were absorbed by the 7th SS. At this time, the 14th SS Mountain Infantry Regiment was given the honorary title "Skanderberg." The division ended the war in the Balkans as part of Army Group F. It surrendered to the Yugoslavs in the Cilli vicinity at the end of the conflict.

Its commanders included SS Major General/SS Lieutenant General Artur Phelps (January 13, 1942), SS Major General Reichsritter Karl von Oberkamp (May 15, 1943), SS Colonel/SS Oberführer August Schmidhuber (November 28, 1943), Oberkamp (December 11, 1943), SS Major General Otto Kumm (January 30, 1944), and Schmidhuber (January 20, 1945).

Notes and Sources: The division's motorcycle battalion was dissolved in the summer of 1943. Phelps was promoted to SS lieutenant general on April 20, 1942. August Schmidhuber was promoted to SS Oberführer on June 21, 1944. He was hanged by the Yugoslavians in Belgrade on February 19, 1947.

Keegen: 100, 158; Kursietis: 259; Lexikon; Stein: 170, 200, 204, 221, 274; Tessin, Vol. 3: 83–84; OB 43: 218; OB 44: 328; OB 45: 340; Yerger 1999: 201–3.

8TH SS CAVALRY DIVISION "FLORIAN GEYER"

Composition (1943): 15th SS Cavalry Regiment, 16th SS Cavalry Regiment, 17th SS Cavalry Regiment, 18th SS Cavalry Regiment, 8th SS Artillery Regiment, 8th SS Bicycle Battalion, 8th SS Tank Destroyer Battalion, 8th SS Assault Gun Battery, 8th SS Engineer Batallion, 8th SS Signal Battalion, 8th SS Anti-Aircraft Battalion, 8th SS Field Replacement Battalion, 8th SS Divisional Supply Troops

Home Station: Debica, General Gouvernement

Originally formed near Warsaw as an SS cavalry brigade in late 1941, this unit first saw action against the Russian winter offensive of 1941–42, and remained in more or less continuous contact until September 1942, when it was upgraded to divisional status as the SS Cavalry Division. At that time, it included the 1st, 2nd, and 3rd SS Cavalry Regiments, the SS Cavalry Artillery Regiment, the SS Reconnaissance Battalion (Cavalry Division), the SS Tank Destroyer Battalion (Cavalry Division), as well as a flak battalion, an engineer battalion, a signal battalion, a field replacement battalion and an assault gun battery (company). The division was soon back in the line and fought at Rzhev and Orel on the central sector of the Eastern Front until the spring of 1943, when it was transferred to the Bobruisk area. It was engaged in anti-partisan operations in the rear of Army Group Center until September 1943, when it was transferred to the south and fought in the retreat to the Dnieper.

The division was then sent to Hungary and was redesignated the 8th SS Cavalry Divison on October 22, 1943, with the composition shown above. (In June 1944, the 17th SS Cavalry Regiment was transferred to the 22nd SS Volunteer Cavalry Division and the tank destroyer and assault gun battalions were combined. The reconnaissance battalion became a panzer reconnaissance battalion in March 1944.) Following its reorganization, the 8th SS Cavalry Division was sent to the Brod area of Croatia (Yugoslavia). By April 1944, it was in Hungary and in September was sent into action in Transylvania, after the German front in Romania collapsed. The 8th SS Cavalry was encircled in Budapest with the IX SS Mountain Corps on December 29, 1944. At the time, it had 8,000 men, twenty-nine tanks and assault guns, thirty pieces of artillery, and seventeen heavy anti-tank guns. It put up a fierce resistance in bitter house-to-house fighting, but was finally destroyed by the Russians during the final breakout attempt on February 11, 1945. Of the estimated 30,000 Axis soldiers surrounded in the Hungarian capital and still available for action that day, only about 800 succeeded in breaking out and making their way back to German lines.

Commanders of the division included SS Colonel/SS Oberführer/SS Major General/SS Lieutenant General Hermann Fegelein (May 15, 1940), SS Colonel/SS Major General Gustav Lombard (March 1942), Fegelein (returned April 1942), SS Major General Wilhelm Bittrich (August 1942), Lombard (December 1942), SS Colonel Fritz Freitag (February 15, 1943), Fegelein (May 14, 1943), SS Lieutenant Colonel of Reserves/SS Oberführer Bruno Streckenbach (September 13, 1943),

Fegelein (October 22, 1943), Streckenbach (January 1, 1944), and SS Lieutenant Colonel/SS Colonel/SS Oberführer/SS Major General Joachim Rumohr (April 1, 1944).

Notes and Sources: Florian Geyer (1490–1525) was a Franconian knight and a supporter of Martin Luther's religious views during the Peasant Wars (1522–25). Freitag was hospitalized in the spring of 1943, and apparently turned command of the division over to SS Colonel August Zehender, who reportedly commanded it for a few days before Fegelein returned. Fegelein was wounded on September 9 and again on September 13, 1943, and had to turn command of the division over to Streckenbach. Streckenbach was promoted to SS colonel of reserves on August 28, 1943, and to SS Oberführer of reserves on January 30, 1944. Rumohr was promoted to SS colonel on April 20, 1944, to SS Oberführer on November 11, 1944, and to SS major general on January 15, 1945. During the breakout from Budapest, he committed suicide to prevent capture on February 12, 1945.

Keegan: 156; Lexikon; Pipes, web site accessed 2006; Seaton: 419–20; Tessin, Vol. 3: 119–20; OB 43: 218; OB 44: 328; OB 45: 341; Yerger 1997: 80, 171; Yerger 1999: 184, 278. For Fegelein's story, see William L. Shirer, *The Rise and Fall of the Third Reich* (1960): 1114, 1121–22.

9TH SS PANZER DIVISION "HOHENSTAUFEN"

Composition: 9th SS Panzer Regiment, 19th SS Panzer Grenadier Regiment, 20th SS Panzer Grenadier Regiment, 9th SS Panzer Artillery Regiment, 9th SS Panzer Reconnaissance Battalion, 9th SS Tank Destroyer Battalion, 9th Assault Gun Battalion, 9th SS Engineer Battalion, 9th SS Panzer Signal Battalion, 9th SS Anti-Aircraft Battalion, 9th SS Rocket Launcher Battalion, 9th SS Divisional Supply Troops

Home Station: Berlin-Lichterfelde

The formation of this division was authorized by Hitler in December 1942, and it was officially activated at Berlin-Lichterfelde as the 9th SS Panzer Grenadier Division on February 1, 1943. It was sent to northeastern France the following month. It spent several months training in the Amiens and Ypres areas, before being sent to the Mediterranean coast area of France in February 1944. Hohenstaufen was hastily sent into combat on the Eastern Front in March, where it took part in the Tarnopol counteroffensive that helped save the 1st Panzer Army. Soon after it was shifted to Poland to prevent a possible Russian advance through that sector. The 9th SS was quickly returned to France in June and was soon heavily engaged in the Normandy fighting. It suffered heavy losses in the battles west of Caen (against the British), in the Montain counterattack (against the Americans), and in the Falaise breakout. Although it had inflicted severe losses on the Allies, it was down to a strength of 460 men, twenty guns, and twenty to twenty-five tanks by August 21. (It had 15,849 men on June 30.)

Transferred to the rear at Arnhem, the 9th SS, with its sister division, the 10th SS Panzer, was in an ideal position to counter the British 1st Airborne Division's parachute assault on Arnhem in September 1944. Under the command of the II SS Panzer Corps, they virtually destroyed the elite Allied paratrooper unit. After resting and refitting in the Arnhem vicinity, the Hohenstaufen Division took part in the Battle of the Bulge and was sent to Hungary in February 1945. It ended the war fighting in Austria on the southern sector of the Eastern Front, although it managed to escape Soviet captivity by surrendering to the U.S. Army at Linz on May 8, 1945.

The division's commanders included SS Major General/ Lieutenant General Willi Bittrich (February 15, 1943), SS Colonel Thomas Mueller (June 28, 1944), SS Oberführer/SS Major General Sylvester Stadler (July 10, 1944), SS Oberführer Friedrich Wilhelm Bock (August 1, 1944), SS Colonel Walter Harzer (August 29, 1944), and Stadler (returned October 10, 1944)

Notes and Sources: The noble German family Hohenstaufen produced several kings and emperors between 1138 and 1254. Bittrich was promoted to SS lieutenant general on May 1, 1943. Stadler was severely wounded by Allied artillery fire on July 29 or 30, 1944. He was promoted to SS Oberführer on August 1, 1944, and to SS major general on April 20, 1945.

Blumenson 1960: 190, 577; Carell 1971: 523; Carell 1973: 209–10; Chant, Volume 14: 1811; Keegan: 90–91; Kursietis: 260; Hastings: 215; *Kriegstagebuch des OKW*, Volume I: 1146; Kursietis: 260; Pipes; Stein: 218; Tessin, Vol. 3: 156–57; OB 44: 329; OB 45: 341, Yerger 1999: 253–54.

10TH SS PANZER DIVISION "FRUNDSBERG"

Composition: 10th SS Panzer Regiment, 21st SS Panzer Grenadier Regiment, 22nd SS Panzer Grenadier Regiment, 10th SS Panzer Artillery Regiment, 10th SS Motorcycle Regiment, 10th SS Panzer Reconnaissance Battalion, 10th SS Tank Destroyer Battalion, 10th Assault Gun Battalion, 10th SS Panzer Engineer Battalion, 10th SS Panzer Signal Battalion, 10th SS Anti-Aircraft Battalion, 10th SS Rocket Launcher Battalion, 10th SS Divisional Supply Troops

Home Station: Bruenn

Formed in southwestern France in the winter of 1942–43, the 10th SS was the sister division of the 9th SS Panzer. At first designated SS Panzer Division "Karl der Grosse" (Karl the Great), it was activated on February 1, 1943, and was transferred to southeastern France in the summer of 1943. By autumn it was in Normandy and, on October 3, 1943, was remustered in as a panzer division. It had 19,513 men at the end of the year. Hastily sent to the Eastern Front in March 1944, "Frundsberg" took part in the Tarnopol offensive that saved the 1st Panzer Army. By April, the 10th SS was in Poland as part of the reserve, and in June it returned to France. The Frundsberg Division was badly hurt in the Normandy fighting and subsequent encirclement in and breakout from the Falaise Pocket. By August 21 its strength had been reduced to that of a weak infantry battalion, and all of its tanks had been destroyed; nevertheless, the division took part in the withdrawal from France. Sent to the Arnhem area to regroup, the 10th SS helped crush the British 1st Airborne Division in September. Later that month, the division was part of Colonel General Student's 1st Parachute Army in the Albert Canal and Siegfried Line battles.

Shifted back to Germany, the division was transferred to the Aachen area in November, fought at Dueren and then in the Saar, where it replaced the 9th Panzer Division, which was earmarked for the Battle of the Bulge. The Frundsberg Division did not fight in the Ardennes offensive but took part in the unsuccessful attempt to take Strasbourg in January 1945. The survivors of the 10th SS Panzer Division were returned to the

The Panzer Mark VI "Tiger" tank. With its thick frontal armor and heavy 88-mm gun, the Tiger terrorized Allied formations late in the war. U.S. WAR COLLEGE PHOTO

Eastern Front (Pomerania) in February and were defending east of Berlin until late March, when they were transferred from Army Group Vistula to Army Group Center. The division fought its last battles in Saxony (eastern Germany) and Czechoslovakia in 1945. On April 19, it was encircled and largely destroyed at Spremberg, together with the 344th Volksgrenadier Division and the Führer Begleit Division. Remnants of the 10th SS broke out of the pocket on April 21, but were surrounded again at Kausche within hours. They broke out again on April 22 and headed west. Most of the survivors of the division surrendered to the Russians near Teplitz-Schoenau on May 9, although a number of small groups and individual soldiers reached the Elbe River between May 10 and 12. These men surrendered to the U.S. 102nd Infantry Division at Tangermünde.

The commanders of the 10th SS Panzer Division included SS Colonel Michel Lippert (January 1, 1943), SS Major General Lothar Debes (February 15, 1943), SS Major General/ Lieutenant General Karl von Treuenfeld (November 12, 1943), SS Colonel/SS Oberführer/SS Major General Heinz Harmel (April 27, 1944), and SS Lieutenant Colonel Franz Roestel (April 27, 1945).

Notes and Sources: Karl von Treuenfeld was promoted to lieutenant general on January 30, 1944. He seriously wounded in the Tarnopol battles on or about April 22, 1944. Harmel was promoted to SS Oberführer on May 18, 1944, and to SS major general on September 7, 1944.

Blumenson 1960: 190, 539, 577; Carell 1971: 523, 529; Chant, Volume 14: 1859–61; Volume 17: 2277, 2372; Keegan: 90–91; Kursietis: 261; Lexikon; MacDonald 1963: 110, 548, 567; Pipes; *www.ritterkreuztraeger-1939–1945.de/Waffen-SS/Harmel-Heinz.htm*; Stein: 218–19; Tessin, Vol. 3: 188–89; OB 45: 342; Yerger 1997: 223; Ziemke 1966: 469.

11TH SS VOLUNTEER PANZER GRENADIER DIVISION "NORDLAND"

Composition: 11th SS Panzer Battalion "Hermann von Salza," 23rd SS Panzer Grenadier Regiment "Norge," 24th SS Panzer Grenadier Regiment "Danemark," 11th SS Panzer Artillery Regiment, 11th SS Panzer Reconnaissance Battalion, 11th SS Motorcycle Battalion, 11th SS Tank Destroyer Battalion, 11th SS Assault Gun Battalion, 11th SS Panzer Engineer Battalion, 11th SS Signal Battalion, 11th SS Flak Battalion, 11th SS Field Replacement Battalion, 11th SS Divisional Supply Troops

Home Station: Graz

The 11th SS was formed in Troop Maneuver Area Grafenwoehr in July 1943, by the merger of three Germanic legions: "Niederlande," or Netherlands (1,600 men); "Danemark," or Denmark (700 men); and "Norwegen," or Norway (600 men). At first designated *SS-Panzergrenadier-Division 11 (germanisch)*, its ranks were rounded out by Volksdeutsche volunteers from the Balkans and by transfers from the "Nordland" Regiment of the 5th SS Panzer Division "Viking." Initially, it consisted of the SS Panzer Grenadier Regiments "Norge" and "Danemark," which were redesignated the 23rd SS Panzer Grenadier Regiment "Norge" and the 24th SS Panzer Grenadier Regiment "Danemark" on October 22, 1943. That same day, it was renamed the 11th SS Volunteer Panzer Grenadier Division "Nordland."

Meanwhile, in the autumn of 1943, it was sent to northern Crotia, apparently engaged in training, but in December 1943, it was transferred to Army Group North, which was unsuccessfully trying to prevent the Russians from breaking the Siege of Leningrad. The 11th SS took part in the retreat across the old Baltic states region and suffered heavy casualties in the Narva area. From September 18–22, 1944, "Nordland" force-marched 250 miles in four days from the Narva sector to Riga, arriving just in time to prevent a major Russian breakthrough and save the 18th Army and Army Detachment Narva from encirclement and annihilation. It withdrew into the Courland Pocket in October 1944 but was returned to Germany via ship in early 1945. It fought in Pomerania and on the Oder, and in April 1945, took part in the Battle of Berlin, where the bulk of the division was destroyed. Elements of the division, however, managed to escape the Berlin encirclement. They joined the 12th Army and surrendered to the Americans on May 5, 1945.

The commanders of the 11th SS included SS Colonel Franz Augsberger (March 22, 1943), SS Major General Fritz Scholz (May 1, 1943), SS Oberführer/SS Major General Joachim Ziegler (July 27, 1944), and SS Major General Dr. jur. Gustav Krukenberg (April 26, 1945).

Notes and Sources: Fritz von Scholz was killed in action on the Narva on July 28, 1944. Ziegler was promoted to major general on August 1, 1944. He was relieved of his command by General Weidling, the commander of the LVI Panzer Corps and commandant of Berlin, on April 26, and committed suicide when the city fell.

Chant, Volume 18: 2381; Keegan: 96, 129, 157; Kursietis: 262; Seaton: 581; Stein: 162–63, 208; OB 45: 342; Ziemke 1966: 406, 487.

12TH SS PANZER DIVISION "HITLER JUGEND"

Composition: 12th SS Panzer Regiment, 25th SS Panzer Grenadier Regiment, 26th SS Panzer Grenadier Regiment, 12th SS Panzer Artillery Regiment, 12th SS Panzer Reconnaissance Battalion, 12th SS Tank Destroyer Battalion, 12th SS Panzer Engineer Battalion, 12th SS Panzer Signal Battalion, 12th SS Flak Battalion, 12th SS Rocket Launcher Battalion, 12th SS Divisional Supply Troops

Home Station: See below

As its name implies, this unit was formed mainly from Hitler Youth members and was recruited from military fitness camps of that organization. Its training cadres were supplied by the 1st SS Panzer Division. The average of the soldiers of the 12th SS in 1943 was seventeen. Activated on June 24, 1943, the 12th spent the next year in Belgium, where it served primarily as a training unit for other SS divisions. In April 1944, it was sent to France and was rushed to the threatened Nonnandy sector on June 6, where it helped contain, but could not defeat, the D-Day invasion. Remaining on the line for almost a month, the young men of the Hitler Youth Division fought with fanatical dedication to the Nazi cause; some of its combat units suffered 90 percent casualties before the campaign was over. All totalled, the division's strength dropped from 20,540 to 12,500—with more than 60 percent casualties in most combat units. Despite its losses, the 12th SS fought with great skill and courage, inflicting heavy casualties on their British and Canadian opponents. On June 26, for example, it played a major role in checking Montgomery's "Epsom" offensive and destroyed more than fifty British tanks in the process; the Hitler Youth Division, however, lost more than 700 men in the fighting, including most of its engineer battalion. On July 4, the 150 survivors of the 27th SS Panzer Grenadier Regiment, supported by the divisional reserve (two or three tanks and one 88mm antiaircraft gun) repulsed the entire Canadian 8th Infantry Brigade, two battalions of the British 78th Armored Division, and associated Allied support units in the Battle of the Carpiquet Airfield. The 12th SS evacuated Caen on July 15, but on August 8 they saved the day at Falaise by preventing a British breakthrough. Eventually encircled, the Hitler Youth Division broke out but, by August 21, could assemble only 300 combat effectives and ten operational tanks, and all its artillery had been lost or destroyed. By September, it still had fewer than 2,000 men.

By October, the 12th SS Panzer was temporarily defunct; its few survivors were in Aachen, fighting the Americans as Combat Group Diefenthal of the 1st SS Panzer Division. Withdrawn and hastily rebuilt, using naval and Luftwaffe personnel, the division permanently lost its eliteness. The 12th SS nevertheless fought in the Ardennes, where it was still understrength. In February 1945, it took part in the Lake Balaton offensive in Hungary and in April was part of the 6th SS Panzer Army in the Battle of Vienna. Its strength at that time was 7,731 men. It ended the war on the southern sector of the Eastern Front but managed to surrender to the Americans near Enns, Austria, on May 8, 1945.

Commanders of the Hitler Jugend included SS Oberführer/SS Major General Fritz Witt (June 24, 1943), SS Colonel/SS Oberführer Kurt "Panzer" Meyer (June 14, 1944), SS Major/SS Lieutenant Colonel Hubert Meyer (September 6, 1944), SS Oberführer Fritz Kraemer (October 24, 1944), and

SS Colonel/SS Oberführer/SS Major General Hugo Kraas (November 13, 1944).

Notes and Sources: Fritz Witt was promoted to SS Oberführer on July 1, 1943, and to SS major general on April 20, 1944. He was killed in Normandy by Allied naval gunfire on June 14, 1944. Panzer Meyer was promoted to SS Oberführer on August 1, 1944. He was sentenced to death by a Canadian military court in 1945, but his sentence was commuted to life imprisonment in 1946, and he was released on September 7, 1954. Hubert Meyer, who was normally the operations officer of the division, was promoted to lieutenant colonel on November 9, 1944. Kraas was promoted to SS Oberführer on January 30, 1945 and to SS major general on April 20, 1945.

Blumenson 1960: 190, 539–40, 577; Carell 1973: 177; Chant, Volume 14: 1863, Volume 17: 2372; Harrison: Map VI; Keegan: 91; Kursietis: 262; Craig W. H. Luther, *Blood and Honor: The History of the 12th SS Panzer Division "Hitler Youth," 1943–1945* (1987); MacDonald 1963: 300; MacDonald 1973: 34; Pipes; OB 44: 329; OB 45: 343.

13TH SS MOUNTAIN DIVISION "HANDSCHAR" (*KROATISCHE #1*)

Composition: Croatian SS Panzer Battalion, 27th SS Volunteer Mountain Infantry Regiment, 28th SS Volunteer Mountain Infantry Regiment, 13th SS Volunteer Mountain Artillery Regiment, 13th SS Mountain Reconnaissance Battalion, Croatian SS Motorcycle Battalion, Croatian SS Bicycle Battalion, 13th SS Tank Destroyer Battalion, 13th SS Mountain Engineer Battalion, 13th SS Mountain Signal Battalion, 13th SS Anti-Aircraft Battalion, 13th SS Divisional Supply Troops

Home Station: Brzko, Croatia

One of the poorer combat units in the Waffen-SS, the 13th was formed on March 1, 1943, as the Croatia SS Volunteer Division. It initially consisted of Bosnian Moslems and Croat volunteers, operating under cadres of the 7th SS Mountain Division "Prinz Eugen." When volunteers lagged, Christian members of the Croatian National Army were forced to join the new SS division. The 13th SS—which reached a maximum strength of 26,000 men—had many of the old trappings of the Muslim reg-

General of Panzer Troops Baron Hasso von Manteuffel, who commanded three different divisions during World War II: the ad hoc Division von Manteuffel, the 7th Panzer Division, and the elite Grossdeutschland Panzer Grenadier Division. NATIONAL ARCHIVES

iments of the former Austrian Army, including the fez and regimental imams, who led prayers. Sent to south-central France in mid-1943 to train, the division promptly mutinied. The rebellion was quelled internally, and fourteen of the ring leaders were executed but the unit, which steadfastly refused to operate outside its own area, had to be returned to Yugoslavia, after brief stays in lower Silesia and Austria in late 1943.

Back in the Balkans, it largely confined itself to massacring defenseless Christian villagers and establishing record desertion rates. Meanwhile, it was designated the 13th SS Volunteer Bosnian-Herzegovinian Mountain Division "Croatian" on October 22, 1943, and the 13th SS Mountain Division "Handschar" in June 1944. In October, during the retreat from the Balkans, the 2nd Panzer Army disarmed the well-equipped but unreliable division and took its arms and supplies for German troops. The division was effectively disbanded in September and October 1944, but the divisional and regimental staffs remained intact, and it was effectively rebuilt that winter. Himmler finally committed it to combat on the Eastern Front in late 1944, but it performed so poorly in Hungary that he withdrew it back to Croatia. The remnants of the division surrendered to the British near Villach in May 1945.

Commanders of the miserable 13th included SS Colonel Herbert von Obwurzer (March 1, 1943), SS Oberführer/SS Major General Karl Sauberzweig (August 9, 1943), and SS Colonel/SS Oberführer/SS Major General Desiderius Hampel (June 1, 1944).

Notes and Sources: Sauberzweig was promoted to SS major general on October 1, 1943. Hampel was promoted to SS Oberführer on November 9, 1944, and to SS major general on January 30, 1945.

Keegan: 104–5, 157; Lexikon; Pipes; Tessin, Vol. 3: 283–84; OB 44: 331; OB 45: 343; Yerger 1997: 209; Ziemke 1966: 378.

14TH SS GRENADIER DIVISION (*GALIZISCHE #1*)

Composition: 29th SS Volunteer Grenadier Regiment, 30th SS Volunteer Grenadier Regiment, 31st SS Volunteer Grenadier Regiment, 14th SS Artillery Regiment, 14th SS

Fusilier Battalion, 14th SS Tank Destroyer Battalion, 14th SS Engineer Battalion, 14th SS Signal Battalion, 14th SS Anti-Aircraft Battalion, 14th SS Field Replacement Battalion, 14th SS Divisional Supply Troops

Home Station: Ukrainian Galicia

Formed in the SS Troop Maneuver Area Heidelager (Debica) in late June 1943, this unit consisted of Ukrainian volunteers with German and Austrian officers and NCOs. The 14th SS was organized and trained in Galicia. In March 1944, it was sent into action on the central sector of the Russian Front, where it was trapped in the Brody-Tarnow Pocket in the Soviet summer offensive in July. Although it fought well, only 3,000 of the division's 14,000 men managed to break out. (Of the missing men, 2,300 infiltrated through Soviet lines and rejoined the division over the next several weeks.) The remnants of the unit were sent to Slovakia (where it helped put down the Slovak Military Mutiny in October) and then to Germany for reforming. The division returned to the Eastern Front (then in southern Poland) in late 1944. By March 1945, the burned out division was fighting Tito's partisans in Slovenia, and the following month was in Steiermark. On April 25, 1945, the 14th SS Division was redesignated 1st Ukrainian Division and was transferred to the 1st Ukrainian National Army. The division surrendered to the British on May 8, 1945. Unlike the case with certain other units, the Allies did not turn these captives over to Stalin. A surprisingly large number of these men eventually settled in Canada.

The commanders of the division included SS Major General Walter Schimana (June 30, 1943), SS Oberführer/SS Major General Fritz Freitag (November 20, 1943), SS Colonel Friedrich Beyerdorff (late January 1944), Freitag (returned February 1944), SS Colonel Sylvester Stadler (April 22, 1944), Freitag (May 1944), SS Colonel/SS Oberführer Nikolaus Heilmann (August 1944), Freitag (September 5, 1944), and Ukrainian Waffen Major General Pavlo Schandruk (April 24, 1945–end).

Notes and Sources: The 14th SS Grenadier was described by Colonel Seaton as well equipped but poorly trained and inexperienced. Freitag was an arrogant and racially prejudiced German who was a poor choice to command this division. He committed suicide on May 20, 1945.

Keegan: 157; Kursietis: 263; Richard Landwehr, *Fighting for Freedom: The Ukrainian Volunteer Division of the Waffen-SS* (1985); Richard Landwehr, "The Waffen-SS and the Crushing of the Slovak Military Mutiny," *Siegrunen,* Volume 5, Number 6: 23–30; Lexikon; Seaton: 447; Tessin, Vol. 3: 313–14; OB 45: 344.

15TH SS GRENADIER DIVISION (*LETTISCHE #1*)

Composition: 32nd SS Volunteer Grenadier Regiment, 33rd SS Volunteer Grenadier Regiment, 34th SS Volunteer Grenadier Regiment, 15th SS Artillery Regiment, 15th SS Bicycle (later Fusilier) Battalion, 15th SS Tank Destroyer Battalion, 15th SS Engineer Battalion, 15th SS Signal Battalion, 15th SS Anti-Aircraft Battalion, 15th SS Divisional Supply Troops

Home Station: Latvia

This division consisted almost exclusively of Latvian volunteers and police battalions, with a few German officers and NCOs added. It was formed shortly after the German Army overran Latvia in the summer of 1941 as *SS-Brigade 2 "Reichsführer-SS"* and included the 4th, 5th, and 14th SS Infantry Regiments "Reichsführer-SS." Apparently there were not enough volunteers to form an entire three-regiment brigade, however, and the 14th SS Infantry Regiment was disbanded before the year was out. In March 1943, the 2nd Brigade was reorganized as the Latvian SS Volunteer Brigade and was upgraded to divisional status in August. Later redesignated *15th Waffen-Grenadier-Division der SS (lettische Nr. 1)*—or 15th SS Grenadier Division—it was soon in action with Army Group North, fighting in all its major campaigns from late 1943 until January 1945, including the retreat through the Baltic States and the first battles of the Courland Pocket. Evacuated by sea to Germany, the remnants of this unit took part in the defense of West Prussia, the northern Vistula and Pomerania, where it suffered heavy casualties. It was finished off in the Battle of Berlin. Many of its survivors were later executed by the Soviets.

Commanders of the 15th SS included SS Major General Peter Hansen (February 25, 1943), SS Major General Count Carl-Friedrich von Puchler-Burghaus, Baron of Groditz (May 1943), SS Oberführer Nikolaus Heilmann (February 17, 1944), SS Oberführer Herbert von Obwurzer (July 21, 1944), SS Oberführer Adolf Ax (January 26, 1945) and SS Oberführer Karl Burk (February 15, 1945).

Notes and Sources: Obwurzer was missing in action near Nakel, West Prussia, on January 26, 1945. He was promoted to SS major general on January 30, four days after he disappeared. SS Oberführer Dr. Eduard Deisenhofer was named permanent commander of the 15th SS Division on January 26, 1945. While traveling to take command, he was killed in Arnswalde on January 31. He never actually commanded the division.

Keegan: 104–5, 129, 157; Lexikon; Stein: 179; Tessin, Vol. 2: 145–46; OB 44: 331; OB 45: 344.

16TH SS PANZER GRENADIER DIVISION "REICHSFÜHRER SS"

Composition: 16th SS Panzer Battalion, 35th SS Panzer Grenadier Regiment, 36th SS Panzer Grenadier Regiment, 16th SS Panzer Artillery Regiment, 16th SS Panzer Reconnaissance Battalion, 16th SS Assault Gun Battalion, 16th SS Engineer Battalion, 16th SS Signal Battalion, 16th SS Anti-Aircraft Battalion

Home Station: See below.

This division was formed in Slovenia in October 1943, by expanding the Reichsführer SS Assault Brigade, which had been engaged in Corsica. It consisted of German and Volksdeutsche troops. By January 1944, elements of the 16th SS had returned to the Mediterranean sector, and these were committed to the Anzio fighting in February 1944; other units were involved in the occupation of Hungary in March. By May, the entire division had been sent to Germany and was reunited as part of the OKW reserve. It was sent back to Italy in June, after the Allies successfully attacked the Gustav Line and took Rome. The division was continuously engaged on the Italian Front until December, fighting in the Gothic Line and the battles around Bologna. In December 1944, it was transferred to the Hungarian sector and spent the rest of the war on the southern sector of the Eastern Front. It fought its last battle at Vienna in April 1945, and ended the war in Steiermark. The division surrendered to the British at St. Veith (west of Graz) and to the Americans at Radstadt in May 1945.

The division's commanders were SS Major General Max Simon (October 3, 1943) and thirty-four-year-old SS Oberführer Otto Baum (November 1, 1944).

Sources: Blumenson 1969; 313, 344–45; Fisher: 80, 302, 321, 382, 420; Keegan: 157; Sydnor: 489–90; Stein: 184; OB 45: 344–45.

17TH SS PANZER GRENADIER DIVISION "GOETZ VON BERLICHINGEN"

Composition: 17th SS Panzer Battalion, 37th SS Panzer Grenadier Regiment, 38th SS Panzer Grenadier Regiment, 17th SS Panzer Artillery Regiment, 17th SS Reconnaissance Battalion, 17th SS Tank Destroyer Battalion, 17th SS Engineer Battalion, 17th SS Signal Battalion, 17th SS Anti-Aircraft Battalion, 17th Divisional Supply Troops

Home Station: Brünn (Brno), the Protectorate; Iglau after August 15, 1944.

This elite division, named for a German robber baron of the Middle Ages, was formed in western France in October 1943, and was activated on November 15. It included Germans, Volksdeutsche, Belgians, and Romanians, built around cadres provided by the 10th SS Panzer Division "Frundsberg." By June 6, 1944, it was stationed southwest of Tours in southwestern France as part of OKW's reserve. It was quickly rushed to Normandy, and on June 11 was counterattacking at Carentan against the U.S. 82nd and 101st Airborne Divisions. Remaining in the line, it slowed the American advance considerably and defended in the St. Lo sector against heavy odds, while both inflicting and sustaining heavy casualties. In late July, 7th Army commander SS Colonel General Hausser reported that it was practically destroyed.

In early August, the remnants of the 17th SS were temporarily absorbed by the 2nd SS Panzer Division. Withdrawn from the combat zone soon after, it rebuilt and refitted at Chartres in eastern France, absorbing the 49th and 51st SS Panzer Grenadier Brigades, which had been transferred from Denmark and intended for use in forming the new 26th and 27th SS Panzer Divisions; instead, they were absorbed by the 37th and 38th SS Panzer Grenadier Regiments, respectively. By November, when it was thrown into the Battle of Metz, the 17th SS Division had almost 16,000 men; however, it only had four tanks and six assault guns, and lacked mobile equipment of all kinds. Moreover, its replacements were of marginal quality, and its former elitism was gone. The 17th SS was mauled at Metz, and on December 4, 1944, had a strength of only 4,000 men, of which only 1,700 were infantry effectives. After Metz fell, the remnants of the 17th SS fought in the Saar battles. Still west of the Rhine on March 22, 1945, it collapsed under repeated Allied attacks. Nevertheless, the surviving fragments of the division fought in the unsuccessful defense of Franconia and Nuremberg in April. It surrendered to the U.S. 101st Airborne Division on May 6 and 7, 1945, near the Achensee.

Divisional commanders of the Goetz von Berlichingen Division included SS Colonel Otto Binge (October 1943), SS Oberführer/SS Major General Werner Ostendorff (October 30, 1943), SS Colonel Fritz Klingenberg (January 1944), Ostendorff (March 1944), Binge (June 17, 1944), SS Colonel Otto Baum (June 20, 1944), Binge (August 1, 1944), SS Colonel Dr. Eduard Deisenhofer (August 30, 1944), SS Colonel Thomas Müller (September 30, 1944), SS Colonel Gustav Mertsch (October 1944), Ostendorff (returned October 21, 1944), Colonel Hans Lingner (November 15, 1944), Colonel

Gerhard Lindner (January 9, 1945), SS Colonel Fritz Klingenberg (January 21, 1945), SS Lieutenant Colonel Vinzenz Kaiser (March 22, 1945), SS Colonel Jakob Fick (March 24, 1945), and SS Colonel Georg Bochmann (March 27, 1945–end).

Notes and Sources: The division was named after Goetz von Berlichingen (1480–1563), a warrior hero about whom Goethe wrote a play. He lost a hand in the Siege of Landshut (1504) and created an iron (prosthetic) hand, which became the symbol of the division. Werner Ostendorff was promoted to SS major general on April 20, 1944. He was seriously wounded on June 16, 1944. He returned to duty on October 21 but was wounded again on November 15, 1944. He finally succumbed to these wounds on May 1, 1945. Deisenhofer was missing in action in September 1944. Hans Lingner was captured on January 21, 1945. Fritz Klingenberg was killed by an American tank on March 22, 1945. He was posthumously promoted to SS Oberführer.

Blumenson 1960: 422, 442, 570; Carell 1973: 145–46; Cole 1960: 48–49, 422–23, 526–27; Harrison: 244, Map VI; Keegan: 91; Lexikon; MacDonald 1973: 263, 412, 415, 423; Hans Stoeber, *Die Eiserne Faust—Bildband der 17. SS-Panzergrenadier-Division "Goetz von Berlichingen"* (1966); Tessin, Vol. 4: 77; OB 45: 345; Yerger 1997: 315–16.

18TH SS VOLUNTEER PANZER GRENADIER DIVISION "HORST WESSEL"

Composition: 18th SS Panzer Battalion, 39th SS Panzer Grenadier Regiment, 40th SS Panzer Grenadier Regiment, 18th SS Panzer Artillery Regiment, 18th SS Panzer Reconnaissance Battalion, 18th SS Tank Destroyer Battalion, 18th SS Engineer Battalion, 18th SS Signal Battalion, 18th SS Anti-Aircraft Battalion, 18th SS Divisional Supply Troops

Home Station: Breslau

The 18th SS Division was formed in Hungary in the spring of 1944, by expanding the 1st SS Motorized Infantry Brigade, which had been fighting on the Eastern Front since 1942. The new division, which consisted mainly of Hungarian *Volksdeutsche* (ethnic Germans), was named after the author of the Nazi Party Anthem. Unlike many so-called panzer grenadier units in the fifth year of the war, it was properly equipped. In August 1944, a battle group from the division was sent to Army Group Center and helped stem the tide of the Soviet summer offensive. The rest of the unit was sent to Hungary in November and fought on the southern sector of the Eastern Front. By January 1945, it was fighting in Slovakia. The following month it fought in Upper Silesia as part of the 1st Panzer Army, where it suffered heavy casualties. It was in remnants in April, when it joined the 17th Army in Silesia. It surrendered to the Russians from May 8 to 10, 1945, in the zone northeast of Melnik/Elbe.

Its commanders were SS Colonel/SS Oberführer Wilhelm Trabandt (January 25, 1944), SS Colonel Josef Fitzthum (January 3, 1945), SS Colonel Georg "Schorsch" Bochmann (January 10, 1945) and SS Colonel Heinrich Petersen (March 27, 1945).

Notes and Sources: Trabandt was commander of the 1st SS Motorized Infantry Brigade since October 18, 1943. He was promoted to SS Oberführer on July 1, 1944. Field Marshal Schoerner relieved Bochmann of his command on March 27, 1945, after he refused to lead a suicide attack.

Keegan: 100; Tessin, Vol. 4: 108–9; OB 45: 345.

19TH SS GRENADIER DIVISION (*LETTISCHE* #2)

Composition: 42nd SS Grenadier Regiment, 43rd SS Grenadier Regiment, 44th SS Grenadier Regiment, 19th SS Artillery Regiment, 19th SS Fusilier Battalion, 19th SS Tank Destroyer Company, 19th SS Engineer Battalion, 19th SS Signal Battalion, 19th SS Anti-Aircraft Battalion, 19th SS Divisional Supply Troops

Home Station: Latvia

This division was formed in the Soviet Union behind the lines of Army Group North on January 7, 1944. Its parent unit was the 2nd SS Volunteer Infantry Brigade "Reichsführer-SS" (later designated 2nd Latvian SS Volunteer Brigade), which had been involved in combat on the Eastern Front since 1941. The division—which reached full strength—was involved in heavy fighting in the retreat from Leningrad and through the Baltic States. It suffered heavy casualties before retiring into the Courland Pocket, where it fought six more major battles and where it was when Germany surrendered. Most of the surviving Latvians surrendered on May 8, 1945, and were subsequently executed by the Soviets.

The 19th SS Grenadier Division's commanders included SS Colonel/SS Oberführer Hinrich Schuldt (January 7, 1944), SS Colonel Friedrich-Wilhelm Bock (March 15, 1944), SS Oberführer/SS Major General/SS Lieutenant General Bruno Streckenbach (April 13, 1944), Waffen Oberführer Arturs Silgailis (May 12, 1944), and Streckenbach (May 19, 1944–end).

Notes and Sources: Schuldt had assumed command of the 2nd SS Brigade on September 5, 1943. He was promoted to SS Oberführer on November 9, 1943, and was killed in action on the Velikaya River on March 15, 1944. Streckenbach was promoted to SS major general on July 1, 1944, and to SS lieutenant general on November 9, 1944. He was in Soviet prisons until 1954.

Keegan: 103–4, 157; Lexikon; Arthur Silgailis, *Latvian Legion* (1986); Stein: 178; Tessin, Vol. 4: 127; OB 45: 346.

20TH SS GRENADIER DIVISION (*ESTNISCHE #1*)

Composition: 45th SS Volunteer Grenadier Regiment, 46th SS Volunteer Grenadier Regiment, 47th SS Volunteer Grenadier Regiment, 20th SS Volunteer Artillery Regiment, 20th SS Fusilier Battalion, 20th SS Tank Destroyer Company, 20th SS Engineer Battalion, 20th SS Signal Battalion, 20th SS Anti-Aircraft Battalion, 20th SS Divisional Supply Troops

Home Station: Heidelager (Debica), Estonia; later Klooga (near Reval)

The 20th SS Grenadier Division was formed behind the lines of Army Group North on the Russian Front in December 1943. Offically activated on January 24, 1944, many of its soldiers were former members of the 3rd Estonian SS Volunteer Brigade and/or the Estonian Legion, which had been in com-

The Tiger tank, with its deadly 88-mm gun, was probably the most feared German ground weapon of the war. This particular tank belonged to the 1st SS Panzer Division. NATIONAL ARCHIVES.

bat since October 1943 and August 1942, respectively. The 20th SS received 15,000 volunteers—enough to reach full divisional strength. Returning to the front in early 1944, it took part in the retreat from Leningrad, the Battle of Narva, and the early Courland Pocket battles. In mid-September 1944, when Hitler authorized a full withdrawal from Estonia, all troops wishing to remain in the country were released from German service. Many remained behind to conduct guerilla warfare against the Communists.

Meanwhile, the division was evacuated to the Neuhammer Troop Maneuver Area in Germany, where it was reformed. It had a strength of 11,000 Estonians and 2,500 Germans when it was sent to the central sector of the Eastern Front in December. The unit suffered heavy casualties in the Vistula and Oder battles, and was encircled in the Oberglogau-Falkenberg-Friedberg area (along with the army's XI Corps) on March 17, 1945. It broke out on March 19, but lost all of its heavy weapons and heavy equipment in the process. The remnants of the 20th SS retreated into Bohemia and was surrounded with Army Group Center in the Deutsch-Brod Pocket east of Prague, where it was when the war ended. Like many former Soviet citizens who actively opposed the Communists during World War II, most of the division's survivors were put to death after they surrendered.

Commanders of the legion/division included SS Colonel/SS Oberführer/SS Major General Franz Augsberger (August 20, 1942), SS Major Hans-Joachim Muetzelfeldt (March 19, 1945), and SS Oberführer/SS Major General Berthold Maack (March 19, 1945).

Notes and Sources: Augsberger was promoted to SS Oberführer on January 30, 1943, and to SS major general on June 21, 1944. He was killed in action near Neustadt, Silesia, on March 19, 1945. Maack was promoted to SS major general on April 20, 1945.

Keegan: 104–5; Kursietis: 265; Tessin, Vol. 2: 213; OB 45: 346; Yerger 1997: 29.

21st SS MOUNTAIN DIVISION "SKANDERBEG" (*ALBANISCHE #1*)

Composition: 50th SS Volunteer Mountain Infantry Regiment, 51st SS Volunteer Mountain Infantry Regiment, 21st SS Volunteer Mountain Artillery Regiment, 21st SS Mountain Reconnaissance Battalion, 21st SS Mountain Tank Destroyer Battalion, SS Assault Gun Battalion "Skanderbeg," 21st SS Mountain Engineer Battalion, 21st SS Mountain Signal Battalion, 21st SS Anti-Aircraft Battalion, 21st SS Field Replacement Battalion, 21st SS Economic Battalion, 21st SS Divisional Supply Troops

Home Station: Albania

This division was formed on May 1, 1944, from unreliable Albanian Muslims. It attracted more than 11,000 recruits, of which about 9,000 were accepted. The division was never fully developed, however, because it would not operate outside of its own area, but preferred raping, pillaging, and massacring innocent Serbian Christian villagers in Kosovo to fighting the enemies of the Third Reich. Approximately 10,000 Serbs were killed during this early version of ethnic cleansing, and another 75,000 fled the region. Himmler ordered it disbanded on January 20, 1945, before it was ever fully formed, but this did not happen. Elements of the division continued to fight until the fall of the Third Reich and surrendered to the Western Allies in Austria in May 1945. Some of the more reliable members of "Skanderbeg" were transferred to the 14th SS Mountain Regiment of the 7th SS Mountain Division.

SS Major General August Schmidhuber was the only permanent commander the 21st SS ever had. SS Lieutenant Colonel Graf reportedly served briefly as acting division commander.

Notes and Sources: George Kastrioti Skanderberg (1405–1468), for whom the division was named, was an Albanian national hero who fought the Ottoman Empire for twenty-five years. Schmidhuber was tried as a war criminal and was hanged in Belgrade on February 27, 1947.

Keegan: 105, 157; Kursietis: 265; Lexikon; Tessin, Vol. 4: 173; OB 45: 346.

22ND SS VOLUNTEER CAVALRY DIVISION "MARIE THERESIA"

Composition: 17th SS Volunteer Cavalry Regiment, 52nd SS Volunteer Cavalry Regiment, 53rd SS Volunteer Cavalry Regiment, 22nd SS Volunteer Artillery Regiment, 22nd SS Panzer Reconnaissance Battalion, 22nd SS Tank Destroyer Battalion, 22nd SS Engineer Battalion, 22nd SS Signal Battalion, 22nd SS Anti-Aircraft Battalion, 22nd SS Divisional Supply Troops

Home Station: Hungary

The 22nd SS Cavalry was formed in Hungary on April 29, 1944, when the 8th SS Cavalry Division "Florian Geyer" was divided. It took over the 8th SS Cavalry Division's 17th Cavalry Regiment and created the 52nd and 53rd SS Cavalry Regiments from cadres provided by the 8th Cavalry. The new division consisted mainly of Hungarian volunteers, and it soon reached full divisional strength. That October it was sent to northern Transylvania (in Romania), where it fought the Soviets. Eventually surrounded in Budapest with the IX SS Mountain Corps, it had 11,345 men, seventeen assault guns, thirty-seven pieces of artillery, and fourteen heavy anti-tank guns when the siege began on December 25, 1944. The 22nd SS fought bravely in weeks of house-to-house fighting, but was finally destroyed when the city fell on February 12, 1945. Most of the division was slaughtered during the unsuccessful breakout attempt of February 11. SS Colonel/SS Oberführer/SS Major General August Zehender, the division's only commander, was killed that day.

Notes and Sources: Zehender was promoted to SS Oberführer on October 16, 1944, and to *SS* Brigadeführer (SS major general) on January 15, 1945.

Keegan: 157; Lexikon; Seaton: 500; Stein: 233; Tessin, Vol. 4: 188–89; OB 45: 347; Yerger 1999: 347–48.

23RD SS MOUNTAIN DIVISION "KAMA" (*KROATISCHE #2*)

Composition: 55th SS Volunteer Mountain Infantry Regiment, 56th SS Volunteer Mountain Infantry Regiment, 23rd SS Volunteer Mountain Artillery Regiment, 23rd SS Mountain Reconnaissance Battalion, 23rd SS Tank Destroyer Battalion, 23rd SS Mountain Engineer Battalion, 23rd SS Mountain Signal Battalion, 23rd SS Anti-Aircraft Battalion, 23rd SS Divisional Supply Troops

Home Station: Croatia

As with the other two Muslim SS divisions (the 13th and 21st), this unit was an unsuccessful experiment because its soldiers were too difficult to discipline. It was partially formed on June 17, 1944, in Croatia and Bosnia, from Moslem and Croat volunteers with cadres of German officers. It maximum strength, however, was less than 3,800 men. It was nevertheless sent to southern Hungary in August, but the reports on this division were not good, and Reichsführer-SS Heinrich Himmler ordered it disbanded on September 24. It was returned to Croatia, where its men were transferred to the 13th SS Mountain Division on October 1.

Its commanders included SS Colonel Helmuth Raithel (July 1, 1944) and SS Oberführer Gustav Lombard (September 28, 1944).

Sources: Keegan: 105, 158; Kursietis: 265; Lexikon; Pipes; Tessin, Vol. 4: 204–5; OB 45: 347.

23RD VOLUNTEER SS PANZER GRENADIER DIVISION "NEDERLAND"

Composition: 48th SS Volunteer Panzer Grenadier Regiment "General Seyffard," 49th SS Volunteer Panzer Grenadier Regiment "De Ruiter," 54th SS Volunteer Artillery Regiment, 54th SS Reconnaissance Comapny, 54th SS Tank Destroyer Battalion, 54th SS Engineer Battalion, 54th SS Signal Battalion, 54th SS Divisional Supply Troops

This unit began its career as the SS Volunteer Legion "Niederlande." It was formed in Krakow (Krakau), Poland, from Dutch volunteers who joined the SS to fight communism. Initially it consisted of the 1st and 2nd SS Volunteer Panzer Grenadier Regiments "Nederland," as well as a two battalion artillery regiment, tank destroyer, engineer and field replacement battalions, a reconnaissance company and a signal company. It distinguished itself in its first action (on the northern sector of the Eastern Front) where, in June 1942, it attacked and destroyed a much larger Soviet force, taking 3,500 prisoners in the process, including General Andrey Vlasov, the future commander of the Russian Liberation Army (ROA). The Legion was then shifted north, where it took part in the Siege of Leningrad and in the Second Battle of Lake Lagoda.

The Legion was sent back to the Netherlands in early 1943 to rest, recruit and expand. It was upgraded to the 4th SS Volunteer Panzer Grenadier Brigade on October 23, 1943, and its panzer grenadier regiments became the 48th SS Volunteer Panzer Grenadier Regiment "General Seyffardt" and the 49th SS Volunteer Panzer Grenadier Regiment "De Ruiter," respectively. The Dutch Legion/Brigade served in the Balkans until December 1943, when it was sent to the Leningrad sector. It joined the III SS Panzer Corps and fought in the Siege of Oranienbaum, in the retreat from Leningrad, in the fierce battles on the Narva, and in the first battles of the Courland Pocket. The 48th SS Volunteer Panzer Grenadier Regiment and most of the division's artillery regiment were destroyed in Operation Bagration (June–July 1944). The division was transported to Stettin, Pomerania, by ship in early 1945, and, on February 10, was upgraded to divisional status as the 23rd SS Volunteer Panzer Grenadier Division "Nederland," although without any change to its table of organization and equipment and without any reinforcements. (It had only about 1,000 men left at this time, and its 48th SS Volunteer Regiment had been reduced from a strength of 2,000 men to eighty men.) It was sent to the Oder sector and was trapped in the huge Halbe Pocket southeast of Berlin. Here it surrendered to the Soviets on or about April 29, 1945.

SS Oberführer/SS Major General Juergen Wagner, who had been the commander of the 4th SS Panzer Grenadier Brigade "Nederland" since October 1943, was the division's only commander.

Notes and Sources: The Dutch Legion's first commander was Dutch Lieutenant General Hendrik A. Seyffardt, who was assassinated by Dutch partisans in 1943. Wagner was promoted to SS major general on April 20, 1945. The Soviets extradited him to Yugoslavia, where he was hanged in 1947.

Keegan: 139; *Kriegstagebuch des OKW*, Volume IV: 1898; Lexikon; Lucas: 42; Pipes; Tessin, Vol. 2: 276.

24TH SS MOUNTAIN DIVISION "KARSTJÄGER"

Composition: 59th SS Volunteer Mountain Infantry Regiment. 60th SS Volunteer Mountain Infantry Regiment, 24th SS Volunteer Mountain Artillery Regiment. 24th SS Mountain Reconnaissance Battalion, 24th SS Tank Destroyer Battalion, 24th SS Mountain Engineer Battalion, 24th SS Mountain Signal Battalion, 24th SS Anti-Aircraft Battalion, 24th Field Replacement Battalion, 24th SS Divisional Supply Troops

Home Station: Italy

This division was formed in the Istrian area of northern Italy on August 1, 1944, by the expansion of the Karstjaeger Battalion of the Waffen-SS. Its men were Italian Fascists in the service of Mussolini's rump republic, although many of its officers were Austrians who had formerly served with the 7th SS Mountain Division. The 24th SS confined itself to anti-partisan activities (largely against Communists) in northern Italy and never exceeded regimental strength by much. It was downgraded to brigade status in December 1944, and, as the *Waffen-Gebirgs-(Karstjäger) Brigade der SS*, controlled the 59th Mountain Infantry Regiment (three battalions), the I/24th SS Artillery Regiment (three batteries), 1st Company/24th Mountain Engineer Battalion, and one company of the 24th SS Mountain Signal Battalion. Later it was given a company of obsolete tanks.

Infantrymen of the SS Panzer Corps are involved in street fighting in Kharkov, March 1943.

In February 1945, it was against renamed the *24. Waffen-Gebirgs-(Karstjäger) Division der SS*, but without any changes to its table of organization. It surrendered to the British at Isonzo at the end of the war (May 1945).

Its commanders were SS Lieutenant Colonel Karl Marx (assumed command August 1944), SS Colonel Werner Hahn (December 5, 1944), and SS-Oberführer Adolf Wagner (February 10, 1945–end).

Sources: Keegan: 99, 158; Kursietis: 266; Lexikon; Tessin, Vol. 4: 220; OB 45: 347.

25TH SS GRENADIER DIVISION "HUNYADI" (*UNGARISCHE #1*)

Composition: 61st SS Volunteer Grenadier Regiment, 62nd SS Volunteer Grenadier Regiment. 63rd SS Volunteer Grenadier Regiment, 25th SS Volunteer Artillery Regiment, 25th SS Fusilier Battalion, 25th SS Tank Destroyer Battalion, 25th SS Engineer Battalion, 25th SS Signal Battalion. 25th SS Anti-Aircraft Battalion, 25th SS Divisional Supply Troops

Home Station: Hungary

Formed on November 2, 1944, as the Russians invaded Hungary, this division was made up primarily of Hungarians from the rear areas of depots. It never reached anything like full strength. It fought in Silesia in January 1945, and was back in Hungary by February. It reorganized at Roth (near Nuremberg) and fought in last battle in Austria. It surrendered to the Americans in May.

Its commanders were SS Oberführer Thomas Mueller (November 1944) and Hungarian Lieutenant General/*Feldmarschalleutnant* Jozsef Grassy (November 1944–end).

Notes and Sources: General Grassy was hanged in Zsablyla, Yugoslavia on November 5, 1946.

Keegan: 158; Lexikon; Tessin, Vol. 4: 234; OB 45: 348, Yerger 1997: 205–6.

26TH SS GRENADIER DIVISION "GOMBOES" (*UNGARISCHE* #2)

Composition: 64th SS Volunteer Panzer Grenadier Regiment, 65th SS Volunteer Panzer Grenadier Regiment, 85th SS Volunteer Panzer Grenadier Regiment, 26th SS Volunteer Panzer Artillery Regiment, 26th SS Panzer Fusilier Battalion, 26th SS Tank Destroyer Battalion, 26th SS Engineer Battalion, 26th SS Signal Battalion, 26th SS Divisional Supply Troops

Home Station: Hungary

Himmler attempted to form this division in the Neuhammer Troop Maneuver Area of northwestern Germany and in Hungary in late 1944 and January 1945, from Hungarian volunteers. It was officially activated on January 29. The troops were mainly young men (mostly Hungarians) who fled from Transylvania when the Russians overran that province, and men from eastern Hungary. The unit was fighting in Bavaria at the end of the war.

Its commanders were SS Colonel Rolf Tiemann (November 1944), SS Oberführer Zoltan Pisky (November 1944), SS Oberführer Laszlo Deak (January 23, 1945), SS Major General Berthold Maack (January 29, 1945), and Lieutenant General Jozsef Grassy (March 21, 1945).

Notes and Sources: Pisky, Deak and Grassy were all Hungarian Waffen-SS men. Pisky was reportedly killed in action on January 23, 1945. Deak was the commander of the 61st SS Grenadier Regiment (Hungarian # 2). He was either shot by U.S. troops or committed suicide at the end of the war. Grassy simultaneously commanded the 25th and 26th SS Divisions. He was executed in Yugoslavia in 1946.

Keegan: 158; Lexikon; Pipes; Tessin, Vol. 4: 248; OB 45: 348. See *http://philosophy.elte.hu* for the biographies of Hungarian Waffen-SS men.

26TH SS PANZER DIVISION

Composition: 66th SS Panzer Grenadier Regiment, 67th SS Panzer Grenadier Regiment, 49th SS Artillery Battalion, SS Motorcycle Company/26th SS Panzer Division, SS Fla Company/26th SS Panzer Division, SS Engineer Company/26th SS Panzer Division

The formation of the 26th SS Panzer Division was ordered on August 10, 1944. It was to be achieved by expanding the 49th SS Panzer Grenadier Brigade in France. The process had just begun, however, when the Anglo-Saxons overran France. The partially formed division fought in the Champagne district as part of the 1st Army and was withdrawn behind the West Wall, where it was dissolved on September 8. Most of its men were transferred to the 37th SS Panzer Grenadier Regiment of the 17th SS Panzer Grenadier Division "Goetz von Berlichingen."

Notes and Sources: The 66th SS Panzer Grenadier Regiment had two battalions, while the 67th had only one.

Lexikon; Tessin, Vol. 4: 248; *www.diedeutschewehrmacht.de.*

26TH SS GRENADIER DIVISION (*UNGARISCHE* #2)

Composition: 26th (?) SS Panzer Battalion, 64th (?) SS Panzer Grenadier Regiment, 65th (?) SS Panzer Grenadier Regiment, 66th (?) SS Panzer Grenadier Regiment, 26th SS Panzer Artillery Regiment, 26th SS Panzer Reconnaissance Battalion, 26th SS Anti-Tank Battalion, 26th SS Engineer Battalion, 26th SS Signal Battalion, 26th SS Anti-Aircraft Battalion

Home Station: Hungary

Himmler attempted to form this division in northwestern Germany in September 1944, by expanding the 49th SS Panzer Grenadier Brigade. Troops were also taken from the SS Panzer Brigade "Gross," which was disbanded in November 1944, and from young men (mostly Hungarians) who fled from Transylvania when the Russians overran that province. The unit disappeared with the fall of Hungary in early 1945; apparently the 26th SS was destroyed in that campaign.

Sources: Keegan: 158; OB 45: 348.

27TH SS PANZER DIVISION

Composition: 68th SS Panzer Grenadier Regiment, 69th SS Panzer Grenadier Regiment, SS Artillery Bn//27th SS Panzer Division, SS Fla Company//27th SS Panzer Division, SS Engineer Company//27th SS Panzer Division, SS Motorcycle Company//27th SS Panzer Division

Like its sister division, the 26th SS Panzer Division, the formation of the 27th SS was ordered on August 10, 1944. This was to be accomplished by expanding the 51st SS Panzer Grenadier Brigade in France. The process had just begun, however, when the British and Americans broke out of the Normandy bridgehead and overran France. The incomplete division fought in Champagne as part of the 1st Army and was then withdrawn behind the Siegfried Line, where it was absorbed by the 38th SS Panzer Grenadier Regiment of the 17th SS Panzer Grenadier Division.

Notes and Sources: The 68th and 69th SS Panzer Grenadier Regiments each had only one battalion when the order to disband arrived.

Lexikon; Tessin, Vol. 4: 259; *www.diedeutschewehrmacht.de.*

27TH SS VOLUNTEER PANZER GRENADIER DIVISION "LANGEMARCK"

Composition: 66th SS Volunteer Panzer Grenadier Regiment, 67th SS Volunteer Panzer Grenadier Regiment, 68th SS Volunteer Panzer Grenadier Regiment, 27th SS Volunteer Artillery Regiment, 27th SS Panzer Reconnaissance Battalion, 27th SS Tank Destroyer Battalion, 27th SS Engineer Battalion, 27th SS Signal Battalion, 27th SS Field Replacement Battalion, 27th SS Divisional Supply Troops

Home Station: Belgium

The first attempt to form this division was made in September 1944, when Himmler ordered the 51st SS Panzer Grenadier Brigade expanded. There simply were not enough soldiers in this unit, however, so the divisional number 27th SS was given to the 6th SS Storm Brigade "Langemarck" later that year. This brigade was a Belgian SS Legion that had been activated at Troop Maneuver Area Heidelager (near Krakau, Poland) on May 31, 1943, and had distinguished itself on the Eastern Front in the spring of 1944. It was upgraded to the 27th Volunteer Panzer Grenadier Division on October 18, 1944. The new 27th SS never exceeded regimental strength but served on the Russian Front in the retreats from Poland and Pomerania and in the Battle of Berlin. It surrendered to the Red Army near Stettin in Mecklenburg on May 2, 1945.

Commanders of the Langemarck Division were SS Lieutenant Colonel Conrad Schellong (September–October 1944) and SS Oberführer Thomas Mueller (October 1944–end).

Sources: Keegan: 96, 158; Lexikon; Tessin, Vol. 3: 46; OB 45: 348.

28TH SS PANZER DIVISION

Composition: SS Panzer Battalion "Gross," 70th SS Panzer Grenadier Regiment, 71st SS Panzer Grenadier Regiment, 49th SS Artillery Battalion, SS Reconnaissance Battalion//28th SS Panzer Division, SS Motorcycle Company//28th SS Panzer Division, SS Engineer Company//28th SS Panzer Division, Flak Company//28th SS Panzer Division

The formation of the 28th SS Panzer was ordered on August 10, 1944, at the same time the formation of the 26th and 27th SS Panzer Division was ordered. This unit, however, was to be organized at Riga, behind the Eastern Front, and was to be built around the SS Panzer Brigade "Gross," which itself had only recently been formed as an emergency or alarm unit (*Alarmverband*). It apparently included three grenadier battalions and four tank companies from the SS panzer brigade. The formation of the 28th SS Panzer Division had only just begun when the order was rescinded in September 1944.

Sources: Lexikon; Tessin, Vol. 4: 270.

28TH SS VOLUNTEER PANZER GRENADIER DIVISION "WALLONIEN"

Composition: 69th SS Volunteer Panzer Grenadier Regiment, 70th SS Volunteer Panzer Grenadier Regiment, 28th SS Panzer Volunteer Artillery Regiment, 28th SS Panzer Reconnaissance Battalion, 28th SS Tank Destroyer Battalion, 28th SS Engineer Battalion, 28th SS Signal Battalion, 28th SS Anti-Aircraft Battalion, 28th SS Divisional Supply Troops

Home Station: Belgium

This division was formed for political and propaganda reasons from French-speaking Belgians, many of whom had been captured by the Germans in the Western campaign of 1940, and volunteered to serve in the division in order to get out of Nazi prisoner-of-war camps. The unit was originally formed in 1941 as the Walloon Legion (373rd Infantry Battalion) of the German Army, which served on the Russian Front for more than two years. It gradually added more volunteers and units, and by mid-1943 had three panzer grenadier companies, a staff company, a machine gun company, an infantry gun company, a heavy tank destroyer company, an assault gun battery, a Fla (light anti-aircraft) company, and a heavy motorized flak battery. As a result, it was redesignated the 5th SS Volunteer Sturm Brigade "Walloon" on October 22, 1943.

The new brigade fought well but was smashed in the Cherkassy (Korsun) encirclement in February 1944. Sent back to the Heidelager Troop Maneuver Area near Krakau, it was rebuilt and by June had two panzer grenadier battalions and an assault gun battalion. It returned to the front in August, where it fought on the Narva as part of the III (*germ.*) SS Panzer Corps. Again it performed well; as a result, it was sent to southern Hanover and Brunswick and was converted into the 28th SS Volunteer Grenadier Division on October 18, 1944, even though it hardly exceeded regimental strength. It was defending the Bonn area in December 1944, but was sent to Pomerania soon after and fought its last battle before Berlin in April 1945. Most of its men surrendered to the Russians near the Oder in Brandenberg.

Its commanders were SS Colonel Lucien Lippert (February 1, 1944) and SS Captain/SS Major/SS Lieutenant Colonel/SS Colonel Leon Degrelle (February 15, 1944–end).

Notes and Sources: Lucien Lippert was killed in action at Cherkassy on February 15, 1944. Degrelle became an SS major (April 20, 1944), an SS lieutenant colonel (January 1, 1945), and an SS colonel (April 20, 1945). He escaped to Spain after the war.

Keegan: 96, 158; Tessin, Vol. 2: 322; Vol. 4: 270; OB 45: 348; Yerger 1997: 112–14.

29TH SS GRENADIER DIVISION (*RUSSISCHE #1*) (1)

Composition: 72nd SS Volunteer Grenadier Regiment, 73rd SS Volunteer Grenadier Regiment, 74th SS Volunteer Grenadier Regiment, 29th SS Volunteer Artillery Regiment, 29th SS Fusilier Battalion, 29th SS Tank Destroyer Battalion, 29th SS Engineer Battalion, 29th SS Signal Battalion, 29th SS Field Replacement Battalion, 29th SS Supply Regiment

This unit was formed from anti-Communist Russians in the zone of Colonel General Schmidt's 2nd Panzer Army in July 1942. Designated the Kaminski Brigade after its commander, Major General of Waffen-SS Bronislav Kaminski (a former Russian Bürgermeister), the unit performed well until the Red Army overran its home area in the second half of 1943. After that, it became a band of rapists, murderers and plunderers such as Europe had not seen since the Middle Ages. It had 6,000 to 7,000 men and probably twice as many women, children, and assorted camp followers. Himmler nevertheless upgraded it to divisional status on August 4, 1944, and attempted to use it to quell the revolt in the Jewish Ghetto of Warsaw. The division, however, proved to be useless, even against such poorly armed and equipped opponents. Kaminski also proved himself to be a lawless thug. On August 28, 1944, he was invited to a conference at Litzmannstadt (Lodz), but was intercepted en route and murdered by the henchmen of SS Lieutenant

Young SS men, circa 1942.

General von der Bach. He was replaced by German SS Major General Christop Diehm (August 28–September 27, 1944) and German SS Lieutenant General Heinrich Juers (September 27–November 1944). In November, the division was disbanded. The Headquarters, 72nd and 73rd SS Regiments were transferred to SS Sturmbrigade Dirlewanger (later the 36th SS Grenadier Division); most of the men were assigned to the 600th Infantry Division (*russisch*), which was later transferred to General Vlasov's army and served briefly on the Eastern Front. Many of its troops surrendered to the Americans but were subsequently handed over to the Soviets, who slaughtered them.

Sources: Keegan: 158; Lexikon; R. Michaels, *Die Brigade Kaminski* (1999); Tessin, Vol. 4: 280; OB 45: 349.

29TH SS GRENADIER DIVISION (*ITALIENISCHE #1*) (2)

Composition: 81st SS Grenadier Regiment (ital. Nr. 1), 82nd SS Grenadier Regiment (ital. Nr. 2), 29th SS Artillery Regiment, 29th SS Fusilier Battalion, 29th SS Engineer Company, 29th SS Tank Destroyer Battalion, 29th SS Signal Company, 29th SS Divisional Supply Troops

Home Station: northern Italy

The second 29th SS Grenadier Division was formed from Fascist Italians in Mussolini's rump republic from the Waffen-Grenadier-Brigade der SS (*ital. Nr. 1*), which had existed since September 7, 1944. It was not officially activated as a division until March 9, 1945. Its men were recruited mainly from Fascist militia and operated against partisans in northern Italy. The division was destroyed in April 1945, when Army Group C collapsed.

Its commanders were Italian Major General Pietro Mannelli (September 1944), SS Major General Peter Hansen (September 1944), SS Major General Gustav Lombard (October 1944), SS Lieutenant Colonel of Reserves Constantin Heldmann (November 1944), and SS Oberführer Erwin Tschoppe (early 1945).

Sources: Keegan: 99, 158; Kursietis: 267; Tessin, Vol. 2: 77; Yerger 1997: 268.

30TH SS GRENADIER DIVISION (*RUSSISCHE #2*)

Composition: 75th SS Volunteer Grenadier Regiment, 76th SS Volunteer Grenadier Regiment, 77th SS Volunteer Grenadier Regiment, 30th SS Volunteer Artillery Regiment, 30th SS Reconnaissance Battalion, 30th SS Tank Destroyer Battalion, 30th SS Engineer Company, 30th SS Signal Company, 30th SS Flak Battalion, 30th Field Replacement Battalion, 30th SS Divisional Supply Troops

This division was formed near Warsaw on August 1, 1944, from Russian personnel, many of whom had police experience, and with a small number of former German police. Greatly understrength, it was sent to eastern France and fought at Belfort Gap in September but was withdrawn from the Western Front in October and returned to Germany. Most of its personnel were considered unreliable and the division was plagued by insubordination and desertion; nevertheless, the 30th SS was back in combat in Alsace in November and took part in the withdrawal across the Rhine.

Sent to the Grafenwöhr Troop Maneuver Area to reform in January and February 1945, it was downgraded to brigade status on January 15, 1945, and its 76th and 77th SS Grenadier Regiments were disbanded, its artillery regiment became a battalion and its reconnaissance battalion a cavalry squadron. It was nonetheless redesignated 30th SS Grenadier Division (*30. Waffen-Gren. Div. d. SS [wiessruth Nr. 1]*) on March 9, 1945. It was disbanded in April 1945, and its former Soviet citizens were transferred to General Vlasov's Free Russian Army and was sent east. Its German cadres were transferred to the 38th SS Grenadier Division "Nibelungen." The men of the former 30th SS fell into Soviet captivity in 1945, which meant death for most of them.

SS Colonel Hans Siegling was the only commander of the division.

Notes and Sources: Siegling was only thirty-three years old in 1945.

Keegan:158; Kursietis: 267; Pipes; Tessin, Vol. 4: 291; OB 45: 349.

31ST SS VOLUNTEER GRENADIER DIVISION "BATSCHKA"

Composition: 78th SS Volunteer Grenadier Regiment, 79th Volunteer SS Grenadier Regiment, 80th SS Volunteer Grenadier Regiment, 31st SS Volunteer Artillery Regiment, 31st SS Fusilier Battalion. 31st SS Tank Destroyer Company, 31st SS Engineer Battalion, 31st SS Signal Battalion, 31st SS Anti-Aircraft Battalion, 31st SS Field Replacement Battalion, 31st SS Divisional Supply Troops

Home Station: Konitz, later Alfeld

The 31st SS Division, which consisted of Hungarians, Germans and Volksdeutsche, was formed in September 1944, and was activated at Fuenfkirchen, Hungary, on October 1, 1944. It was in action on the Hungarian sector of the Eastern Front by November 1944, but was sent to southern Steiermark in Austria in January 1945, where it was reorganized as a "Division 45"—a 1945-type division. Its grenadier companies were reduced from four to three platoons, and its regiments were reduced from three battalions each to two battalions. Meanwhile, it absorbed Police Regiment Brixen. The following month, it was sent to join the 17th Army in Silesia, which was opposing the Red Army's advance into southeastern Germany. The 31st SS was down to kampfgruppe strength by April. Along with 17th Army and much of Army Group Center, it was surrounded near Koeniggraetz and surrendered to the Soviets in May 1945.

Its commanders were SS Major General Gustav Lombard (end of September 1944) and SS Major General Wilhelm Trabandt (April 1945–end).

Sources: Keegan: 158; *Kriegstagebuch des OKW*, Volume I: 1146; Kursietis: 267; Pipes; Tessin, Vol. 5: 11–12; OB 45: 349.

32ND SS VOLUNTEER GRENADIER DIVISION "JANUARY 30"

Composition: 86th SS Volunteer Grenadier Regiment, 87th SS Volunteer Grenadier Regiment, 32nd SS Volunteer

Artillery Regiment, 32nd SS Fusilier Battalion, 32nd SS Tank Destroyer Battalion, 32nd SS Engineer Battalion, 32nd SS Signal Battalion, 32nd SS Flak Battalion, 32nd SS Field Replacement Battalion, 32nd SS Divisional Supply Troops

Activated on January 30, 1945, in SS Troop Maneuver Area Kurmack, the 32nd SS was formed mainly from the SS NCO School at Lauenburg and the 101st, 102nd and 103rd SS Field Training Regiments. It was later reinforced with the 1236th and 1237th SS Fahnenjunker (Officer-Cadet) Regiments. In February 1945, it was still half-formed and incompletely trained; nevertheless it was sent from Berlin to the Oder Bridgehead near Frankfurt. Attached to the V SS Mountain Corps of Army Group Vistula, it was destroyed in the Battle of Berlin. Most of the division was trapped in the Halbe Pocket and surrendered to the Red Army on April 29. The division staff, along with 150 men, managed to join the 12th Army and surrendered to the Americans at Tangermuende on May 5.

The commanders of the 32nd SS were SS Colonel Rudolf Muehlenkamp (January 30, 1945), SS Colonel Joachim Richter (February 5, 1945), SS Oberführer Adolf Ax (February 17, 1945), and SS Colonel Hans Kempin (March 15, 1945).

Sources: Keegan: 158; Pipes; Tessin, Vol. 5: 22–23; Ziemke 1959b: 34.

33RD SS CAVALRY DIVISION (*UNGARISCHE #3*) (1)

Composition: Various units

Organized in Hungary December 1944, this division was at regimental strength the following month, when it was absorbed by the 26th SS Panzer Grenadier Division (Ungarische # 2). Most of its men were Hungarian volunteers. Its commander was SS Oberführer Laszlo Deak (December 27, 1944–January 23, 1945).

Sources: Chant, Volume 17: 2371; Keegan: 159; Kursietis: 267.

33RD SS GRENADIER DIVISION "CHARLEMAGNE" (*FRANZÖSISCHE #1*) (2)

Composition: 57th SS Volunteer Grenadier Regiment (*franz. Nr. 1*), 58th SS Volunteer Grenadier Regiment (*franz. Nr. 2*), 33rd SS Volunteer Artillery Battalion, 33rd SS Tank Destroyer Battalion, 33rd SS Engineer Company, 33rd SS Signal Company, 33rd SS Fla Company, 33rd Field Replacement Company, 33rd SS Divisional Supply Troops

Home Station: France

The forerunner of this division, the "Legion Volontaire Francaise," was formed in Paris on July 7, 1941, by French-speaking Fascists. They joined the Waffen-SS to fight Bolshevikism. Many of its men were Volksdeutsche, recruited from Alsace and Lorraine. Later it received half-hearted financial support from the Vichy government. It fought on the Russian Front until the spring of 1944, when it was sent to Prague and expanded into the SS Grenadier Brigade "Frankreich." Later designated SS Sturmbrigade "Charlemagne," this unit was sent to the Wildflecken Troop Maneuver Area in West Prussia on February 10, 1945, it became the 33rd SS Grenadier Division. It remained on the Eastern Front and fought in Pomerania, where it was surrounded by the Red Army and lost 4,800 of its 8,000 men. It nevertheless fought with great bravery, reportedly knocking out sixty-two Soviet tanks with *Panzerfausts* (shoulder-fired, single shot, disposable anti-tank weapons) in one week. Hastily reorganized, most of the remainder of the 33rd SS was annihilated in the Battle of Berlin on April 30, 1945—the day Hitler committed suicide. Its survivors went into Russian captivity.

Its commanders were SS Oberführer Edgard Puaud (August 10, 1944), SS Major General Dr. Gustav Krukenberg (March 5, 1945), and SS Colonel Walter Zimmermann (April 24, 1945).

Notes and Sources: Puaud, a former general in the French Foreign Legion, was badly wounded at Stargard by an artillery shell on March 5, 1945. He was with that part of the division which was surrounded and broke out that same day, but his ambulance was lost in the confusion, and he was never heard from again.

Keegan: 96, 159; Richard Landwehr, *Charlemagne's Legionnaires: French Volunteers of the Waffen-SS, 1943–1945* (1989), ff. 1; Lexikon; OB 45: 350; Yerger 1999: 167.

34TH SS VOLUNTEER GRENADIER DIVISION "LANDSTURM NEDERLAND"

Composition: 83rd SS Volunteer Panzer Grenadier Regiment, 84th SS Volunteer Panzer Grenadier Regiment, 60th SS Volunteer Artillery Regiment, 60th SS Reconnaissance Battalion, 60th SS Tank Destroyer Battalion, 60th SS Engineer Company, 604th SS Signal Company, 60th SS Field Replacement Battalion, 60th SS Divisional Supply Troops

Home Station: The Netherlands

The 34th SS was formed in February 1945, from the expansion of the SS Volunteer Grenadier Brigade "Landstorm Nederland," a unit composed of Dutch Fascists, which had previously served in Yugoslavia (1943–44) and on the northern sector of the Eastern Front (1944–45). It was assigned to the 25th Army and was still fighting in the Netherlands at the end of the war.

Commanders of the division included SS Colonel Joachim Ziegler (April 1943), SS Major General Juergen Wagner (April 20, 1944), and SS Oberführer Martin Kohlroser (November 2, 1944).

Sources: Keegan: 99, 159; Kursietis: 268; Lexikon; Tessin, Vol. 5: 42; OB 45: 350.

35TH SS POLICE GRENADIER DIVISION

Composition: 89th SS and Police Regiment, 90th SS and Police Regiment, 91st SS and Police Regiment, 35th SS Police Artillery Regiment, 35th SS Police Fusilier Battalion, 35th SS Tank Destroyer Battalion, 35th SS Police Engineer Battalion, 35th SS Signal Battalion, 35th SS Divisional Supply Troops

This unit was formed on the Oder Front from Police Brigade Wirth (the 1st and 2nd Special Purposes Police Regiments). Each grenadier regiment had only two battalions. It fought in the Berlin campaign and was largely destroyed in the Halbe Pocket on April 24, 1945. Its survivors were absorbed by nearby army units and were later taken into Soviet captivity.

Its commanders were SS Oberführer Johannes Wirth (February 1945) and SS Colonel Rüdiger Pipkorn (March 1, 1945–end).

Notes and Sources: Pipkorn was an army officer involuntarily transferred to the SS. He was killed on April 24, 1945, during the Battle of Halbe.

Keegan: 159; *Kriegstagebuch des OKW,* Volume IV: 1896; Hans von Luck, *Panzer Commander* (1989).

36TH SS GRENADIER DIVISION "DIRLEWANGER"

Composition: 72nd SS Volunteer Grenadier Regiment, 73rd SS Volunteer Grenadier Regiment, 1244th Grenadier Regiment (attached), Panzer Detachment 1/36th SS Grenadier Division (two assault gun companies), 681st Tank Destroyer Battalion (attached), 687th Army Engineer Brigade (attached), divisional fusilier, engineer and signal companies

Formed on February 20, 1945, this unit is better known as the Dirlewanger Brigade, which was its name before it was upgraded in the last weeks of the war. Most of its members were men taken from concentration camps; a few of its "soldiers" were Communists or political prisoners, but most were common criminals. Its commander, SS Colonel/SS Oberführer Dr. Oscar Dirlewanger, was a brutal drunkard who had once been expelled from the SS on a morals offense. (He was involved in pederasty.)

The brigade was responsible for a number of atrocities, especially against the Poles and Jews during the Warsaw Ghetto uprising during the autumn of 1944. It also fought on the Hungarian sector of the Russian Front in late 1944. As of early October, the brigade had 4,000 men—5 percent poachers, 65 percent Waffen-SS/Army/Luftwaffe convicts, and 30 percent political prisoners and civilian convicts. Both the division and its commander were considered notoriously unreliable by the German Army. General Friessner, commander-in-chief of Army Group South Ukraine, once gave Dirlewanger orders on how to defend a sector against Russian attack. Returning later to check on how those orders were being carried out, he found that the brigade had departed the area without informing his headquarters or anybody else's and that the Soviets had occupied the positions he had assigned Dirlewanger to defend. Friessner himself narrowly avoided capture by the Russians by taking to his heels. The 36th SS ended the war on the Eastern Front, although Dirlewanger himself fled on May 1, 1945, to escape capture by the Allies. SS Major General Fritz Schmedes surrendered the division to the Russians.

Notes and Sources: Dirlewanger was promoted to SS Oberführer of Reserve on August 15, 1944. He ended up in a French prison camp at Altshausen, under an assumed name. Some of the inmates recognized him, however, and beat him to death on June 7, 1945.

Keegan: 159; Lexikon; French MacLean, *The Cruel Hunters: SS Sonderkommando Dirlewanger* (1998); Seaton: 456, 498–99; Tessin, Vol. 5: 62; Ziemke 1966: 344. Also see Johannes Friessner, *Verratene Schlachten* (1956).

37TH SS VOLUNTEER CAVALRY DIVISION "LUETZOW"

Composition: 92nd SS Cavalry Regiment, 93rd SS Cavalry Regiment, 94th SS Cavalry Regiment, 37th SS Artillery Battalion, 37th SS Reconnaissance Battalion, 37th SS Engineer Battalion, 37th SS Signal Battalion, 37th SS Field Replacement Battalion, 37th SS Divisional Supply Troops

This unit was formed in the vicinity of Pressburg from those elements of the 8th and 22nd SS Cavalry Divisions which had not been encircled and destroyed in Budapest during the siege of the Hungarian capital (November 26, 1944–February 12, 1945), plus the handful of SS cavalrymen who managed to break out. The 37th SS inherited the horses of the two annihilated divisions, as both the 8th and 22nd were fighting dismounted when Budapest was surrounded. The new division never exceeded regimental strength. En route to Army Group South in western Hungary on March 1, 1945, the 37th SS fought on the southern sector of the Eastern Front until May 1945. It surrendered to the Americans at the end of the war.

Its commanders were SS Oberführer Waldemer Fegelein (February 26, 1945) and SS Colonel Karl Gesele (early March 1945–end).

Sources: Keegan: 159; *Kriegstagebuch des OKW,* Volume IV: 1895; Kursietis: 268; Tessin, Vol. 5: 70; Yerger 1997: 185.

38TH SS GRENADIER DIVISION "NIBELUNGEN"

Composition (April 1945): 95th SS Grenadier Regiment, 96th SS Grenadier Regiment, 97th SS Grenadier Regiment, Tank Destroyer Battalion "Niberlungen," 38th SS Engineer Company, 38th SS Signal Company, 38th SS Divisional Supply Troops

Home Station: Bad Tölz

This unit was originally formed on March 27, 1945. It included four infantry battalions (mainly from the SS Junker School at Bad Tölz) and never exceeded a strength of 6,000 men. It was sent to the 19th Army on the Upper Rhine and initially fought in the Black Forest on April 12. The 38th SS Grenadier Division fought in the Battle of Nuremberg on April 16, at Neumarkt (April 18–23) and at Landshut (April 28–30). Placed in OKW reserve, it was behind the Western Front when the war ended. It surrendered to the Americans in southern Germany on May 8, 1945.

Commanders of the Nibelungen Brigade/Division were SS Lieutenant Colonel Richard Schulz-Kossens (March 27, 1945) and SS Lieutenant General Martin Stange (April 12, 1945–end).

Notes and Sources: "Nibelungen" comes from the famous medieval poem, the *Nibelungenlied,* which was put to music by Richard Wagner in his opera *Ring des Nibelungen.* The 97th SS Grenadier Regiment was authorized but apparently never formed. In early April 1945, SS Major General Hans Lammerding was appointed divisional commander, but he was unable to reach the division and his appointment was rescinded. A few days later, the same thing happened to SS Major General Reichsritter Karl von Oberkamp.

Keegan: 159; *Kriegstagebuch des OKW,* Volume I: 1147; Lexikon; Pipes; Tessin, Vol. 5: 77; Stoves, *Gepanzerten*: 240.

SS DIVISION VERFÜGUNGSTRUPPE (SS-VT)

See the beginning of this chapter.

SS DIVISIONS PLANNED BUT NEVER FORMED

39th SS Mountain Division "Andreas Hofer"
40th SS Panzer Grenadier Division "Feldherrnhalle"
41st SS Grenadier Division "Kalevala" (*Finnische #1*)
42nd SS Grenadier Division "Niedersachsen"
43rd SS Grenadier Division "Reichsmarschall"
44th SS Grenadier Division "Wallenstein"
45th SS Grenadier Division "Warager"

APPENDIX 1

Table of Equivalent Ranks

U.S. Army	German Army
General of the Army	Field Marshal (Generalfeldmarschall)
General	Colonel General (Generaloberst)
Lieutenant General	General (General)
Major General	Lieutenant General (Generalleutnant)
Brigadier General	Major General (Generalmajor)
Colonel	Colonel (Oberst)
Lieutenant Colonel	Lieutenant Colonel (Oberstleutnant)
Major	Major (Major)
Captain	Captain (Hauptmann)
First Lieutenant	Lieutenant (Oberleutnant)
Second Lieutenant	Lieutenant (Leutnant)

SS Rank	German Army Equivalent
Reichsführer S.S. (Himmler)	Commander in Chief of the Army*
None	Field Marshal
Oberstgruppenführer	Colonel General
Obergruppenführer	General
Gruppenführer	Lieutenant General

* Held by Field Marshal Werner von Blomberg (1933–38), Field Marshal Walter von Brauchitsch (February 4, 1938–December 1941), and Hitler (December 1941–April 1945).

SS Rank	**German Army Equivalent**
Brigadeführer	Major General
Oberführer	None
Standartenführer	Colonel
Obersturmbannführer	Lieutenant Colonel
Sturmbannführer	Major
Hauptsturmführer	Captain
Obersturmführer	First Lieutenant
Untersturmführer	Second Lieutenant

APPENDIX 2

The Individual Wehrkreise

WEHRKREIS I

This Wehrkreis consisted primarily of East Prussia until 1939. Later it was expanded to include the microstate of Memel, and the Zichenau, Sudauen, and Bialystok districts of Poland. It gave up the Elbing district of West Prussia when Wehrkreis XX was created in late 1939. The Wehrkreis had an area of 48,921 square miles (78,731 square kilometers) in 1944, with a populalion of 4,667,000. Wehrkreis Headquarters was located in Königsberg.

When the war broke out, the Wehrkreis created Replacemenl Division Staffs 141 and 151 to control its replacement-training units. From September 1940 to July 1941 these staffs conducted their training operations in Poland but then returned to East Prussia. When the Replacement Army was reorganized in the fall of 1942, Wehrkreis I lost much of its training mission. The 141st and 151st were upgraded to reserve division status, given training responsibilities separate from the Wehrkreis, and placed directly under the Home Army; in other words, Wehrkreis I lost them. The 141st was transferred to Lithuania and the 151st went to White Russia. Meanwhile, the Wehrkreis's replacemenl functions were laken over by Replacement Division Staffs 401 and 461, located at Königsberg and Bialystok, respectively. In 1944 the Wehrkreis regained its training mission, but all of its operations were disrupted when the Soviets invaded East Prussia in January 1945. The 401st Replacement Division, for example, went into combat in the Baltic States in late 1944. The Wehrkreis ceased to exist in March 1945 when Königsberg fell to the Soviets.

WEHRKREIS II

This Pomeranian and Mecklenburger military district, which was headquartered at Stettin, had an area of 33,635 square miles (54,131 square kilometers) and a population of about 3,251,000.

When the war broke out, Wehrkreis II created Replacement Division Staffs 152 and 192 to control its replacement-training units. When the replacement and training functions were divided in the fall of 1942, the 152nd and 192nd went to Graudenz and Gnesen, Poland, respectively, and Wehrkreis II lost them and their subordinate training regiments. Meanwhile, the Wehrkreis created Replacement Division Staff 402 to control its replacement units. By late 1944 the military district had reassumed its training mission.

This Wehrkreis was noted for its largely nondivisional artillery and antiaircraft schools and units.

WEHRKREIS III

Consisting of the Berlin area and Brandenburg, Wehrkreis III had an area of 24,334 square miles (39,161 square kilometers) and a population of about 7,250,000. It included a large number of school units, as well as special units and service organizations centering on the Third Reich's capital city.

Immediately after the outbreak of the war, Wehrkreis Headquarters at Berlin set up Replacement Division Staffs 143, 153, and 233 to control the military district's replacement-training units. The 233rd directed motorized and panzer training and replacement units and was upgraded to a panzer reserve division in the fall of 1942. Some of the Wehrkreis's affiliated units were stationed in Poland, beginning in 1941. After the partial separation of the Replacement Army's training and replacement functions in the fall of 1942, the Wehrkreis's training units were sent to the northwestern Ukraine with the 143rd and to the Crimea with the 153rd; both of these units were upgraded to reserve divisions. The 233rd was transferred to Denmark and remained there until the end of the war. It was one of the few reserve divisions still conducting training in 1945. Meanwhile, Wehrkreis III formed Replacement Division Staff 463, in late 1942, to assume control of the remaining non-motorized replacement units, and Replacement Division Staff 433 was later added to direct the motorized replacement units. These new divisions headquartered at Potsdam and Frankfurt-on-the-Oder, respectively.

As the reserve divisions of the German Army were committed to combat in 1943–44, it became necessary for the Wehrkreis to reassume training responsibilities. Wehrkreis III met this problem initially by sending recruits to training units in Wehrkreis XX and then, in early 1944, by gradually added training companies to its organic replacement battalions. The replacement and training units of the elite Grossdeutschland Panzer Division, the Fuehrer Begleit Brigade, and the Fuehrer Grenadier Brigade were all controlled by the Grossdeutschland Motorized Replacement Brigade, which was subordinate to the III Military District from its (the brigade's) inception.

WEHRKREIS IV

Wehrkreis IV included Saxony, most of the Prussian Province of Merseburg (the southern part of the former Prussian province of Saxony), a small district in eastern Thuringia and a small part of western Lower Silesia. In 1938 it was extended to include the former Czechoslovakian Sudetenland. It had an estimated population of 7,875,000 and an area of 18,863 square miles (30,357 square kilometers).

After the invasion of Poland in 1939, the Wehrkreis formed Replacement Division Staffs 154 and 174, to control its replacement and training units. In autumn 1941, some of these units were transferred to the Czechoslovakian Protectorate. The replacement elements of these units returned to Wehrkreis IV in the fall of 1942, when the Home Army divided the military districts' training and replacement functions. The 174th (now a reserve division) left for central Poland, and the 154th, which was also upgraded, followed shortly afterward. Wehrkreis Headquarters (which was located at Dresden) upgraded Special Administrative Division Staff 404 to a replacement division staff and created Replacement Division Staff 464 to replace them. In March 1944, elements of the 154th and 174th Reserve Divisions went into combat on the Eastern Front, but these divisions were not entirely committed to action until the end of the year. Wehrkreis IV meanwhile resumed its training missions under its new replacement division staffs and the IV Panzer Command, a brigade-sized headquarters that was also subordinate to the Wehrkreis. The military district was overrun by the Russians in the spring of 1945.

WEHRKREIS V

This military district included all of Hohenzollern and all but the northern sections of Wuettemberg and Baden. After the fall of France in 1940 it absorbed Alsace. In mid-1944 it had an area of 24,118 square miles (38,814 square kilometers) and a population of about 5,340,000 people. Stuttgart was the headquarters of the Wehrkreis.

After the outbreak of hostilities, V Military District established Replacement Division Staffs 155 and 165 to control its replacement-training units. The 155th consisted of motorized and panzer elements. From November 1939 until September 1940, these units were stationed in the Protectorate (formerly Czechoslovakia). In early 1942, the replacement units were transferred to Alsace, and Special Administrative Division Staff 405 was upgraded to replacement division status to control them. Meanwhile, Colonel General Fromm, the commander-in-chief of the Replacement Army, partially divided the replacement and training missions of the Wehrkreis in early 1942, in an experimental measure that was later adopted in all the Wehrkreise. Replacement Division Staff 165 became the original reserve division and moved to the Epinal area of eastern France with approximately half of Wehrkreis V's training units. Later it was transferred to Holland.

Meanwhile, the Wehrkreis created Replacement Division Staff 465 to take over the non motorized replacement elements left by the 165th. In late 1943 the military district also lost its panzer and motorized training units when the 155th Reserve Panzer Division was created from the former replacement division, and was sent to northwestern France. In May 1944, the 155th Reserve Panzer was absorbed by the 9th Panzer Division; two months later the 165th Reserve Division was disbanded, its personnel sent to several divisions on the Western Front and its Headquarters used to form the 70th Infantry Division. The loss of these two divisions meant that Wehrkreis V had to resume its own training operations under the 465th and newly formed Replacement Division Staff 405. Parts of these divisions were in action in September 1944, when the Western Allies invaded Alsace. Elements of the 405th Replacement Division worked on fortifications in the Vosges Mountains and later held defensive positions on the eastern bank of the Rhine, before withdrawing into the interior. The entire V Military District was overrun by the Americans and the French in the spring of 1945.

WEHRKREIS VI

This large military district encompassed almost all of Westphalia, the northern half of Rhenish Prussia, and part of western Hanover. It had an area of just over 40,000 square miles and a population of 12,100,000. Wehrkreis Headquarters was located in Münster.

When the war broke out, the VI Military District set up Replacement Division Staffs 156, 166, and 176. Most of the subordinate replacement-training units of these divisions were posted in Wehrkreis XX from November 1939 until September 1940. When the Home Army split the Wehrkreis's training and replacement functions in the autumn of 1942, the training units in the southwestern part of the District moved into eastern Belgium under the 156th Reserve Division, which eventually became the 47th Infantry. The training units in the northeastern part of the Wehrkreis were transferred to Denmark under Replacement Division Staff 166 (later 166th Reserve Division) early the following year. The rest of the training elements of the Wehrkreis remained subordinate to the

Münster headquarters and generally concentrated in western Westphalia, although some of them operated as far away as the Netherlands. Within the Wehrkreis, the 176th Replacement Division absorbed the remaining replacement units of the 166th and the 526th Frontier Guard Division Headquarters was converted to a replacement division staff to replace the 156th Division. The VI Panzer Command, a brigade-sized headquarters that was probably formed prior to the start of the war, remained at Warendorf and never gave up its training units, although it did set up bases in eastern Holland.

After the British and Canadians entered Belgium in August and September 1944, the 176th and 526th Replacement Divisions were both committed to combat, although their unfit, convalescent, and untrained personnel remained behind under Wehrkreis control. The 526th also left a "reserve" or cadre staff behind at Wuppertal-Vohwinkel and possibly at Cologne as well. The 526th was eventually dissolved and its personnel distributed among several divisions. On the other hand, the 176th was upgraded to an infantry division in November 1944, while the VI Panzer Command also sent a battle group into action in the Low Countries. The Wehrkreis was still performing its mission on a reduced scale until just before the end of the war, when it was overrun by Montgomery's armies.

WEHRKREIS VII

The VII Military District, which had an area of 20,000 square miles (32,000 square kilometers) and a population of 3,200,000, included Upper Bavaria, the southern parts of lower (northern) Bavaria, the Upper Palatinate, most of Swabia, and minor parts of Upper and Central Franconia. Its headquarters was in Munich.

Replacement Division Staffs 147 and 157 were established after the outbreak of the war to control the rapidly growing number of replacement-training units in the district. The infantry and mountain training elements of the Wehrkreis went to eastern France under the 157th, when it was upgraded to a mountain reserve division in the fall of 1942. In early 1943, the

147th was also upgraded to reserve division status and was transferred to the Ukraine by the Home Army. Wehrkreis VII formed Replacement Division Staffs 407 and 467, at Augsburg and Munich, respectively, to replace them. The 147th Reserve Division became the 147th Field Training Division in 1943 and was destroyed in 1944. The 157th became a mountain division in 1944, and was engaged in combat in southern France by August. It thus became necessary for the Wehrkreis to begin training its own recruits, and its replacement units became replacement and training formations once more. The VII District continued to conduct operations until it was overrun—mainly by the Americans—at the end of the war.

WEHRKREIS VIII

The VIII Military District consisted of almost all of Silesia. In 1938 it absorbed part of the Sudetenland, and the next year it was extended to include Polish Eastern Upper Silesia and the Teschen district of Poland. In 1944 this Wehrkreis had a population of 8,441,000 and an area of 34,800 square miles (56,000 square kilometers). The headquarters was located at Breslau.

Replacement Division Staffs 148, 158, and 178 were formed in 1939 to control the replacement-training units of this Wehrkreis. The 178th was a motorized/panzer unit. In February 1941, the 148th moved to Lorraine and the 158th was posted in Alsace, but both remained subordinate to the VIII. In the latter part of 1942, these divisions returned their replacement elements to Wehrkreis VIII, were upgraded to reserve divisions, and separated from the District. Special Administrative Division Staffs 408 and 432 were converted to replacement division headquarters to control the replacement units released by the new reserve divisions. The 178th Panzer Replacement Division retained both its training and replacement missions to the end and never left the Wehrkreis. After D-Day, the 158th and 189th were both committed to battle on the Western Front, and the Wehrkreis reassumed training responsibilities for its non motorized recruits. Wehrkreis VIII ceased operations in early

1945, and committed its units to action against the Russians when Breslau came under siege. The city held out until May 7, more than a week after Berlin had fallen.

WEHRKREIS IX

This military district consisted of almost all of Thuringia, the Prussian province of Hesse, northern and eastern Hesse, eastern Nassau, a part of western Merseburg, and small sections of southern Westphalia, southern Hanover, and western Lower Franconia. Its area was 23,397 square miles (37,654 square kilometers) and its population was estimated at 5,427,000 in early 1945. District Headquarters was located at Kassel.

Wehrkreis IX set up Replacement Division Staffs 159,179, and 189 when the war broke out in 1939. After the separation of the District's replacement and training elements in 1942, the 159th and 189th became reserve divisions and left for France with the non-motorized training units that had formerly belonged to the Wehrkreis. The 179th was upgraded to a reserve panzer division and left for France with its subordinate training units in autumn 1943. Wehrkreis IX did not have primary training responsibility again until 1944, when the 159th and 189th became engaged in combat on the Western Front, and the 179th was merged with the depleted 16th Panzer Division to form the 116th Panzer. Replacement Division Staff 409 and IX Panzer Command assumed the missions formerly conducted by the three reserve divisions. In 1945 the Soviets occupied the eastern sectors of this district, and the Western Allies overran the rest.

WEHRKREIS X

Located just south of Denmark, this Wehrkreis included Schleswig-Holstein, Oldenburg, Hamburg, Bremen, and northern Hanover. It had an area of 24,322 square miles (39,143 square kilometers) and a population of about 5.5 million. Hamburg was the district headquarters.

After the invasion of Poland began, the X formed Replacement Division Staffs 160, 180, and 190 to control its replacement-training units. From 1940 to 1942, most of the Wehrkreis's subordinate units were billeted in Denmark, except for those elements native to Oldenburg, which were mainly stationed in the Netherlands. After the Home Army reorganized in 1942, the 160th became a reserve division, while the 180th and 190th returned to Wehrkreis control, directing the district's replacement units. By 1944, they included substantial numbers of combined replacement-training units.

In mid-September 1944, the 180th and 190th were hastily committed to combat as infantry units against Allied ground forces that were driving on the Arnhem area, where the British 1st Airborne Division was trying to hold off the II SS Panzer Corps. By delaying the Allied advance, the 180th and 190th probably contributed more to the success of a major operation than did any other units that were affiliated with a Wehrkreis. These divisions never returned to Hanover, for they were both upgraded to infantry divisions in November 1944. The X Military District was not completely overrun until May 1945 and seems to have operated (with declining intensity) until the very end.

WEHRKREIS XI

Consisting of Brunswick, Anhalt, the southern part of Hanover, the Province of Magdeburg and the small region of Schaumburg-Lippe, this Wehrkreis covered 20,530 square miles (33,040 square kilometers) and had a population of 4,149,000. The city of Hanover was the district capital.

In 1939, the XI formed Replacement Division Staffs 171 and 191, which stayed within the Wehrkreis until the fall of 1942, when they were upgrade to reserve division status and sent to the coast of the English Channel. Replacement Division Staff 471 was formed in late 1942, to control the replacement units left behind by the reserve divisions. By early 1944, the 171st and 191st Reserve Divisions had ceased training operations and were redesignated the 48th and 49th Infantry Divisions, respectively. The Wehrkreis, therefore, had to resume training within its borders. To do this, it converted most of its replacement units to replacement-training units. These forces continued in operation until the end of the war.

WEHRKREIS XII

The XII Military District, which headquartered at Wiesbaden, included the southern part of Rhenish Prussia, the western parts of the State of Hesse and Prussian Nassau, the Bavarian Palatinate, the vital Saar Industrial District, and a small part of northern Baden. It was expanded after the fall of France to include Lorraine and Luxembourg. The Wehrkreis's area was 22,662 square miles (36,471 square kilometers), with a population of 6,240,000.

The District created Replacement Division Staffs 172 and 182 to direct its replacement-training units when the war broke out. These divisions went to Poland in November 1939, but returned to the Wehrkreis in September 1940. In 1941 and 1942, elements of these units were stationed in the Nancy area of eastern France. In the fall of that year, these elements returned their replacement components to Germany and were joined by other training battalions under the headquarters of the 182nd, which had been redesignated a reserve division. Later these forces were transferred to the Channel coast. Meanwhile, Wehrkreis XII created Replacement Division Staff 462, to control the returning replacement battalions.

In August 1944, the 182nd Reserve was disbanded and its personnel scattered among a number of combat divisions. Wehrkreis XII thus regained its training responsibilities, which it met by expanding its existing regiments. The 462nd Replacement Division was upgraded to a field (Volksgrenadier) division in September 1944, went into action in eastern France, and was subsequently destroyed at Metz. Shortly thereafter, the entire Wehrkreis became a battleground and the district's operations were seriously disrupted. Until this time the motorized and panzer units were trained and administered by Replacement Division Staff 172 and the XII Panzer Command, which had ceased to exist by early 1945. The 999th Replacement Brigade, which consisted mainly of political prisoners and ordinary criminals, was also administered by this Wehrkreis until the Western Allies overran it in 1945.

In April 1945, Headquarters, Wehrkreis XII was redesignated XII Corps and fought on the middle Rhine and Thueringen as part of the field army.

WEHRKREIS XIII

This district consisted of most of Franconia, Lower Bavaria, the Upper Palatinate, and small sections of southern Thuringia, northern Baden, Wuerttemberg and Swabia. In 1938 it annexed part of Czechoslovakia. The Wehrkreis, which had its headquarters in Nuremberg, had an area of 31,006 square miles (49,900 square kilometers) and a population of 4,771,000.

When the war started, the XIII established Replacement Division Staffs 173 and 193 to control its replacement-training units. In the fall of 1943, the 173rd was redesignated a reserve division, transferred to eastern Croatia with most of the Wehrkreis's training units, and placed directly under the control of the Home Army. The 193rd Replacement Division, which was now in Bohemia, remained under Wehrkreis control with some of the training units. Replacement Division Staff 413 was created at Nuremberg in 1943, to assume command of the replacement units left behind by the 173rd. The district's motorized and panzer training units were assigned to the 273rd Reserve Panzer Division in late 1943 and lost to the Wehrkreis.

By the spring of 1944, both the 173rd Reserve and 273rd Reserve Panzer Divisions had been dissolved, and the Wehrkreis regained all the training responsibilities it had lost the year before. To meet these responsibilities, the Wehrkreis enlarged its existing replacement regiments, which continued operating until the end of the war. In 1945, the eastern parts of this Wehrkreis were overrun by the Soviets, and the western sections were captured by the Americans and the French.

WEHRKREIS XVII

With an area of 24,192 square miles (38,934 square kilometers) and an estimated population of 4,604,000 in 1944, this Wehrkreis consisted of the northeastern part of what had once been Austria. It was headquartered in Vienna.

The district, which was formed in 1938, set up Replacement Division Staffs 177 and 187 shortly after the invasion of Poland, to control its replacement-training units. Many of these were transferred to Moravia in 1941, under the HQ of the 177th or the XVII Panzer Command, both of which remained under Wehrkreis control. The western part of Slovakia was also used by the Wehrkreis as a training area.

In the fall of 1942, the XVII District lost much of its training mission, as well as the 187th Division, which was redesignated a reserve unit and sent to Croatia with the training units. Replacement Division Staff 487, however, was formed at Linz to control the replacement units left behind by the 187th. When the 187th ceased training and was redesignated a jaeger division in autumn 1943, Wehrkreis XVII, which had never completely ceased training (unlike some other districts), simply enlarged its existing replacement-training facilities and expanded its capabilities with a minimum of difficulty. The Wehrkreis was overrun by the Russians in April 1945.

WEHRKREIS XVIII

Created with the annexation of Austria in 1938, this mountainous district included most of the territory of what was formerly Austria, but less than half of its population. It consisted of southern and western Austria, the Tyrol region, and (as of 1941) the Upper Carniola and Lower Styria districts of what had been Yugoslavia. It had a population of 3,000,000 and an area of almost 59,000 square kilometers (36,660 square miles) in 1944.

With the outbreak of hostilities, the XVIII set up Replacement Division Staff 188 to control its replacement-training units, which were almost all mountain forces. In autumn 1943, this division was transferred to northern Italy as a reserve division, and its training units were lost to the Wehrkreis. To control the remaining replacement units, the XVIII set up Replacement Division Staff 418 at Salzburg, which was also the headquarters of the Wehrkreis. When the 188th was upgraded to a regular mountain division in late 1944, Wehrkreis XVIII reassumed its normal training duties, in so far as that was possible in the fifth year of the war. The district was occupied, largely by the Western Allies, in the spring of 1945.

WEHRKREIS XX

This Wehrkreis, which consisted of Danzig, the Elbing area of West Prussia, and sections of northern Poland, was created in the winter of 1939–40. Its Danzig headquarters administered an area of 26,000 square kilometers (16,156 square miles), which were inhabited by 2,259,000 people, most of whom were Poles.

The XX never set up any replacement or reserve divisions of its own, although Replacement Division Staff 152 of Wehrkreis II was attached to it in the fall of 1942. The XX Military District also controlled the "Feldherrnhalle" Motorized Replacement Brigade, which provided replacements for the 60th Panzer Grenadier and 13th Panzer Divisions. Most of these men were former S.A. (Brownshirt) members. General of Artillery Bodewin Keitel, the younger brother of Field Marshal Wilhelm Keitel, was the commander of this Wehrkreis for most of its existence. The District was overrun by the Russians in January 1945.

WEHRKREIS XXI

The XXI Military District was created in northern Poland in 1939–40. Headquartered at Posen, it controlled an area of 27,340 square miles (44,000 square kilometers) and had a population of 4,635,000, most of which were Poles.

Because of its foreign composition, the XXI never set up its own units but did provide facilities for other Wehrkreise training elements, principally the 192nd Replacement Division of Wehrkreis II.

The XXI District was overrun by the Russians in late 1944 and early 1945.

WEHRKREIS GENERAL GOUVERNEMENT

Officially formed in central and southern Poland on November 1,1943, this District had, in fact, been functioning since 1939. With 88,363 square miles (142,207 square kilometers) and 18 million people, it was easily the largest and probably the least German of the Wehrkreise. Warsaw was the District Headquarters.

The Wehrkreis's main function in World War II was to provide training facilities for the reserve divisions. It had a limited internal organization and no affiliated divisions.

WEHRKREIS BOHEMIA AND MORAVIA

With an area of 30,386 square miles (48,902 square kilometers) and a population of 7,500,000, this Czechoslovakian district was headquartered at Prague. It was created in 1939 but never produced a field division; however, it provided facilities, administrative support, and training areas to no less than five Wehrkreise, as well as Luftwaffe and Waffen-SS units, which tended to concentrate here. It did not cease operations until Czechoslovakia became a battleground in 1945.

APPENDIX 3

The Higher Headquarters

The German divisions in the field were, generally speaking, controlled by three types of higher headquarters: the army group, the army, and the corps or corps command. The corps command differed from the corps in that it was usually formed as special headquarters for defensive missions, mainly in occupied territories. Most of the corps commands were upgraded to corps as the war progressed, and, indeed, there was little difference in them and corps headquarters. As early as 1942, for example, U.S. Intelligence reported of them: "While not composed of a high percentage of offensive combat arms, they can give a good account of themselves in battle. In some cases, they have been used for offensive missions" (OB 42: 52).

An army group headquarters usually controlled two or more armies, but never more than seven. Armies directed the operations of two or more corps, and corps controlled two or more divisions. Each headquarters had various combat and support units organic to it, as well as attached combat divisions. An army group, for example, included a commander of the Army Group Rear Area (*Befehlshaber des ruckwartigen Heeresgebiets*), and each army had a commandant of Army Rear Area (*Kommandant des ruckwartigen Armeegebiets*), whose task was to supervise the administration of the communications zone so that the army group or army commander could concentrate on field operations. Both commandants were in charge of security units (divisions or regiments), as well as administrative and supply units, and GHQ (General Headquarters) formations.

General Headquarters units organic or attached to armies and army groups included special duty infantry battalions, security and motorized security regiments or brigades, special

Jagdkommandos (raiding detachments), motorized machine gun battalions, antiaircraft units, reconnaissance battalions, and special disciplinary battalions (*Sonderbataillons*) units to which insubordinate soldiers were sent. Usually they were employed in areas of the Russian Front where heavy fighting was expected.

Each army also had an infantry equipment park, as well as other parks for medical and veterinary services, heavy transport equipment parks (one per army), and other maintenance detachments. Independent tank, heavy anti-tank, and tank flame-thrower battalions were also organic to some army and army group headquarters and were often attached to corps or divisions, in accordance with the tactical judgment of the army or army group commander. Other GHQ units included (but were not limited to) artillery regimental staffs (all fully motorized, except for coastal defense artillery), super heavy artillery units, all varieties of artillery, artillery observation battalions (i.e., forward observers), armored assault gun battalions, survey and mapping units, observation balloon units, meteorological platoons, artillery parks, chemical units (including projector, or rocket launcher units), decontamination battalions, gas defense units, combat, fortress, and railway engineer unts, engineer landing companies (amphibious), assault boat companies, briding units, technical battalions (used for the production and treatment of oil, coal mining, etc.), signal units, motor transport regiments and battalions, tank repair battalions, motor maintenance workshops, field workshops, motor transport park companies, supply battalions and special supply staffs, GHQ or army medical battalions, hospital detachments, veterinary parks and units, construction staffs, military police battalions (one per army), and local defense units—which were usually assigned to guard prisoners of war.

Corps-type units varied with the type of corps, of which there were several, including infantry (or *Armeekorps*), panzer, mountain, reserve, parachute, SS, and corps commands. They contained fewer GHQ units than army or army group headquarters, but included supply, signal, military police, artillery, security, field postal, and other units.

One other type of major headquarters must be mentioned, and that is the *Oberbefehlshaber,* or OB. It frequently controlled army groups, although sometimes it just controlled armies. OB West was the most famous Oberbefehlshaber, and it was responsible to OKW and to Hitler for directing the war on the Western Front in 1944–45.

OB EAST

October 8, 1939:	formed in Poland to guard Germany's eastern territories against a possible Russian surprise attack while Hitler overran France and the Benelux countries. It controlled a dozen third- and fourth-wave divisions plus a cavalry brigade
July 1940:	dissolved

OB NORTHWEST

April 6, 1945:	created to control the remnants of the 1st Parachute and 25th armies, plus naval and Luftwaffe units, in Holland and northwestern Germany
May 1945:	surrendered

OB SOUTH (ALSO KNOWN AS OB SOUTHWEST)

late 1941:	formed to direct German military activities in Italy and North Africa
August 1943:	included Rommel's Army Group B in northern Italy, Hube's forces fighting the Allies in Sicily, and a few German units in central Italy, Sardinia, and Corsica
May 1944:	directed the 10th and 14th armies on the Italian Front, plus Army Detachment von Zangen in northern Italy
April 1945:	in charge of army groups G, C, and E

OB SOUTHEAST (AND SIMULTANEOUSLY ARMY GROUP F)

August 1943:	created at the time of the Italian surrender. Included Army Group F (in Yugoslavia and Albania) and Army Group E (in Greece and the Mediterranean islands)
March 1945:	dissolved

OB WEST

1940:	formed in Paris (also known as Army Group D, a headquarters it eventually absorbed)
1944–45:	controlled army groups B, G, and H on the Western Front

ARMY GROUP A

October 26, 1939:	formed when Headquarters, Army Group South was redesignated
May–June 1940:	played the major role in the conquest of France
June 1941:	designated Army Group South for the invasion of Russia
July 1942:	reactivated on the southern sector of the Russian Front, when Army Group South was divided
1942–43:	directed the drive on and retreat from the Caucasus; fought on the southern flank of the Russian Front
April 1944:	redesignated Army Group South Ukraine; eventually renamed Army Group South and, on January 25, 1945, Army Group Center
May 1945:	surrendered

ARMY GROUP B

July 9, 1942:	formed to control armies advancing on Stalingrad

June 1943:	deactivated
August 1943:	reformed in southern Germany under Rommel
late 1943:	controlled German units in northern Italy
January 1944:	sent to France; controlled 7th and 15th armies and Armed Forces Netherlands HQ
June 1944:	Normandy
August 1944:	crushed at Falaise
December 1944:	commanded Ardennes counteroffensive
April 1945:	destroyed in the Ruhr Pocket

ARMY GROUP C

August 26, 1939:	formed upon mobilization to control units on the Western Front
May–June 1940:	France; attached Maginot Line
April 20, 1941:	redesignated Sector Staff East Prussia
June 22, 1941:	redesignated Army Group North for the invasion of Russia
November 26, 1943:	reactivated in Italy under OB Southwest
1943–45:	directed German combat operations in Italy, controlling 10th Army and later 14th Army
May 2, 1945:	surrendered

ARMY GROUP CENTER

1939:	formed as Army Group North; invaded Poland
1940:	overran Low Countries as Army Group B
1941:	redesignated Army Group Center; invaded Russia; defeated at Moscow
1943:	Kursk
1944:	crushed in Vitebsk-Minsk area: retreated through Poland
January 26, 1945:	redesignated Army Group North; fighting in East Prussia

April 2, 1945:	disbanded

ARMY GROUP COURLAND

1939:	formed as Army Group C on Siegfried Line
1940:	opposed French forces in Maginot Line
June 22, 1941:	redesignated Army Group North for Russian invasion; conquered Baltic States
1941–January 1944:	maintained siege of Leningrad and fought in the Lake Ilmen area
1944:	withdrew to Narva River–Lake Peipus line
September 1944:	retreated into Courland Pocket
late 1944:	redesignated Army Group Courland (Kurland)
May 1945:	surrendered to the Soviets

ARMY GROUP D

October 26, 1940:	formed to control German armies stationed in France, Belgium, and Holland
April 15, 1941:	absorbed by OB West

ARMY GROUP DON

November 21, 1942:	formed from HQ, 11th Army; directed Stalingrad relief operation
February 12, 1943:	redesignated Army Group South; later renamed Army Group North Ukraine, Army Group A, and Army Group Center
April 1945:	surrounded in Czechoslovakia; surrendered to the Russians early the following month.

ARMY GROUP E

January 1, 1943:	formed in the Balkans by the expansion of the 12th Army
1944:	withdrew from southern Balkans

1945:	surrendered in Croatia

ARMY GROUP F

August 12, 1943:	formed to control German occupation forces in the Balkans
autumn 1944:	retreated from southern Balkans
winter 1944:	gave up control of most of the units of Army Group E
March 25, 1945:	dissolved

ARMY GROUP G

April 28, 1944:	formed in southern France
1944–45:	retreated across southern France and southern Germany
May 6, 1945:	surrendered

ARMY GROUP H

November 11, 1944:	formed on northern sector, Western Front
1945:	retreated across northwestern Germany
April 6, 1945:	became OB Northwest

ARMY GROUP NORTH

See Army Group Courland

ARMY GROUP NORTH UKRAINE

March 30, 1944:	activated when Army Group South was redesignated Army Group North Ukraine
September 29, 1944:	redesignated Army Group A

ARMY GROUP SOUTH

1939:	formed to control German forces invading southern Poland
1940:	as Army Group A, played the major role in the conquest of France
1941:	once again designated Army Group South; overran the Ukraine, the

	Donets, and most of the Crimea; turned back at Rostov
July 9, 1942:	divided into army groups A and B; ceased to exist
September 23, 1944:	reactivated when Army Group South Ukraine was redesignated
March 1945:	redesignated Army Group Ostmark

ARMY GROUP SOUTH UKRAINE

March 30, 1944:	activated when Army Group A was redesignated Army Group South Ukraine
September 29, 1944:	redesignated Army Group South

ARMY GROUP VISTULA

January 25, 1945:	created for the defense of western Prussia, Pomerania, and Berlin
April 1945:	crushed in Battle of Berlin
May 2, 1945:	surrendered

1ST ARMY

August 26, 1939:	mobilized
1940:	French campaign
1940–44:	occupation duties, southwestern France
1944:	withdrew across southern France; fought along the Loire and upper Seine
early 1945:	fought in the Saar; retreated across southwestern Germany
May 1945:	surrendered south of Munich

1ST PANZER ARMY

August 26, 1939:	formed in Lueneburg (Wehrkreis X) as XXII Corps
September 1939:	Poland
1940:	fought in Western campaign as Group von Kleist
1941:	fought in Balkans as 1st Panzer Group

late 1941:	redesignated 1st Panzer Army
1941–45:	fought on Eastern Front

1ST PARACHUTE ARMY

early 1944:	formed in eastern France as a training headquarters from HQ, XI Air Corps
autumn 1944:	became operational; fought in Belgium and Holland
early 1945:	in eastern Holland
May 1945:	surrendered in Oldenburg area, northwestern Germany

2ND ARMY

1939:	formed
1940:	Western campaign
1941:	Balkans
1941–44:	Russian Front
autumn 1944:	Poland
1945:	fought in East Prussia and Vistula delta
May 1945:	last elements surrendered to the Russians on the Hela penmsula

2ND PANZER ARMY

May 1939:	formed as XIX Motorized Corps
September 1939:	Poland
1940:	Western campaign; redesignated Group Guderian
1941:	redesignated 2nd Panzer Group; upgraded to panzer army status in December
1941–43:	Eastern Front
late 1943:	transferred to Balkans
late 1944:	engaged in Croatia and subsequently fought the Russians in Hungary
1945:	ended the war on the southern sector of the Eastern Front

3RD ARMY

1939:	formed from elements of HQ, I Corps and Wehrkreis I
1939:	Poland
late 1939:	disbanded; the bulk of its staff used to form the new HQ, 16th Army

3RD PANZER ARMY

1937:	formed in Jena as XV Corps. to control the original three German light divisions
1939:	Poland
1940:	Western campaign (as XV Motorized Corps and later as Group Hoth)
1941:	Eastern Front as 3rd Panzer Group
January 1, 1942:	redesignated 3rd Panzer Army
1941–45:	fought on central sector, Russian Front, and in Poland, East Prussia and north-eastern Germany
1945:	Surrendered to the Anglo-Americans

4TH ARMY

1939:	Poland
1940:	Western campaign
1941–44:	Central sector. Russian Front
1944:	crushed by Soviet summer offensive
1945:	East Prussia; mostly destroyed at and in vicinity of Königsberg
April 7, 1945:	Disbanded; staff used to form 21st Army

4TH PANZER ARMY

1937:	formed in Berlin as XVI Corps to control the original panzer divisions
1939:	Poland
1940:	West
1941:	Russia (as 4th Panzer Group)
January 1, 1942:	upgraded to panzer army status

1941–45:	central and southern sectors, Eastern Front. Retreated across the northern Ukraine, Poland, and Silesia
May 8, 1945:	ended the war in eastern Germany

5TH ARMY

August 25, 1939:	controlled units along the western German frontier during the Polish campaign
October 1939:	transferred to occupied Poland
November 4, 1939:	redesignated 18th Army

5TH PANZER ARMY

December 8, 1942:	formed in Tunisia from LXXXX Corps
May 12, 1943:	surrendered
January 24, 1944:	HQ, Panzer Group West established in France
August 6, 1944:	Panzer Group West redesignated 5th Panzer Army
1944:	fought in Normandy, Falaise, the retreat through France and in the Ardennes
April 17, 1945:	surrendered in the Ruhr Pocket

6TH ARMY

1939:	formed as 10th Army; Poland
October 10, 1939:	redesignated 6th Army
May 1940:	destroyed Belgian Army
1941–43:	southern sector, Russian Front
January 31–February 2, 1943:	surrendered at Stalingrad
early 1943:	reformed in southern Russia
1943–45:	on Eastern Front; suffered heavy losses on lower Dnieper and in Hungary; ended war on southern sector

6th PANZER (LATER SS PANZER) ARMY

September 24, 1944:	formed as 6th Panzer Army in the vicinity of Paderborn, northwestern Germany; in charge of refitting panzer divisions smashed in French campaign
late 1944:	Ardennes offensive
1945:	Hungary, Austria; defeated by the Russians in the Battle of Vienna
May 1945:	surrendered to the U.S. Army

7th ARMY

August 25, 1939:	formed in Stuttgart, Wehrkreis V
1940:	Western campaign
1940–44:	occupation duties, western France
1944–45:	fought in Normandy, at Falaise, in the Ardennes offensive, and in the defense of Germany
May 8, 1945:	surrendered to the Americans in Czechoslovakia

8th ARMY

August 25, 1939:	formed from HQ, Army Group 3 (Dresden)
1939:	Poland
October 20, 1939:	redesignated 2nd Army
July 1943:	reformed on southern sector, Russian Front, from Army Detachment Kempf, which had been formed on February 21, 1943
February 1944:	smashed west of the lower Dnieper
1944:	retreated through eastern Carpathians, lower Dnestr, Transylvania, and Hungary
1945:	ended the war on the southern sector, Eastern Front

9th ARMY

May 15, 1940:	formed from Staff, OB East
1940:	Western campaign
1941–44:	central sector, Russian Front

summer 1944:	smashed by Soviets
1944–early 1945:	retreated across southern and central Poland
late April–May 1, 1945:	destroyed in the Halbe Pocket, east of Berlin

10TH ARMY

1939:	formed from Staff, Army Group 4 in Leipzig; Poland
early 1940:	redesignated 6th Army (see 6th Army)
August 15, 1943:	reformed in southern Italy
1943–45:	Italian campaign

11TH ARMY

October 5, 1939:	formed in Leipzig
1941–42:	southern sector, Russian Front; conducted siege of Sevastopol
August 1942:	shifted to northern sector, Eastern Front
December 1942:	redesignated Army Group Don
November 26, 1944:	formed in Pomerania (also called 11th SS Panzer Army)
February 1945:	Eastern Front; launched futile counter-attack at Stargard
April 1945:	Overrun by Western Allies following the collapse of the Ruhr Pocket; continued to operate in northern Germany until the end of the war

12TH ARMY

October 13, 1939:	formed from Staff, 14th Army
1940:	Western campaign
1941:	Sent to Balkans; remained there
January 23, 1943:	expanded into Army Group E
April 10, 1945:	reactivated in Harz Mountains from Staff, Army Group North; ordered to relieve Berlin
May 3, 1945:	surrendered to Western Allies

14TH ARMY

August 1, 1939:	formed from Headquarters, Army Group 5 in Vienna
1939:	Poland
late 1939:	redesignated 12th Army
November 18, 1943:	formed in northern Italy to control forces formerly under Army Group B
February 1944:	committed to battle at Anzio
1944–45:	Italian Front
April 29, 1945:	surrendered

15TH ARMY

January 15, 1941:	formed to control units in northern France and Belgium
September 1944:	in action on Western Front; retreated into Holland
late 1944:	shifted to Aachen sector
April 1945:	destroyed in Ruhr Pocket

16TH ARMY

October 22, 1939:	formed from Staff, 3rd Army
1940:	Western campaign
1941–45:	northern sector, Eastern Front
May 1945:	surrendered in Courland Pocket

17TH ARMY

December 20, 1940:	formed in Schneidemühl, Wehrkreis II
1941–43:	southern sector, Eastern Front; in Caucasus campaign
late 1943:	withdrew into Crimea
April 1944:	largely destroyed at Sevastopol; HQ evacuated
September 1944:	reappeared in the Krakow sector, Poland
1944–45:	fought on the southern sector of the Eastern Front for the rest of the war
May 8, 1945:	surrendered to Red Army

18TH ARMY

November 4, 1939:	formed from Headquarters, 5th Army
1940:	Western campaign; took Paris
1941–45:	northern sector, Eastern Front; besieged Leningrad
May 1945:	surrendered in Courland Pocket

19TH ARMY

August 26, 1943:	formed at Avignon, southern France, absorbing Headquarters, LXXXIII Corps, as well as Army Detachment Felber, which had occupied Vichy France in November, 1942
1944–45:	Western Front

20TH MOUNTAIN ARMY

January 14, 1942:	formed as the Army of Lapland
1941–late 1944:	Far North sector, Eastern Front
June 22, 1942:	redesignated 20th Mountain Army
1944–45:	northern Norway; surrendered to the British

21ST ARMY

April 27, 1945:	formed from the Staff, 4th Army, which had been recalled from East Prussia
1945:	Eastern Front. Surrendered to Anglo-Americans in May

24TH ARMY

November 1944:	formed
March–May 1945:	Fortress Alps

25TH ARMY

November 10, 1944:	formed in the Netherlands from the Staff, Armed Forces Netherlands and Staff, Army Detachment Narva
April 7, 1945:	renamed Headquarters, Fortress Holland

ARMY OF NORWAY

December 19, 1940:	created
1940–44:	administered occupied Norway
December 18, 1944:	absorbed by 20th Mountain Army

PANZER ARMY AFRIKA

June 1941:	formed as Panzer Group Afrika
1941–43:	directed Axis operations in Libya and Egypt; retreated to Tunisia
late 1942:	redesignated 1st Italian-German Army
May 1943:	destroyed

I CAVALRY CORPS

May 25, 1944:	formed as the Cavalry Corps in the Generalgouvernement (Poland) from Staff, LXXVIII Corps
August–October 1944:	Narev sector, Eastern Front
November–December 1944:	East Prussia
January–May 1945:	Hungary, Austria. Surrendered to the British

I CORPS

1921:	formed as an integral part of Headquarters, Wehrkreis I
1939:	Poland
1940:	France
1941–45:	northern sector, Eastern Front
1945:	surrendered in Courland Pocket

I FLAK CORPS

October 1939:	formed in Berlin
1940:	Western campaign, supporting 12th and 16th Armies and Panzer Group von Kleist
June 1940:	disbanded

April 1, 1941:	reformed in Berlin from Staff, I Flak Brigade
1941–45:	Eastern Front
May 1945:	surrendered to the Russians at Koeniggraetz

I LUFTWAFFE FIELD CORPS

winter 1942–43:	formed
1943–1944:	France
January 1944:	disbanded; used to form Headquarters, II Parachute Corps

I PARACHUTE CORPS

January 1944:	formed in central Italy from Staff, II Luftwaffe Field Corps
1944–end:	fought on Italian Front

I SS PANZER CORPS

July 27, 1943:	formed in Berlin-Lichterfelde
late 1943:	northern Italy
1944:	Western Front (Normandy, Falaise. Ardennes)
January 1945:	sent to Eastern Front; fought in Hungary and Austria

II CORPS

1921:	formed as a part of Headquarters, Wehrkreis II
1939:	Poland
1940:	West
1941–45:	northern sector, Eastern Front
1945:	surrendered in Courland Pocket

II FLAK CORPS

October 1943:	formed in central Russia from Staff, III Luftwaffe Field Corps
1943–45:	Eastern Front

II LUFTWAFFE FIELD CORPS

early 1943:	formed
1943–early 1944:	Eastern Front, mainly on central sector
early 1944:	disbanded; part of staff used to form I Parachute Corps

II PARACHUTE CORPS

January 1944:	formed in France from the I Luftwaffe Field Corps and the XIII Air Corps; responsible for forming new Luftwaffe Field and parachute divisions
June 1944:	committed to combat in Normandy; almost continuously in action on the Western Front thereafter
1945:	fought in Holland and northwestern Germany

II SS PANZER CORPS

May 1942:	formed in Germany; sent to northern France in July
November 1942:	helped overrun Vichy France; took Toulon
January 1943:	sent to southern sector, Eastern Front
August 1943:	transferred to Italy
December 1943:	returned to France
March 1944:	returned to Eastern Front; fought at Tarnopol on southern sector
June 1944:	rushed to Normandy sector of France
August 1944:	surrounded at Falaise and Mons; broke out with heavy casualties; sent to Arnhem, The Netherlands, to reform
September 1944:	smashed British 1st Airborne Division at Arnhem
Decetnber 1944:	in Ardennes counteroffensive
1945:	Eastern Front; fought in Hungary and Austria

III FLAK CORPS

February 22, 1944:	formed in France from Staff, 11th Flak Division (Motorized)
1944–45:	Western Front; supported Panzer Group West (later 5th Panzer Army) in Normandy
1945:	Destroyed in Ruhr Pocket

III LUFTWAFFE FIELD CORPS

January 1943:	formed
1943:	Eastern Front, mainly on northern sector
October 1943:	dissolved. Staff used to form II Flak Corps

III PANZER CORPS

1921:	formed as an integral part of Headquarters, Wehrkreis III
1939–40:	fought in Poland and France as an infantry corps
March 21, 1941:	redesignated III Motorized Corps
1941–45:	Eastern Front, mainly on southern sector
June 21, 1942:	upgraded to III Panzer Corps

III (GERMANIC) SS PANZER CORPS

April 1943:	formed to control the training and subsequent operations of new Scandinavian and Dutch SS divisions
Sept.–Dec. 1943:	in Croatia
December 1943–1945:	northern sector, Eastern Front

IV LUFTWAFFE FIELD CORPS

See XC Corps.

IV FLAK CORPS

June 1944: formed in Breslau
1944–45: Supported Army Group G on the Western Front
May 1945: Surrendered in southern Germany

IV CORPS

1921: formed as part of Headquarters, Wehrkreis IV
1939–40: Poland and France as an infantry corps
1941–43: Eastern Front; destroyed at Stalingrad
December 1942: reformed from Group Mieth
July 20, 1943: redesignated IV Corps
1943–44: southern sector, Eastern Front
September 2, 1944: destroyed in Romania

IV PANZER CORPS

October 10, 1944: formed as a panzer corps to replace the IV Corps
1944–45: southern sector, Eastern Front

IV SS PANZER CORPS

August 8, 1943: formed in France to control SS divisions forming at that time
August 1944–45: southern sector, Russian Front

V CORPS

1921: formed as part of Headquarters, Wehrkreis V
August 26, 1939: mobilized as a field corps
1940: Western campaign
1941–44: southern sector, Eastern Front
May 1944: evacuated from Crimea
July 24, 1944: disbanded; remnants used to form XI SS Corps
January 26, 1945: a new V Corps Headquarters was formed from the remains of the staffs of the

	221st Security and 20th Luftwaffe Field Divisions.
1945–end:	central sector, Eastern Front

V FLAK CORPS

November 15, 1944:	formed from Staff, General of Flak Artillery
1944–45:	supported OB Southeast and Army Group E in the Balkans and later in Austria

V SS MOUNTAIN CORPS

July 1, 1943:	formed in Berlin and Prague
1943–44:	engaged in anti-partisan operations in Bosnia
late 1944:	transferred to Germany
1945:	destroyed in the Battle of Berlin

VI CORPS

1921:	formed as part of Headquarters, Wehrkreis VI
August 26, 1939:	mobilized
1939–40:	Poland and Western campaign
1941–45:	Eastern Front (southern sector until early 1944); surrendered in East Prussia

VI SS CORPS

October 8, 1943:	organized to control Latvian SS divisions and smaller units
1944–45:	northern sector, Eastern Front

VII CORPS

1921:	formed as part of Headquarters, Wehrkreis VII
August 26, 1939:	mobilized as a field corps
1939–40:	Poland and Western campaign

1941–44:	Russian Front, mainly on central sector
August–September 1944:	destroyed in Romania

VII PANZER CORPS

December 18, 1944:	formed from Staff, 49th Infantry Division
1945:	Eastern Front (West Prussia)

VII SS PANZER CORPS

April 1944:	formed in Germany
June 30, 1944:	disbanded; used to form corps troops for the IV SS Panzer Corps

VIII CORPS

October 1934:	formed in Breslau as a corps HQ and a Wehrkreis from HQ, 2nd Cavalry Division
August 26, 1939:	mobilized
1939–40:	Poland and West
1941–43:	Eastern Front; destroyed at Stalingrad
March 1943:	reformed under 16th Army
1943–45:	Eastern Front, southern, northern, and central sectors

IX CORPS

1935:	formed as a corps headquarters and a Wehrkreis from HQ, 3rd Cavalry Division
August 26, 1939:	mobilized as a field corps
1939–40:	Polish and Western campaigns
1941–45:	Eastern Front
1945:	East Prussia

IX SS MOUNTAIN CORPS

July 1944:	formed in Croatia
late 1944:	transferred to Hungary; in action, Eastern Front

February 12, 1945:	destroyed in Siege of Budapest

X CORPS

1935:	formed as a corps headquarters and a Wehrkreis from Headquarters, Cavalry Corps
August 26, 1939:	mobilized as a field corps
1939–40:	Poland and Western campaigns (the Netherlands and Dunkirk)
1941–45:	northern sector, Eastern Front

XI CORPS

1936:	formed as a corps headquarters and a Wehrkreis
August 26, 1939:	mobilized as a field corps
1939–40:	Poland and Western campaigns
April 1941:	Balkans campaign (Serbia)
1941–43:	Eastern Front; destroyed at Stalingrad
summer 1943:	reformed; back to southern sector
February 1944:	smashed at Cherkassy
1944:	reformed in Poland; still in southern Poland in August
1945:	Upper Silesia; surrendered to the Russians in Czechoslovakia

XI AIR CORPS

summer 1940:	formed to control expanding parachute units
1941:	Crete
1942:	in southern France
April 1943:	Italy (in Rome area)
March 1944:	upgraded to 1st Parachute Army at Nancy, France

XI SS CORPS

July 24, 1944:	formed near Neisse, Wehrkreis VIII, from the remnants of the army's V Corps

1944–45:	central (Vistula) sector, Eastern Front

XII CORPS

October 1, 1936:	formed in Wiesbaden as a corps and a Wehrkreis
August 26, 1939:	mobilized as a field corps
1940:	France
1941–44:	central sector, Eastern Front
August 21, 1944:	remnants used to from Staff, 6th Panzer Army
April 1945:	Headquarters, Wehrkreis XII became the new XII Corps; served on the Western Front (middle Rhine and Thueringen)

XII SS CORPS

August 1, 1944:	formed in Silesia
August 1944:	Courland, Eastern Front
October 1944:	Western Front (Aachen, Roehr, Rhine)
April 1945:	destroyed in Ruhr Pocket

XIII CORPS

October 1, 1937:	formed in Nuremberg as Wehrkreis XIII
August 1, 1939:	mobilized; field components became XIII Corps
1939–40:	Poland and France
1941–44:	Eastern Front
July 1944:	destroyed at Brody
January 19, 1945:	reformed from Higher Command Vosges (formerly Corps Felber)
May 1945:	Surrendered to the Western Allies in Saxony

XIII SS CORPS

August 1, 1944:	formed in Breslau from the remnants of Headquarters, XXXV Corps and Staff, 312th Special Purposes Artillery Division
1944–45:	Western Front (Saar and Danube)

XIV PANZER CORPS

April 1, 1938:	formed in Magdeburg as XIV Motorized Corps
1939–41:	Poland, France and the Balkans (Yugoslavia)
1941–43:	Eastern Front
June 21, 1942:	redesignated XIV Panzer Corps
February 1943:	destroyed at Stalingrad
April 1943:	rebuilt in France
1943–45:	Italian Front

XIV SS CORPS

November 1944:	formed
January 1945:	Western Front (Upper Rhine)
January 1945:	dissolved; Staff used to form the X SS Corps in Pomerania

XV MOTORIZED (LATER PANZER) CORPS

October 10, 1938:	formed in Jena to control Germany's light divisions
1939–40:	Poland and France
November 16, 1940:	upgraded to 3rd Panzer Group (later Army)

XV MOUNTAIN CORPS

August 12, 1943:	formed in the Balkans from Staff, German Commander in Croatia
1943–45:	Croatia; surrendered to Yugoslavs

XV SS COSSACK CAVALRY CORPS

February 1, 1945:	formed in Croatia
1945:	Eastern Front

XVI CORPS

July 1944:	formed under Army Group North as Special Purposes Command Kleffel
October 30, 1944:	upgraded to XVI Corps
1944–end:	northern sector, Eastern Front

XVI MOTORIZED CORPS

February 1938:	formed in Berlin to control Germany's three panzer divisions
1939–40:	Poland and France
February 17, 1941:	upgraded to 3rd Panzer Group (later Army)

XVII CORPS

April 1, 1938:	formed in Vienna as Wehrkreis XVII
August 26, 1939:	field components mobilized as XVII Corps
1939–41:	Poland
1941–45:	Eastern Front; surrendered to Red Army in Silesia

XVIII MOUNTAIN CORPS

April 1, 1938:	formed as Wehrkreis XVIII
August 26, 1939:	mobilized as XVIII Corps
1939–40:	Poland and the West
October 30, 1940:	became XVIII Mountain Corps
1941:	Balkans campaign
1942–45:	Lapland and northern Norway
1945:	East Prussia; surrendered to Red Army

XVIII SS CORPS

1944:	created
1945:	southern sector, Western Front
May 1945:	surrendered to I st French Army near Swiss border

XIX MOTORIZED CORPS

July 1, 1939:	formed in Vienna
1939–40:	Poland and France
June 1, 1940:	redesignated Panzer Group Guderian
November 16, 1942:	upgraded to 2nd Panzer Group (later Army)

XIX MOUNTAIN CORPS

July 1, 1940:	formed as Mountain Corps Norway
November 10, 1942:	redesignated XIX Mountain Corps
1941–44:	fought on Murmansk (Far North) sector of Eastern Front
1944–45:	retreated across northern Finland to Norway; ended the war there

XX CORPS

1939:	formed in Danzig
1939:	Poland
1941–45:	Eastern Front, mainly on central sector
May 5–7, 1945:	surrendered to the Americans

XXI CORPS

See Army of Norway

XXI MOUNTAIN CORPS

August 12, 1943:	formed in Balkans from staffs in Serbia
1943–44:	Serbia and Croatia
late 1944:	heavily engaged against partisans; withdrew to Sarajevo
1945:	southern sector, Eastern Front

XXII CORPS

See 1st Panzer Army

XXII MOUNTAIN CORPS

August 20, 1943:	formed in Greece
September 1944:	withdrew through Yugoslavia
December 1944:	Hungary
1945:	southern sector, Eastern Front

XXIII CORPS

1938:	part of peacetime army as Frontier Command Eifel, headquartered at Bonn

August 26, 1939:	mobilized
September 18, 1939:	redesignated XXIII Corps
1940:	West
1941–45:	central sector, Eastern Front; ended the war in West Prussia

XXIV PANZER CORPS

1938:	part of the peacetime army as Frontier Command Saarpfalz, headquartered at Kaiserslautern
1939:	redesignated XXIV Corps; Poland
1940:	West
November 16, 1940:	redesignated XXIV Motorized Corps
June 21, 1942:	redesignated XXIV Panzer Corps
1941–45:	Eastern Front
1945:	surrendered in Czechoslovakia

XXV CORPS

1938:	part of peacetime army as Frontier Command Oberrhein at Baden-Baden
October 1939:	redesignated XXV Corps; sent to the Upper Rhine
1940:	West
1940–44:	occupation duties in France
August 1944:	isolated in Brittany
May 1945:	surrendered

XXVI CORPS

August 22, 1939:	formed in East Prussia as Operational Staff z.b.V.
October 1, 1939:	redesignated XXVI Corps
1939–40:	Poland and the West
1941–44:	northern sector, Eastern Front
early 1944–45:	central sector, Eastern Front; ended the war in East Prussia

XXVII CORPS

August 26, 1939:	formed in Munich
1940:	West
1941-44:	Eastern Front
July 1944:	destroyed near Minsk
July 27, 1944:	reformed
1944–45:	Eastern Front (Oder)

XXVIII CORPS

May 20, 1940:	formed
1941–45:	Eastern Front
January 1945:	temporarily redesignated Army Detachment Samland
May 1945:	surrendered in Courland Pocket

XXIX CORPS

May 20, 1940:	formed in Wehrkreis IV
1941–45:	southern sector, Eastern Front

XXX CORPS

August 26, 1939:	formed in Brunswick, Wehrkreis XI
1939–40:	Poland and the West
1941:	Greece
1941–44:	Eastern Front
February 1944:	suffered heavy losses during evacuation of Nikopol bridgehead on the lower Dnieper
August 1944:	destroyed in Romania
October 1944:	rebuilt from LXV z.b.V. and Staff, Commandant of Bonn
1944–45:	Western Front (Holland)

XXXI CORPS COMMAND

See LXXX Corps

XXXII CORPS COMMAND

See LXXXI Corps

XXXIII CORPS

October 18, 1939:	formed as the XXXIII Corps Command from Frontier Guard Sector Command 3 at Oppeln, Upper Silesia
summer 1940:	sent to Trondheim area, central Norway; remained there throughout the war
January 23, 1943:	redesignated XXXIII Corps

XXXIV CORPS COMMAND

October 23, 1939:	formed in Kuestrin, Wehrkreis II from Frontier Sector Guard Command 12
January 31, 1942:	absorbed by XXXV Corps
November 13, 1944:	reformed in northern Yugoslavia from part of the Staff, Commandant of Crete
1944–45:	in Balkans withdrawal; fought between the Drava and Sava

XXXV CORPS

October 15, 1939:	formed in Poland as XXXV Corps Command from Frontier Guard Sector Command 13
January 20, 1942:	upgraded to XXXV Corps
1942–44:	central sector. Eastern Front
July 1944:	destroyed at Bobruisk; remnants assigned to XIII SS Corps

XXXVI MOUNTAIN CORPS

October 5, 1939:	formed as XXXVI Corps Command in Breslau from Frontier Guard Sector Command 14
February–May 1940:	designated Guard Sector Command Center (in Poland)
Fall 1940:	Norway
June 1941:	transferred to northern Finland and northern Russia; fought in the Murmansk sector
November 18, 1941:	upgraded to XXXVI Mountain Corps

autumn 1944:	withdrew through northern Finland to Norway

XXXVII CORPS COMMAND

See LXXXII Corps

XXXVIII CORPS

January 27, 1940:	formed in Schneidemuehl, Wehrkreis II
1940:	West
1941–45:	northern sector, Eastern Front
January 1945:	redesignated XXXVIII Panzer Corps

XXXIX PANZER CORPS

January 27, 1940:	formed as XXXIX Motorized Corps
1940:	France
1941–44:	Eastern Front
July 9, 1942:	redesignated XXXIX Panzer Corps
July 8, 1944:	surrendered to Soviets near Minsk
autumn 1944:	reconstituted
December 1944:	on Western Front in Ardennes counter-offensive
1945:	Pomerania and Silesia
May 1945:	surrendered to Western Allies

XXXX PANZER CORPS

January 26, 1940:	formed as XXXX Corps
1940:	West
September 15, 1940:	redesignated XXXX Motorized Corps
1941:	Balkans
1941–45:	Eastern Front, mainly on southern sector
July 9, 1942:	upgraded to XXXX Panzer Corps
May 1945:	surrendered to the Red Army in middle Silesia

XXXXI PANZER CORPS

February 24, 1940:	formed in Silesia as XXXXI Motorized Corps

1940:	West
1941:	Balkans
1941–44:	central sector, Eastern Front
July 10, 1942:	upgraded to XXXXI Panzer Corps
July 1944:	destroyed at Bobruisk
August 1944:	reconstituted
1944–45:	Eastern Front
May 1945:	surrendered to the Western Allies near Magdeburg

XXXXII CORPS

January 29, 1940:	formed: Poland
1940:	West
1941–44:	Eastern Front (northern and southern sectors)
February 1944:	smashed at Cherkassy during the Dnieper withdrawals
April 1944:	reorganized in Poland
January 1945:	destroyed near the Vistula during the Battle of the Baranov Bridgehead

XXXXIII CORPS

April 15, 1940:	formed in Hanover
1940:	West
1941–45:	Eastern Front; ended the war in Linz, Austria

XXXXIV CORPS

April 15, 1940:	formed
1940:	West
1941–44:	Eastern Front
August 1944:	destroyed in Romania

XXXXV CORPS COMMAND

See LXXXIII Corps

XXXXVI PANZER CORPS

June 20, 1940:	formation began as XXXXVI Corps
July 1, 1940:	formation cancelled
October 25, 1940:	formed as XXXXVI Motorized Corps
1941:	Balkans
June 14, 1942:	redesignated XXXXVI Panzer Corps
1941–45:	Eastern Front
August 1944:	cited for distinguished defensive action on Vistula and northeast of Warsaw
early 1945:	heavily engaged in Silesia
April 1945:	with 3rd Panzer Army in Pomerania; surrendered to Anglo-Americans in May

XXXXVII PANZER CORPS

June 20, 1940:	formed in Danzig as an infantry corps
July, 1940:	formation cancelled
November 25, 1940:	formed as the XXXXVII Motorized Corps
1941–44:	Eastern Front
June 21, 1942:	renamed XXXXVII Panzer Corps
June 1944:	transferred to France
1944–45:	fought in Normandy, at Falaise, and in the Ardennes
April 1945:	destroyed in Ruhr Pocket

XXXXVIII PANZER CORPS

June 20, 1940:	formation began as an infantry corps
July 1, 1940:	formation cancelled
December 14, 1940:	formed as XXXXVIII Motorized Corps in Koblenz, Wehrkreis XII
June 21, 1942:	redesignated XXXXVIII Panzer Corps
1941–45:	Eastern Front
1945:	surrendered to Western Allies on the Elbe

XXXXIX MOUNTAIN CORPS

June 20, 1940:	formation began as an infantry corps

July 1, 1940: formation cancelled
October 25, 1940: formed in Bavaria as a mountain corps
1941: Balkans
1941–45: southern sector, Eastern Front; suffered heavy losses in the Crimea 1944
May 1945: surrendered to Soviets in Czechoslovakia

L CORPS

October 8, 1940: formed in Baden, Wehrkreis V
1941: Balkans
1941–45: Eastern Front
October 1944: isolated in the Courland Pocket; remained there

LI MOUNTAIN CORPS

November 25, 1940: formed in Austria as an infantry corps
1941: Balkans (Yugoslavia)
1941–43: Eastern Front; destroyed at Stalingrad
September 12, 1943: reformed in Austria as a mountain corps
1943–45: Italian Front; destroyed in Po River campaign

LII CORPS

October 25, 1940: formed in Cologne, Wehrkreis VI
1941–44: southern sector, Eastern Front
August 1944: destroyed in Romania

LIII CORPS

February 15, 1941: formed in Innsbruck, Austria (Wehrkeis XVIII)
1941–44: central sector, Eastern Front
July 1944: destroyed at Vitebsk
November 11, 1944: reformed in Danzig; subsequently fought on Western Front
April 1945: destroyed in Ruhr Pocket

LIV CORPS

June 1, 1941:	formed from the Staff, German Military Mission to Romania
1941–44:	Eastern Front (southern, then northern sector)
1944:	upgraded to Headquarters, Army Detachment Narva, then Grasser, then Kleffel
November 10, 1944:	combined with Staff, Armed Forces Netherlands, to form 25th Army

LV CORPS

January 6, 1941:	formed
1941–45:	central sector, Eastern Front
May 1945:	surrendered in East Prussia

LVI PANZER CORPS

February 15, 1941:	formed as LVI Motorized Corps
1941–45:	Eastern Front
March 1, 1942:	upgraded to LVI Panzer Corps
May 1945:	surrendered in Berlin

LVII PANZER CORPS

February 15, 1941:	formed in Augsburg, Bavaria, as the LVII Motorized Corps
June 21, 1942:	redesignated LVII Panzer Corps
1941–45:	Eastern Front

LVIII PANZER CORPS

July 28, 1943:	formed in Wehrkreis V as LVIII Reserve Panzer Corps in France
September 1943:	sent to France
July 6, 1944:	upgraded to LVIII Panzer Corps
August 1944:	southern France
December 1944:	fought in the Ardennes
April 1945:	surrendered in Ruhr Pocket

LIX CORPS

October 10, 1940:	formed in Luebeck, Wehrkreis X, as Corps Command LIX z.b.V.
1941–45:	Eastern Front
January 20, 1942:	upgraded to LIX Corps
March 1944:	cited for distinguished action on the southern sector
May 1945:	surrendered to the Russians in Czechoslovakia

LX CORPS COMMAND

See LXXXIV Corps

LXI RESERVE CORPS

September 2, 1942:	formed in Königsberg to control reserve divisions in Poland
February 21, 1944:	dissolved

LXII RESERVE CORPS

September 15, 1942:	formed in Berlin to control reserve divisions in the Ukraine
January 1944:	transferred to southern France
August 5, 1944:	upgraded to LXII Corps
August 18, 1944:	destroyed in Marseilles, southern France

LXIII CORPS

November 14, 1944:	formed in southern France
1944–45:	Western Front
April 1945:	surrendered in Ruhr Pocket

LXIV CORPS

September 24, 1942:	formed as LXIV Reserve Corps
early 1944:	in southeastern France
August 5, 1944:	upgraded
early 1945:	in southern Alsace
March 1945:	largely destroyed in Colmar Pocket
April 1945:	finished off by French in the Black Forest

LXV CORPS Z.B.V.

May 21, 1941:	formed
June 1941–April 1942:	at Belgrade, Serbia
1942:	dissolved to form the Staff, Military Governor Serbia
November 28, 1943:	reformed
1943–44:	controlled artillery staffs connected with use of the "V" weapons
October 20, 1944:	dissolved; used to form XXX Corps

LXVI CORPS

September 21, 1942:	formed in Frankfurt/Main as LXVI Reserve Corps
1942–44:	on Eastern Front
August 1944:	took part in the withdrawal from the Mediterranean coast
autumn 1944:	upgraded to LXVI Corps
late 1944:	fought in the Ardennes
April 1945:	destroyed in Ruhr Pocket

LXVII CORPS

September 24, 1942:	formed in France as LXVII Reserve Corps
1942–44:	Brussels
January 20, 1944:	Upgraded to LXVII Corps
summer 1944:	took part in the withdrawal from France
late 1944:	in Aachen sector
early 1945:	smashed at Eifel and Remagen

LXVIII CORPS

April 9, 1943:	formed in Greece from Special Staff Felmy (the Military Mission to Iraq)
September 1944:	evacuated Athens and withdrew through Yugoslavia
late 1944:	sent into action on Eastern Front; fought at Lake Balaton and on the Drava

LXIX CORPS

July 8, 1943:	formed as LXIX Reserve Corps
1943–45:	served in Croatia
January 20, 1944:	upgraded to LXIX Corps

LXX CORPS

May 4, 1941:	formed in southern Norway as LXX Corps Command
January 25, 1943:	upgraded to LXX Corps
1941–45:	Stationed in Oslo throughout the war

LXXI CORPS

March 1, 1942:	formed as LXXI Corps Command from Sector Staff Northern Norway
January 26, 1943:	upgraded to LXXI Corps
1945:	ended the war in Norway

LXXII CORPS

February 13, 1944:	formed in southern Russia
1944–45:	Eastern Front; surrendered in Czechoslovakia

LXXIII CORPS

November 25, 1944:	created from Staff, Military Commander Venetian Coast (Italy)
1944–end:	Venetian Coast

LXXIV CORPS

July 26, 1943:	formed under OB West
1943–45:	West; destroyed in Ruhr Pocket

LXXV CORPS

December 15, 1943:	formed as Corps Walkuere from the Staff, 255th Infantry Division
January 15, 1944:	upgraded to LXXV z.b.V.; sent to northern Italy
June 6, 1944:	upgraded to LXXV Corps
1944–end:	with the Ligurian Army, northern Italy

LXXVI PANZER CORPS

June 29, 1943: formed as LXXVI Corps from elements of the LXVI Reserve Corps
July 27, 1943: upgraded to LXXVI Panzer Corps
1943–45: Italy

LXXVIII CORPS

March 6, 1944: formed
April 1944: Bessarabia, Romania
May 25, 1944: absorbed by I Cavalry Corps

LXXX CORPS

August 1939: formed in Schwerin, Wehrkreis II, from the Frontier Guard Sector Command 1 as Corps Kaupisch. Fought in Poland
September 19, 1939: redesignated Military Commander, Danzig-West Prussia
November 7, 1939: redesignated Corps Command XXXI
April 1940: conquered Denmark
1940–45: West
May 27, 1942: redesignated LXXX Corps

LXXXI CORPS

October 15, 1939: formed at Deutsch-Krone, Pomerania, as Corps Command XXXII z.b.V.
July 1940: on the English Channel coast, northern France
May 28, 1942: reorganized in France from the XXXII Corps Command
1942–45: West; destroyed in Ruhr Pocket

LXXXII CORPS

October 23, 1939: formed as Corps Command XXXVII from Headquarters, Frontier Guard Sector Command 30 in western Germany
July 1940: sent to the Netherlands
May 27, 1942: upgraded to LXXXII Corps

1942–45: West

LXXXIII CORPS

March 8, 1940: formed in Königsberg, Wehrkreis I, as XXXXV Corps Command
1940: Saar and Vosges sectors
1940–42: on Vichy France/occupied France Demarkation Line
May 27, 1942: upgraded to LXXXIII Corps
1942–43: France
August 26, 1943: upgraded to Army Detachment Felber; later became Staff, 19th Army

LXXXIV CORPS

October 15, 1940: formed in Prague as Corps Command LX z.b.V. to control the replacement-training units of Wehrkreis I
1940–44: France
May 27, 1942: upgraded to LXXXIV Corps
August 1944: destroyed in the Falaise Pocket

LXXXV CORPS

October 1943: formed in southern France as Corps Kniess
July 10, 1944: upgraded to LXXXV Corps
1943–45: West

LXXXVI CORPS

November 19, 1942: formed by OB West
1942–45: West

LXXXVII CORPS

November 5, 1942: formed in France
March 1943: upgraded to Army Detachment von Zangen
August 1944: redesignated Ligurian Army
1943–45: northern Italy

LXXXVIII CORPS

April 16, 1942:	formed as Division Staff 240 z.b.V. ("for special purposes")
June 15, 1942:	redesignated Staff, Armed Forces Netherlands
1942–45:	the Netherlands
July 1944:	upgraded to LXXXVIII Corps

LXXXIX CORPS

August 2, 1942:	formed as Corps "Y"
August 9, 1942:	redesignated Corps Schaldt
October 25, 1942:	redesignated LXXXIX Corps
1942–45:	West
April 1945:	disbanded

LXXXX CORPS

November 17, 1942:	formed in Tunisia
December 8, 1942:	became 5th Panzer Army
November 19, 1944:	formed from IV Luftwaffe Field Corps
1944–end:	Western Front

LXXXXI CORPS

August 7, 1944:	formed under OB Southeast
1944–45:	Greece, Croatia, Austria

LXXXXVII CORPS

August 28, 1944:	formed in Italy
1944–end:	Adriatic coast, Italy

CI CORPS

February 9, 1945:	formed from Corps Staff Berlin
February 1945–End:	with 9th Army, Eastern Front

AFRIKA KORPS

February 16, 1941:	formed as Staff, Commander of German Troops in Libya

February 21, 1941: redesignated Deutsches Afrikakorps or DAK
1941–43: fought in Libya and Egypt
May 12, 1943: surrendered in Tunisia

CORPS EMS

April 1945: formed from Headquarters, Wehrkreis X
May 1945: surrendered to the British

PANZER CORPS "FELDHERRNHALLE"

November 27, 1944: formed
1945: southern sector, Eastern Front

PANZER CORPS "GROSSDEUTSCHLAND"

September 28, 1944: formed from Staff, 18th Artillery Division and the remnants of the XIII Corps
1945: Poland and East Prussia

PARACHUTE PANZER CORPS "HERMANN GOERING"

late 1944: formed
1944–45: fought in East Prussia; destroyed there

MOUNTAIN CORPS NORWAY

See XlX Mountain Corps

APPENDIX 4

Chronology of the Second World War

1939

September 1:	Germany invades Poland; World War II begins
September 2:	Polish Corridor is cut; East Prussia is linked with the rest of the Reich
September 6:	Krakow falls
September 9:	Poles launch major counterattack across the Bzura at Radom
September 16:	Warsaw is surrounded
September 27:	Warsaw falls. Germans take 150,000 prisoners
September 29:	Polish fortress of Modlin falls
October 6:	Last Polish resistance ends. 800,000 Poles killed or captured by the Germans. German losses: 13,111 killed or missing, 27,278 wounded.
October:	The "Phony" War phase of the war begins. The Germans wait behind the West Wall, the French wait behind the Maginot Line, and neither side takes any major aggressive action against each other until the spring.

1940

April 9:	Germany invades Denmark and Norway; Denmark capitulates and every major city in Norway is captured. The British soon join

	the battle, however, and fighting continues in the Narvik sector until June 10.
May 10:	Western Campaign begins as Germany invades Luxembourg, Belgium, the Netherlands and France.
May 11:	Belgian fortress of Eben Emael falls.
May 13:	The major German armored thrust under General Guderian crosses the Meuse and captures Sedan, breaking the main Allied line. The Anglo-French command has already committed its mobile reserve forces to Belgium and will be unable to prevent the panzers from pushing to the sea.
May 13:	Secondary German attacks breach the Meuse at Dinant.
May 13:	Liege falls.
May 15:	The Dutch Army surrender.
May 17:	Brussels falls
May 18:	Antwerp falls.
May 20:	The panzers reach the English Channel near Abbeville.
May 21:	Anglo-French counterattack at Arras.
May 24:	Hitler issues halt order to panzer forces advancing on Dunkirk.
May 28:	The Belgian Army surrenders.
June 4:	Dunkirk evacuation ends. 224,585 British and 112,546 French and Belgian soldiers escape. British leave behind 1,200 guns, 1,250 anti-aircraft and anti-tank guns, and 75,000 vehicles. Dunkirk occupied the next day.
June 5:	German attack on France proper and the Battle of the Weygand Line begin
June 9:	Anglo-French forces complete the evacuation of Narvik. End of Norwegian campaign.
June 10:	Italy declares war on Paris and London.

June 14:	Fall of Paris.
June 14–16:	Russia invades and occupies the Baltic States of Lithuania, Latvia and Estonia.
June 18:	Cherbourg falls.
June 19:	Brest falls.
June 20:	Lyons and Vichy are captured.
June 22:	France surrenders. Germany lost 27,074 killed, 111,034 wounded and 18,383 missing. Allies lost 90,000 killed, 200,000 wounded, and 1,900,000 captured or missing.
July 2:	Hitler orders the preparation of Operation "Sealion," the invasion of Great Britain.
July 9:	Romania placed under the military protection of Germany.
July 21:	Hitler announces to OKH that he intends to invade Russia in 1941.
December 9:	British launch offensive in North Africa.

1941

February 7:	British complete the conquest of Cyrenaica. Italian 10th Army destroyed, 130,000 men lost.
February 14:	First German forces, the vanguard of the Afrika Korps, land in Tripoli, Libya.
March 26–27:	Pro-Axis government of Yugoslavia overthrown.
March 31:	Rommel and Afrika Korps begin First Cyrenaican campaign.
April 4:	Afrika Korps captures Benghazi.
April 6:	Germany invades Yugoslavia and Greece.
April 9:	Greek Metaxas Line collapses.
April 10:	Zagreb, Yugoslavia, is captured.
April 11:	Rommel isolates Tobruk, beginning a 242 day siege.
April 12:	Belgrade falls.
April 13:	Rommel encircles Tobruk.
April 17:	Yugoslavia surrenders.

April 23:	Greece surrenders.
April 27:	Athens occupied.
April 28–29:	Last British forces evacuate Greek mainland.
May 20:	Crete invaded.
June 1:	Conquest of Crete completed.
June 15–17:	Operation "Battleaxe," a British attempt to relieve Tobruk, is defeated.
June 22:	Germany invades the Soviet Union; Operation "Barbarossa" begins.
June 23–24:	Battle of Raseiniai (Rossieny). 300 Soviet tanks and 100 guns destroyed by 3rd Panzer Group. Appearance of Klim Voroshilov (KV-1) heavy tanks surprise the Germans.
June 24:	Vilna and Kaunas, Lithuania, fall to Germans.
June 26:	Manstein's LVI Panzer Corps seizes the Daugavils crossings over the Dvina.
June 27:	2nd and 3rd Panzer Groups begin encirclement of Minsk Pocket.
June 28:	Minsk, the capital of Belorussia and a city 200 miles from the border, falls.
June 30:	Lvov and Brest-Litovsk captured. Guderian's panzers cross the Berezina River.
July 1:	Riga is captured.
July 3:	Resistance ends in Minsk Pocket. Soviets lost 324,000 men, 3,332 tanks and 1,809 guns.
July 4:	Ostrov captured.
July 5:	Germans reach the Dnieper east of Minsk.
July 6:	1st Panzer Group breaks Stalin Line.
July 8:	Pskov (on Lake Peipus) captured.
July 9:	Vitebsk captured. Smolensk encirclement begins.
July 10:	Panzer division spearheads cross the Dnieper.
July 16:	Smolensk falls. To the south, large Soviet forces are encircled at Uman.

July 17:	More than 300,000 Reds trapped east of Smolensk.
August 2:	Heavy fighting around Staraya Russa (south of Lake Ilmen) as Army Group North drives on Leningrad.
August 5:	End of the Battle of the Smolensk Pocket. Soviets lost 310,000 captured, 3,205 tanks, and 3,120 guns.
August 3–8:	Uman Pocket cleared. 103,000 Russians captured, 317 tanks and 1,100 guns captured or destroyed.
August 8:	Guderian encircles several Soviet divisions at Roslavl, southeast of Smolensk and 110 miles south of Moscow; 38,000 Reds captured, 250 tanks and 359 guns captured or destroyed.
August 9:	Army Group South begins to attack across the Bug River.
August 12:	Hitler sends 2nd Panzer Group toward Kiev and 3rd Panzer Group toward Leningrad—both away from Moscow.
August 17:	Novgorod (in zone of Army Group North) captured. Army Group South captures Dnepropetrovsk on the Dnieper.
August 23:	Army Groups Center and South begin offensive aimed at encircling Kiev.
August 24:	Soviet pocket at Gomel collapses. 84,000 Russians captured, 144 tanks and 848 guns captured or destroyed.
August 30:	Germans capture Mga and cut the major railroad connections between Leningrad and the rest of Russia.
September 8:	Heavy fighting at Vyazma and Bryansk.
September 12:	Schluesselburg (Petrokrepost) on the southern shore of Lake Lagoda is captured, Leningrad isolated.

September 15:	Kiev encircled.
September 19:	Kiev falls.
September 21:	Germans reach the Sea of Azov, cutting off the Crimea.
September 26:	End of the Battle of the Kiev Pocket. 667,000 Soviets captured, 3,718 guns, 884 armored vehicles captured or destroyed.
September 30:	2nd Panzer Group begins offensive against Orel and Bryansk; 1st Panzer Group reaches the Dnieper River in the Ukraine. Two days later, 3rd and 4th Panzer Groups launch offensive toward Vyazma.
September 30–October 17:	Double Battle of Vyazma-Bryansk. Soviets lose 663,000 men, 1,242 tanks and 5,412 guns.
October 5–10:	Battle of the Chernigovka Pocket on the Sea of Azov. More than 100,000 Soviet soldiers captured, 212 tanks and 672 guns captured or destroyed by 1st Panzer Group.
October 7:	First snow falls in Russia.
October 8:	Orel falls.
October 14:	Vyazma Pocket collapses.
October 15–16:	Red Army and Navy evacuate Odessa.
October 20:	Rostov and Stalino (Donetsk) captured.
October 24:	Kharkov, the main industrial city of the Ukraine, captured.
October 28:	German advance toward Moscow is halted by the weather.
October 30:	Siege of Sevastopol (the major Soviet Black Sea base, located at the southern tip of the Crimea) begins.
November 3–9:	Army Group North captures Tikhvin, an important railroad center 100 miles east of Leningrad.
November 16:	Army Group Center launches its last drive on Moscow.
November 17:	Soviet Rostov counteroffensive begins.

November 18: British 8th Army begins Operation "Crusader," an attempt to relieve Tobruk. After an extremely fluid battle, the garrison's isolation is finally broken.

November 25: Final push toward Moscow begins.

November 27: 3rd Panzer Group reaches Volga Canal, 19 miles from Moscow.

November 27: In the southern sector, a Soviets counteroffensive recaptures Rostov.

December 5: Hitler finally agrees to halt the Moscow offensive.

December 6: Stalin's massive Winter Offensive begins on central sector with 100 division attack along a 500 mile front.

December 9: British forces break the Siege of Tobruk after 242 days.

December 11: Germany declares war on the United States.

December 15: Russians recapture Klin and Istra.

December 16: Russians recapture Kalinin.

December 19: Hitler sacks Field Marshal von Brauchitsch and names himself commander-in-chief of the Army; also issues his first "stand or die" order.

December 23: Panzer Group Afrika evacuates Benghazi.

December 26: Red Army launches amphibious assault on Kerch peninsula on the eastern Crimea.

1942

January 21: Rommel begins 2nd Cyrenaican campaign.

January 23: Russians launch major offensive along a 250-mile front between Smolensk and Lake Ilmen.

January 26: Rommel recaptures Benghazi.

February 7: Soviets launch heavy but unsuccessful attacks on the German 9th Army in Rzhev Salient west of Moscow. This battle will continue until March 1943.

February 8:	German II Corps isolated in the Demyansk Pocket with 103,000 men.
February 23:	Russians recapture Dorogobuzh on the Dnieper.
April 9:	Russians recapture Orel.
April 21:	Demyansk Pocket is relieved.
May 12:	Russians launch major spring offensive aimed at Kharkov and Kursk. This offensive will be known as the Battle of Izyum (Isjum).
May 15:	Field Marshal von Manstein's 11th Army recaptures Kerch and inflicts 176,000 casualties on Stalin's armies.
May 17:	Russians suspend Kharkov offensive due to counterattack by 1st Panzer Army.
May 20:	Kerch peninsula overrun by German 11th Army. 100,000 Soviets surrender.
May 24:	Russian Kharkov forces trapped in huge pocket at Izyum, west of the Donets River.
May 26:	In North Africa, Panzer Army Afrika begins an offensive against the Gazala Line and Tobruk.
May 29:	End of the Battle of Izyum (Kharkov). Russians lose 239,000 men, 1,250 tanks and 2,026 guns. Germany loses 20,000 men.
June 7:	Manstein's 11th Army begins offensive against Sevastopol.
June 13–14:	British evacuate the Gazala Line.
June 21:	Tobruk captured by Panzer Army Afrika.
June 23:	Rommel invades Egypt.
June 28:	German summer offensive begins in Russia.
July 1:	First Battle of El Alamein begins; Panzer Army Afrika checked 60 miles west of Alexandria, Egypt.
July 2:	Sevastopol falls. Russians lose 90,000 men, 460 guns.

July 4:	Germans advance along a broad front toward the Don River.
July 6:	Germans capture Voronezh.
July 23:	Rostov recaptured. Germans take 240,000 prisoners.
July 27–August 11:	Battle of Kalach (on the west bank of the Don) begins; Soviets retreat toward the Volga and Stalingrad
July 29:	Caucasus offensive begins.
August 9:	Maikop oilfields captured.
August 11:	Germans smash Soviet 4th Tank Army near Kalach, in the bend of the Don River. The German 6th Army captures the place and pushes on in the direction of Stalingrad.
August 19:	Major British-Canadian raid on Dieppe ends in an Allied disaster. They lose 3,600 men, 30 tanks and 33 landing craft. Germans lose 600 men.
August 20:	Panzers reach the Volga north of Stalingrad.
August 23:	Germans capture the town of Elbrus on the east coast of the Black Sea; the 6th Army reaches the Volga north of Stalingrad along a five-mile front.
August 30–31:	Panzer Army Afrika launches its last major offensive aimed at breaking the British El Alamein Line. It fails at Alam Halfa.
August 31:	1st Panzer Army crosses the Terek River in the Caucasus sector.
September 6:	Heavy fighting in the Black Sea port of Novorossiysk.
September 7:	6th Army attacks city center in Stalingrad.
September 17:	Hitler fires Franz Halder as chief of the General Staff. Gen. Kurt Zeitzler formally suceeds him on September 24.
October 23:	The Second Battle of El Alamein begins.

November 1:	In the Caucasus sector, German efforts to take the Grozny oilfields are repulsed.
November 4:	Panzer Army Afrika crushed, begins withdrawal from El Alamein and Egypt.
November 8:	In Operation "Torch," Allied forces land in Algeria and Morocco, recapture French North Africa.
November 9:	Germans land in Tunisia, begin forming 5th Panzer Army.
November 11:	Hitler occupies Vichy France.
November 13:	Tobruk falls to British.
November 19:	Soviet winter offensive begins in the Don sector north of Stalingrad. The southern wing of the offensive jumps off the following day.
November 23:	Red Army forces link up at Kalach, 50 miles west of Stalingrad, encircling 6th Army in Stalingrad Pocket.
December 7:	The Soviet offensive reaches the Chir River.
December 12:	Manstein launched Operation "Winter Storm," the attempt to relieve of Stalingrad.
December 16:	Reds attack and rout Italian 8th Army on the middle Don. The Italian Army practically ceases to exist as an organized fighting force by December 19.
December 19 :	6th Panzer Division reaches a point within 30 miles of Stalingrad.
December 20:	Red Army cuts the Rostov-Voronezh railroad.
December 23:	Soviets halt Stalingrad relief effort.
December 26:	German "Winter Storm" forces begin a full retreat.
December 27:	Fearing that he will be cut off, Field Marshal von Kleist begins to withdraw from the Caucasus.

1943

January 1:	Soviets retake Velikiye Luki in the central sector after bitter street fighting.
January 12:	Red Army attacks and crushes Hungarian 2nd Army and pushes toward Kharkov.
January 22:	Panzer Army Afrika abandons Tripoli.
January 23–25:	Russians attack and capture Voronezh.
January 25:	Stalingrad Pocket cut in two.
January 30:	Soviets clear Maikop oilfields.
January 31:	Field Marshal Paulus and 6th Army staff captured in Stalingrad.
February 2:	Northern pocket surrenders; end of resistance in Stalingrad. 90,000 Germans surrender. Total German and Romanian losses: 240,000 men. Only about 6,000 of the captured Germans ever see home again.
February 4:	Russians cut off 17th Army in the Kuban. It must now be supplied via the Crimea.
February 5:	Soviet forces reach the Donetz.
February 11:	Battle of Kharkov begins.
February 14:	Reds recapture Rostov.
February 14:	Rommel launches Kasserine Pass offensive in Tunisia.
February 16:	Soviets recapture Kharkov.
February 19:	Manstein counterattacks toward Kharkov and Belgorod.
February 28:	Kasserine counteroffensive ends.
March 1:	Soviets recapture Demyansk.
March 2:	Rzhev evacuated by German 9th Army.
March 6:	Red Army recaptures Gzhatsk on the central sector (on the road to Vyazma, south of Rzhev).
March 6:	Panzer Army Afrika launches an offensive at Medenine but is easily defeated.
March 9–14:	Heavy street fighting inside Kharkov.
March 12:	Germans abandon Vyazma.

March 15:	Kharkov falls to Manstein's panzer troops. Soviets lose 615 tanks and 354 guns.
March 18:	Grossdeutschland Division retakes Belgorod.
May 6:	Allies launch final offensive in Tunisia.
May 7:	Tunis and Bizerte fall.
May 13:	Last German forces in Tunisia surrender. Army Group Afrika, including the 5th Panzer Army and 1st Italian-German Panzer Army (formerly Panzer Army Afrika) surrender. More than 230,000 Axis troops captured.
July 5:	Operation "Citadel," the Battle of Kursk and the largest tank battle in history, begins.
July 10:	Allies land in Sicily
July 12:	Russians counterattack in rear of Model's 9th Army; largest tank clash in history takes place near the village of Prochorovka.
July 12:	Hitler orders the Kursk offensive ended.
July 22:	Palermo, Sicily falls to the Americans.
July 24–August 3:	Hamburg is fire-bombed. About 50,000 civilians are killed and 800,000 made homeless.
July 25:	Mussolini overthrown and arrested. Hitler vows to restore Fascism, occupy Italy.
August 3:	Red Army launches offensive toward Kharkov.
August 4:	Soviets recapture Orel.
August 5:	Belgorod falls to Red Army.
August 13:	Stalin launches an offensive aimed at Smolensk. Spas-Demensk is captured.
August 17:	Last German troops evacuate Sicily.
August 23:	Reds recapture Kharkov.
August 30:	Reds smash Army Group A, capture Taganrog.
September 3:	Russians cross the Desna.

September 7:	Stalino (on the Black Sea) falls to the Russians.
September 8:	Italian surrender to the Western Allies made public; Germans disarm Italian Army.
September 9:	Hitler finally approves a withdrawal from the Ukraine to the Dneiper
September 9:	Allied forces land in Italy at Salerno.
September 10:	German troops seize Rome.
September 12–October 9:	German 17th Army evacuates the Kuban. 255,000 soldiers escape.
September 17:	Reds recapture Bryansk.
September 21:	Russians reach the Dnieper along a 300-mile front.
September 22:	Reds establish a bridgehead on the west bank of the Dnieper.
September 24:	Germans abandon Smolensk and Roslavl, which the Reds occupy the next day.
October 1:	Allies capture Naples.
October 1–6:	The Red Army establishes bridgeheads across the Dnieper north and south of Kremenchug.
October 4:	Corsica is liberated by the Free French.
October 7:	Soviets recapture Nevel in the northern sector of the Eastern Front.
October 9:	The Kuban evacuation is successfully completed.
October 9–23:	Soviets take Melitopol (on the northern flank of Field Marshal von Kleist's Army Group A) in bitter house-to house fighting.
October 12:	U.S. 5th Army starts its attacks on the Volturno Line.
October 15:	Germans retreat north of the Volturno. They will skillfully fall back to two intermediate lines (the Barbara and the Reinhard) before reaching their main defensive line, the Gustav Line, behind the Garigliano, Rapido and Sangro Rivers.

October 19–25:	Red Army pushes out of the Kremenchug bridgehead to the edge of Krivoy Rog.
October 23:	Melitopol finally falls.
October 25:	Russians push across the Dnieper and recapture Dnepropetrovsk.
October 27:	Manstein's Army Group South launches a counteroffensive in the Krivoy Rog sector.
October 29:	A series of major Soviet attacks in the Orsha and Vitebsk sectors begin. They are skillfully defeated by the 4th Army (Heinirci) and the 3rd Panzer Army (Reinhardt).
October 30:	Soviets capture the Perekop on the northern edge of the Perekop Isthmus.
October 30:	Manstein's counteroffensive in the Krivoy Rog sector ends. Red Army pushed back 20 miles. Soviets lose 15,000 men, 350 tanks and 350 guns.
October 30:	Battle of the Nikopol Bridgehead (east of the Dnepr River) begins.
November 1:	Last German land link to the Crimea cut by Soviets.
November 5:	In Italy, the U.S. 5th Army attacks the Reinhard Line.
November 6:	Kiev falls to the Russians.
November 9–13:	Zhitomir falls.
November 14–19:	Germans launch counteroffensive, recapture Zhitomir.
November 26:	Soviets take Gomel.
December 21:	Red Army eliminates the German bridgehead east of the Dnieper at Kherson.
December 29:	Manstein orders the withdrawal of all his forces to the Dnieper.
December 31:	Reds retake Zhitomir.

1944

January 10:	Soviet offensive to clear the east bank of the Dnestr River (including the Nikopol Bridgehead) begins.
January 12:	Soviets launch major offensive to relieve Leningrad.
January 18:	Siege of Leningrad broken after 900 days.
January 20:	Army Group North retreats from Leningrad; Novgorod falls.
January 21:	Soviets capture Mga.
January 22:	Allied forces land at Anzio.
January 25:	In Italy, the Allies continue to unsucessfully attack the Gustav Line.
February 3:	60,000 Germans encircled at Korsun (Cherkassy).
February 7:	The last German troops successfully evacuate the Nikopol Bridgehead.
February 12:	German relief forces halted 10 miles from Korsun.
February 15:	Allies bomb the abbey at Monte Cassino.
February 16:	German 14th Army launches major attacks against the Anzio Beachhead.
February 16–17:	Encircled German forces break out of the Cherkassy Pocket, losing about 21,000 men. About 35,000 escape but without their heavy weapons or equipment.
February 18:	Red Army retakes Staraya Russa.
February 21–22:	Reds recapture Krivoy Rog in heavy fighting.
March 1:	Red forces drive across the Narva River.
March 4–9:	The Russians capture Uman from the 8th Army of Kleist's Army Group A.
March 6:	Stalin launches offensive in the Ukraine along a 100-mile front.
March 9:	Uman falls. Left flank of German 8th Army collapses. Army Group A retreats toward the Bug River.

March 15:	Russians break through German defenses on the Bug River.
March 15:	Allies again unsuccessfully attack Cassino.
March 18:	Reds reach Romanian border, capture Yampol on the eastern bank of the Dniester (Dnestr).
March 19:	German forces occupy Hungary.
March 23:	Reds encircle Tarnopol.
March 26:	Red Army reaches the Prut River in the Ukraine along a 50-mile front.
March 26:	1st Panzer Army encircled in "Hube Pocket"
April 2:	Soviets enter Romania.
April 8:	Russian offensive begins in the Crimea.
April 9:	1st Panzer Army escapes.
April 10:	Black Sea port of Odessa falls to Russians after a bitter battle.
April 16:	Tarnopol falls after a fight of several weeks.
April 18:	Battle of Sevastopol begins.
May 11:	Allies armies in Italy launch major offensive against the Gustav Line.
May 6–12:	Remnants of 17th Army in the Crimea destroyed at Sevastopol. 151,500 Germans and Romanians evacuated by sea and air, 78,000 killed or captured since mid-April.
May 18:	In Italy, Monte Cassino falls to Allies.
June 4:	American forces enter Rome.
June 6:	D-Day; Allies land in Normandy.
June 22:	Russian summer offensive (Operation "Bagration") begins against Army Group Center. Soviets attack along a line from north of Vitebsk to south of Mogilev. By early July, Army Group Center will lose 28 divisions, 300,000 men, 215 tanks and 1,500 guns.
June 24:	Soviets reach the Dvina River in the Baltic sector.

June 25:	LIII Corps breaks out of Vitebsk but is destroyed two days later. 80,000 Germans captured.
June 26:	Vitebsk falls.
June 27:	Last German resistance in Cherbourg ends.
June 28:	Reds capture Mogilev.
June 29:	Bobruisk falls.
July 1:	Reds cross the Berezina.
July 3:	Minsk falls.
July 6:	Kovel falls.
July 11:	German pocket east of Minsk is destroyed.
July 13:	After five days of street fighting, the Russians capture Vilna.
July 14:	Germans abandon Pinsk; Red offensive extended into northern Ukraine.
July 17:	Russians cross Bug River and swing into Poland.
July 18:	Americans capture St. Lo in Normandy.
July 19:	German XIII Corps (five divisions) surrounded at Brody in Ukraine; only remnants escape.
July 19:	Russians cross in Latvia near Dvinsk (Daugavpils).
July 19:	In Italy, American forces take Leghorn.
July 20:	Anti-Nazi conspirators, led by Colonel Count Claus von Stauffenberg, attempt to kill Hitler and overthrow the Nazi government. They narrowly miss.
July 22:	End of the fighting in the Brody Pocket.
July 24:	Lublin falls to Stalin's forces.
July 25:	American heavy bombers blast Panzer Lehr Division in Normandy.
July 25:	Russians reach the Vistula.
July 26:	U.S. armored forces launch major offensive which breaks the deadlock in Normandy.
July 27:	Reds take Lwow (Lvov) and Bialystok.

July 28:	Brest-Litovsk falls.
August 1:	Russians reach the Gulf of Riga, isolating Army Group North in the Baltic States. They also capture Kaunas, the capital of Lithuania.
August 1:	The non-Communist Polish Home Army revolts, seizes most of Warsaw.
August 2:	Patton's U.S. 3rd Army, which was activated the day before, advances into Brittany.
August 4:	Rennes, France, falls. In Italy, the Americans occupy the areas of Florence south of the Arno River.
August 6:	Germans launch disastrous Avranches counteroffensive in Normandy.
August 7:	Russian summer offensive finally checked after an advance of more than 400 miles; German panzer divisions smash Soviet III Tank Corps at Wolomin, northeast of Warsaw.
August 11:	Soviets launch a major offensive south of Lake Peipus, breaking through and gaining up to 15 miles.
August 12:	Florence falls. In France, the Americans capture Alencon.
August 15:	Huge Franco-American forces invade southern France, landing between Toulon and Cannes.
August 17:	Canadians capture Falaise. Orleans falls, St. Malo surrenders.
August 17:	Russians reach the East Prussian border.
August 18:	Falaise gap is closed. Americans enter Versailles.
August 19:	Free French forces begin a revolt in Paris.
August 20:	Simultaneously with a major Soviet offensive, Romania defects to Allies, trapping most of 6th and much of 8th German armies (16 divisions).

August 20:	Americans cross the Seine.
August 22:	Russians capture Jassy (Iasi).
August 24:	Bordeaux and Cannes occupied by Allies.
August 25:	Paris liberated.
August 25:	Germans attempt to retake Bucharest, Romania, but are turned back in heavy fighting. Kishinev falls.
August 25:	Cannes falls.
August 26:	Bulgaria declares its neutrality, begins disarming German forces in the country.
August 26:	Hitler orders the evacuation of Greece.
August 28:	Russian troops enter Transylvania.
August 28:	In southern France, Marseilles and Toulon fall to Franco-American forces.
August 29:	Two pockets cleared on the Prut River in Romania; 180,000 Germans captured. Russians capture the Black Sea port of Constanta, cross into Bulgaria.
August 30:	Ploesti falls. Slovakian military revolts against the Germans.
August 31:	Bucharest falls to Red Army.
September 1:	Nice and Verdun fall.
September 2:	Finland accepts Stalin's armistice terms, leaves the Axis. Lyon falls.
September 2:	Brussels liberated by British.
September 3:	Abbeville, Mons and Lyons are captured.
September 4:	British take Antwerp. Finland defects from thc Axis, signs armistice with the Soviet Union.
September 5:	U.S. forces halted by stiff resistance on Moselle River.
September 8:	Liege and Ostend are liberated.
September 11:	First American forces cross into Germany near Stalzenburg; American liberate the city of Luxembourg; Dijon captured.
September 12:	Le Havre surrendered; 12,000 Germans captured.

September 15:	Americans capture Nancy, attack Siegfried Line; British take Maastricht.
September 16:	Sofia, the capital of Bulgaria, captured by Russians.
September 17:	Allies launch Operation Market-Garden, aimed at capturing Arnhem and outflanking the Siegfried Line.
September 18:	5th Panzer Army launches a series of unsuccessful counterattacks aimed at eliminating American bridgeheads over the Moselle.
September 19:	Last German forces in Brest surrender.
September 19:	The Battle of the Huertgen Forest begins. It will not finish until December 12 and will end in a Pyrrhic victory for the Americans, who will suffer 42,000 casualties, including 9,000 due to illness and exhaustion. The Germans will suffer 12,000 casualties. Most historians now believe that the battle should never have been fought.
September 20:	Nijmegen captured by British forces and American paratroopers driving on Arnhem.
September 21:	British reach Rimini, Italy.
September 22:	Soviets capture Tallinn, the capital of Estonia.
September 24:	Guderian orders Army Group South Ukraine to withdraw to the Danube.
September 25:	British survivors begin withdrawing from Arnhem, their offensive defeated.
September 27:	U.S. forces attack Metz.
September 30:	Calais garrison surrenders to the Canadians.
October 2:	Polish Home Army in Warsaw surrenders.
October 3:	American forces break through Siegfried Line north of Aachen.
October 8:	British capture Corinth, Greece.
October 10:	Tank battle near Debrecen, Poland; three Soviet corps destroyed.

October 10:	Russian forces reach the Baltic Sea north of Memel, cutting off Army Group North in Courland for the last time.
October 13:	Americans capture Aachen after a fierce battle; British enter Athens; Russians capture Riga, the capital of Latvia.
October 14:	Russians and Yugoslav partisans surround Belgrade, the capital of Yugoslavia; British capture Athens and Piraeus.
October 16:	Aachen surrounded.
October 20:	Belgrade falls.
October 21:	Aachen surrenders.
October 31:	Germans evacuate Salonika.
November 7:	Reds cross the Danube.
November 8:	The remnants of the Walcheren garrison surrenders.
November 19:	Americans capture Metz.
November 20:	Germans evacuate Tirana, the capital of Albania. The Albanian resistance occupies it the following day.
November 24:	French forces capture Strasbourg.
November 26:	Soviets reach the outskirts of Budapest.
December 3:	Americans capture an intact bridge over the Saar near Saarlautern, compromising the Siegfried Line.
December 5:	Saarlautern falls.
December 16:	The Battle of the Bulge begins.
December 21:	Bastogne surrounded.
December 24:	German advance in the Ardennes halted.
December 26:	Bastogne encirclement broke, but siege continues.
December 29:	Siege of Budapest begins

1945

January 10:	Germans begin counteroffensive toward Strasbourg.

January 12:	Soviets launch a major offensive from the Baltic to the Carpathians. The main concentration is from the Baranov Bridgehead west of the Vistula, smashing the XXXXVI Panzer and XXXXII Corps; 1,300,000 Reds attack in Poland and East Prussia, smashing Army Group Center.
January 13:	Kielce falls.
January 16:	Ardennes salient eliminated.
January 16:	Radom, Poland, falls to Soviets. Hitler abandons Rastenburg headquarters and moves to the bunker under the Reichschancellery in Berlin.
January 17:	Reds capture Warsaw.
January 19:	Soviets capture Krakow and Lodz.
January 20:	Tilsit falls.
January 22:	German evacuation of Memel begins. Red Army captured Allenstein and Deutsch Eylau.
January 25:	Soviets cross the Oder near Breslau and Steinau.
January 26:	Russians reach the Gulf of Danzig northeast of Elbing (Elblag), cutting off East Prussia from the Reich; 3rd Panzer and 4th Armies cut off in East Prussia.
January 27:	Memel finally falls.
January 29:	Reds enter Pomerania.
February 5:	Heavy fighting in Kuestrin (Kostrzyn), about 50 miles northeast of Berlin.
February 8:	Battle of the Reichswald begins as British begin offensive to clear the area between the Meuse and the Rhine.
February 9:	Colmar Pocket crushed. German forces west of the Rhine from Strasbourg to the Swiss border are eliminated.
February 9:	Elbing falls.

February 11:	Budapest garrison breaks out; of 30,000 men, 800 escape. The IX SS Mountain Corps is destroyed. The German and Hungarian forces lost 38,000 men killed and 51,000 captured during the siege. The Russians lost more than 80,000 killed. Approximately 40,000 civilians were also killed.
February 11:	On the Western Front, Cleve and Pruem are captured.
February 12:	Budapest falls.
February 13:	Pruem is captured; organized resistance ends in the Reichswald.
February 14:	Schneidmuehl and Deutsche Krone taken by the Red Army
February 15:	German Stargard offensive begins in Pomerania; fails.
February 20:	Allies break through Siegfried Line at several points.
February 22:	Americans cross the Saar River.
February 23:	Russians capture Poznan. US Army crosses the Roer in several places.
February 28:	Soviets capture Neustettin.
March 6:	Americans capture the west bank part of Cologne (i.e., most of the city).
March 6:	Germans counterattack around Lake Balaton in Hungary.
March 7:	Americans cross the Rhine at Remagen; other US troops take Cologne.
March 8:	Americans capture Bonn.
March 12:	Kuestrin falls.
March 13:	Russians attack Königsberg, the capital of East Prussia.
March 18:	Kolberg (Kolobrzeg), East Prussia, falls to Soviets.
March 20:	Saarbruecken, Ludwigshafen and Kaiserslautern are captured by U.S. forces.

March 22:	Patton's forces cross the Rhine near Nierstein.
March 25:	The Russians captured the town of Heiligenbeil and crush or destroy several German divisions in the Heiligenbeil Pocket.
March 25:	US forces begin breaking out of the Remagen bridgehead. Darmstadt falls.
March 26:	The "Eastern March of the Goths" begins as most of the Replacement Army is sent to the front.
March 28:	Heinz Guderian replaced as chief of the General Staff; succeeded by General of Infantry Hans Krebs.
March 28:	"Western March of the Goths" begins as those elements of the Replacement Army earmarked for use in the west head for the Western Front.
March 28:	Gdynia falls.
March 29:	Frankfurt/Main falls, Mannheim abandoned.
March 30:	Danzig captured by Russians.
April 1:	Army Group B encircled in the Ruhr.
April 1:	Glogau on the Oder is captured.
April 2:	Münster falls to the British.
April 3:	Wiener Neustadt is captured by the Soviets.
April 4:	Kassel and Karlsruhe are captured by the Americans and French, respectively.
April 4:	Bratislava falls.
April 6:	On the Eastern Front, the Siege of Vienna begins.
April 9:	Heavy fighting in Königsberg, East Prussia.
April 9:	Allied spring offensive begins in Italy.
April 10:	Hanover (Hannover), Lower Saxony, captured by Americans.
April 12:	On the Western Front, American tanks reach the Elbe. Brunswick, Erfurt, Baden-Baden and Essen are all captured.

April 12:	Königsberg falls.
April 12:	U.S. President Franklin D. Roosevelt dies.
April 13:	Vienna falls.
April 15:	The Canadians take Arnhem; the Soviets begin their final offensive against the German troops on the Samland peninsula.
April 16:	East of Berlin, the Russians begin their last offensive.
April 18:	End of the Battle of the Ruhr Pocket. 325,000 Germans surrender. To the north, US forces take Magdeburg.
April 19:	Leipzig captured by Americans; British attack Bremen.
April 20:	Americans capture Nuremberg.
April 21:	French forces take Stuttgart, Poles and Americans capture Bologna in Italy. Soviets encircle the 9th Army at Halbe, southeast of Berlin
April 24:	Berlin encircled; Reds capture Potsdam; Americans take Ulm; British and American forces cross the Po River in Italy in several places.
April 25:	U.S. and Soviet forces link up at Torgau (on the Elbe), cutting Germany in half. Pillau, an East Prussian Baltic Sea port, falls to the Russians.
April 26:	British take Bremen; Russians capture Stettin, Pomerania and Bruenn (Brno), Czechoslovakia.
April 27:	Genoa, Italy, is liberated by the Americans.
April 28:	Mussolini shot; Americans reach Venice, capture Augsburg.
April 29:	German forces in Italy sign the instrument of surrender. Venice is captured by the British.
April 30:	Hitler commits suicide.

April 30:	Munich and Turin occupied by U.S. forces. Trieste and Luebeck are captured by the British.
May 2:	German resistance in Berlin ends. All fighting in Italy ends. British reach the Baltic, sealing off Schleswig-Holstein and Denmark.
May 3:	Hamburg surrenders to the British; Americans take Innsbruck, Brenner Pass.
May 5:	Czech resistance forces stage an uprising in Prague.
May 6:	Patton takes Pilsen in Czechoslovakia.
May 7:	Colonel General Jodl and Admiral Freideburg sign the instrument of surrender in Rennes, France.
May 7:	Breslau surrenders to Soviets.
May 8:	Germany surrenders. V-E Day.
May 9:	Field Marshal Keitel signs the instrument of surrender in Berlin.
May 9:	Soviets capture Prague.
May 9:	Fighting officially ends at 11:01 p.m.
May 11:	Army Group A surrenders to the Red Army at Deutsch-Brod.

Bibliography

Absolon, Rudolf, comp. *Rangliste der Generale der deutschen Luftwaffe nach dem Stand vom 20. April 1945.* Friedberg, Germany: Podzun-Pallas-Verlag, 1984.

Air University Archives.

Air University Files SRGG 1106 (c).

Allmayer-Beck, Baron Christop von, *Die Geschichte der 21. (ostpr./westpr.) Infanterie-Division.* Munich, Germany: Schild, 1990.

Andres, Wladyslaw, and Antonio Munoz. "Russian Volunteers in the German Wehrmacht in World War II." *www.feldgrau.com/rvol.html.*

Barker, A. J. *Afrika Korps.* London: Domus, 1978.

Bartov, Omar. *The Eastern Front, 1941–1945: German Troops and the Barbarisation of Warfare.* New York: St. Martin's Press, 1986.

Baumann, Hans. *Die 35 Infanterie Division im Zweiten Weltkrieg, 1939–1945.* Karlsruhe, Germany: Verlag G. Braun, 1964.

Beck, Alois. *Die 297. Infanterie-Division.* Ulm, Germany: Abt-Verlag, 1983.

Benary, Albert. *Die Berliner Baeran-Division: Geschichte der 257. Infanterie-Division, 1939–1945.* Bad Nauheim, Germany: H. H. Podzun, 1955.

Benoist-Mechin, Jacques. *Sixty Days That Shook the West: The Fall of France, 1940.* Translated by Peter Wiles. London: J. Cape, 1963.

Beyersdorff, Ernst. *Geschichte der 110. Infanterie-Division.* Bad Nauheim, Germany: Podzun, 1965.

Blumenson, Martin. *Breakout and Pursuit.* Washington, DC: Office of the Chief of Military History, Department of the Army, 1961.

———. *Salerno to Cassino.* Washington, DC: Office of the Chief of Military History, Department of the Army, 1969.

Boucsein, Heinrich. *Halten oder Sterben: Die hessisch-thueringische 129. Infanterie-Division in Russlandfeldzug und Ostpreussen, 1941–1945.* Neckargemünd, Germany: Vowinckel Verlag, 1999.

Braake, Guenther. *Bildchronik der 126. rheinisch-westfaelischen 126. Infanterie-Division.* Friedberg, Germany: Podzun-Pallas-Verlag, 1985.

Bradley, Dermot, et al. *Die Generale des Heeres.* 7 vols. Osnabrück, Germany: Biblio, 1993–2004.

Braun, Julius. *Enzian und Edelweiss: Die 4. Gebirgs-Division, 1940–1945.* Bad Nauheim, Germany: H. H. Podzun, 1955.

Brehm, Werner. *Mein Kriegstagebuch, 1939–1945: Mit der 7. Panzer-Division 5 Jahre in West und Ost.* Kassel, Germany: self-published, 1953.

Breithaupt, Hans. *Die Geschichte der 30. Infanterie-Division, 1939–1945.* Bad Nauheim, Germany: H. H. Podzun, 1955.

Brett-Smith, Richard. *Hitler's Generals.* London: Osprey Publishing, 1976.

Breymayer, Helmut. *Das Wiesel: Geschichte der 125. Infanterie-Division, 1940 bis 1944.* Ulm-Langenau, Germany: Armin Vaas Verlag, 1982.

Carell, Paul. *The Foxes of the Desert.* Translated by Mervyn Savill. London: Macdonald, 1960.

———. *Hitler Moves East, 1941–43.* Translated by Ewald Osers. Boston: Little Brown, 1965.

———. *Invasion: They're Coming! The German Account of the Allied Landings and the 80 Days' Battle for France.* Translated by Ewald Osers. New York: Dutton, 1963.

———. *Scorched Earth: Hitler's War on Russia.* Translated by Ewald Osers. London: G. G. Harrap, 1970.

Chandler, David G., and James Lawton Collins, Jr., eds. *The D-Day Encyclopedia.* New York: Simon & Schuster, 1994.

Chant, Christopher, et al. *The Marshall Cavendish Illustrated History of World War II.* 25 vols. New York: Marshall Cavendish, 1979.

Chant, Christopher, et al. *Hitler's Generals and Their Battles.* London: Salamander Books, 1976.

Chapman, Guy. *Why France Fell: The Defeat of the French Army in 1940.* New York: Holt, Rinehart and Winston, 1968.

Clark, Alan. *Barbarossa: The Russian-German Conflict, 1941–45.* New York: W. Morrow, 1965.

Cole, Hugh M. *The Ardennes: Battle of the Bulge.* Washington, DC: U.S. Government Printing Office, 1965.

———. *The Lorraine Campaign.* Washington, DC: Historical Division, Department of the Army, 1950.

Conze, Werner. *Die Geschichte der 291. Infanterie-Division, 1940–1945.* Bad Nauheim, Germany: H. H. Podzun, 1953.

Cooper, Matthew and James Lucas. *Panzer: The Armored Force of the Third Reich.* London: Macdonald and Jane's, 1976.

Denniston, Peter. "Jaeger Kopold." *www.gebirgsjaeger.4mg.com.* 1997 and 1998.

Denzel, Egon. *Die Luftwaffen-Felddivision, 1942–1945, sowie die Sonderverbände der Luftwaffe im Kriege 1939–45.* 3rd ed. Neckargemünd, Germany: K. Vowinckel, 1976.

Desch, John. "The 1941 German Army/The 1944–45 U.S. Army: A Comparative Analysis of Two Forces in Their Primes." In *Hitler's Army: The Evolution and Structure of the German Forces,* edited by the Editors of *Command Magazine.* Conshohocken, PA: Combined Books, 1996.

D'Este, Carlo. *Decision in Normandy.* New York: Dutton, 1983.

Detlev von Plato, Anton. *Die Geschichte der 5. Panzer-Division, 1939–1945.* Regensburg, Germany: Walhalla und Praetoria Verlag, 1978.

Dieckhoff, Gerhard. *3. Infanterie-Division, 3. Infanterie-Division (mot.), 3. Panzergrenadier-Division.* Cuxhaven, Germany: G. Dieckhoff, 1960.

DiNardo, Richard L. *Mechanized Juggernaut or Military Anachronism? Horses and the German Army of World War II.* Westport, CT: Greenwood, 1991.

Dobson, Christopher, et al. *The Cruelest Night.* Boston: Little, Brown, 1979.

Engelmann, Joachim. *Die 18. Infanterie- und Panzergrenadier-Division, 1934–1945: ein Schicksalsbericht in Bildern.* Friedberg, Germany: Pozun-Pallas-Verlag, 1984.

Edwards, Roger. *German Airborne Troops, 1936–45.* Garden City, N.Y.: Doubleday, 1974.

———. *Panzer: A Revolution in Warfare, 1939–1945.* London: Arms and Armour, 1989.

Eisenhower, John S. D. *The Bitter Woods: The Dramatic Story, Told at All Echelons, from Supreme Command to Squad Leader, of the Crisis that Shook the Western Coalition: Hitler's Surprise Ardennes Offensives.* New York: Putnam, 1969.

Ellis, L. F. *Victory in the West.* 2 vols. London: Her Majesty's Stationery Office, 1962–68.

Esteban-Infantes, Emilio. *Die Blaue Division.* Translated by Werner Haupt. Leoni am Starnberger See: Druffel, 1958.

Fisher, Ernest F., Jr. *Cassino to the Alps.* Washington, DC: Center of Military History, United States Army, 1977.

Fletcher, Harry R. "Legion Condor: Hitler's Military Aid to Franco." Unpublished Master's Thesis, University of Wisconsin, Madison, 1961.

Friessner, Hans, *Verratene Schlachten: Die Tragödie der deutschen Wehrmacht in Rumänien und Ungarn.* Hamburg, Germany: Holsten-Verlag, 1956.

Galante, Pierre. *Operation Valkyrie: The German Generals' Plot against Hitler.* Translated by Mark Howson and Cary Ryan. New York: Harper & Row, 1981.

Garland, Albert N. and Howard McG. Smyth. *Sicily and the Surrender of Italy.* Washington, DC: Office of the Chief of Military History, Department of the Army, 1965.

Geyr von Schweppenburg. "Panzer Group West (Mid 43–July 1944)." United States Army Military History Institute *MS # B-258.* Unpublished manuscript on file at the United States Army Military History Institute, Carlilse Barracks, Pennsylvania.

———. "Panzer Group West (Mid 43–July 1944)." United States Army Military History Institute *MS # B-466.* Unpublished manuscript on file at the United States Army Military History Institute, Carlilse Barracks, Pennsylvania.

Goebbels, Joseph. *The Goebbels Diaries, 1942–1943.* Edited by Louis P. Lochner. Garden City, N.Y.: Doubleday, 1948.

Grams, Rolf. *Die 14. Panzer-Division, 1940–1945.* Bad Nauheim, Germany: H. H. Podzun, 1957.

Graser, Gerhard. *Zwischen Kattegat und Kaukasus: Weg und Kämpfe der 198. Infanterie-Division, 1939–1945.* Tübingen, Germany: self-published, 1961.

Greiner, Heinz. *Kampf um Rom—Inferno am Po: Der Weg der 362. Infanterie-Division, 1944/45.* Neckargemünd, Germany: K. Vowinckel, 1968.

Grossmann, Horst. *Geschichte der rheinisch-westfälischen 6. Infanterie-Division, 1939–1945.* Bad Nauheim, Germany: Podzun, 1958.

Grube, Rudolf. *Unternehmen Erinnerung: Eine Chronik über den Weg und den Einsatz des Grenadier-Regiment 317 in der 211. Infanterie-Division, 1935–1945.* Bielefeld, Germany: Ernst und Werner Giesking, 1961.

Gschoepf, Rudolf. *Mein Weg mit der 45. Infanterie-Division.* Linz an der Donau, Austria: Oberösterreichischer Landesverlag, 1955.

Guderian, Heinz. *Panzer Leader.* Translated by Constantine Fitzgibbon. New York: Dutton, 1952.

Gundlach, Georg. *Wolchow-Kesselschlacht der 291. Infanterie-Division (Bildband).* Bingen am Rhein, Germany: self-published, 1995.

Hake, Friedrich von. *Der Schicksalsweg der 13. Panzer-Division, 1939–1945.* Munich, Germany: Traditionsverband e.V. der ehemaligen 13. Panzer-Division, 1971.

Harrison, Gordon A. *Cross-Channel Attack.* Washington, DC: Office of the Chief of Military History, Department of the Army, 1951.

Hartmann, Theodor. *Wehrmacht Divisional Signs, 1938–1945.* Edgware, England: Almark Publishing Co., 1970.

Haslob, Gevert. *Ein Blick zurück in die Eifel—Schicksalsweg der 89. Infanterie-Division.* Emmelshausen, Germany: Condo Verlag, 2000.

Hastings, Max. *Das Reich: The March of the 2nd SS Panzer Division through France.* New York: Holt, Rinehart and Winston, 1981.

Haupt, Werner. *Geschichte der 134. Infanterie-Division.* Tuttlingen, Germany: Werner Groll, 1971.

———. *A History of the Panzer Troops.* Translated by Edward Force. West Chester, PA: Schiffer, 1990.

———. *Die 260. Infanterie-Division, 1940–1944.* Bad Nauheim, Germany: Podzun-Pallas-Verlag, 1970.

Hauschild, Reinhard. *Der springende Reiter—1. Kavallerie-Division—24. Panzer-Division im Bild.* Groß-Umstadt, Germany: Ernst J. Dohany Druck und Verlag, 1984.

Hermann, Carl Hans. *68 Kriegsmonate: Der Weg der 9. Panzerdivision durch zweiten Weltkrieg.* Vienna, Austria: Kameradschaft der Schnellen Division des ehemaligen Österrichischen Bundesheeres, 1975.

———. *Die 9. Panzerdivision, 1939–1945: Bewaffnung, Einsätze, Männer.* Friedberg, Germany: Podzun-Pallas-Verlag, n.d.

Hertlein, Wilhelm, *Chronik der 7. Infanterie-Division.* Munich, Germany: Bruckmann, 1984.

Hildebrand, Hans Friedrich. *Die Generale der deutschen Luftwaffe, 1935–1945.* 3 vols. Osnabrück, Germany: Biblio Verlag, 1990–1992.

Hinze, Rolf. *Geschichte der 31. Infanterie-Division.* Meerbusch, Germany: Verlag Hinze, 1997.

Hoffmann, Dieter. *Die Magdeburger Division: Zur Geschichte der 13. Infanterie- und 13. Panzer-Division, 1935–1945.* Hamburg, Germany: Mittler, 2001.

Hoffmann, Peter. *The History of the German Resistance, 1933–1945.* Translated by Richard Barry. Cambridge, Mass.: MIT Press, 1977.

Hoehne, Heinz. *Canaris.* Translated by J. Maxwell Brownjohn. Garden City, N.Y.: Doubleday, 1979.

Hoppe, Harry. *Die 278. Infanterie-Division in Italien, 1944/45.* Bad Nauheim, Germany: H. H. Podzun, 1953.

Horne, Alister. *To Lose a Battle: France, 1940.* Boston: Little, Brown, 1969.

Hossbach, Friedrich. *Infanterie im Ostfeldzug, 1941/42 (31. Infanterie-Division).* Osterode, Germany: Giebel & Oehlschlägel, 1951.

Hubatsch, Walter. *Die 61. Infanterie-Division 1939–1945. Ein Bericht in Wort und Bild.* Bad Nauheim, Germany: Podzun Verlag, 1958.

Jackson, W. G. F. *The Battle for North Africa, 1940–43.* New York: Mason/Charter, 1975.

Jenner, Martin. *Die 216/272. niedersächsische Infanterie-Division, 1939–1945.* Bad Nauheim, Germany: Podzun, 1964.

Kaltenegger, Roland. *Kampf der Gebirgsjäger um die Westalpen und den Semmering: Die Kriegschroniken der 8. und 9. Gebirgs-Division "Kampfgruppe Semmering".* Graz, Austria: L. Stocker, 1987.

Kameradschaftsbund 8.Jäger-Division. *Die Geschichte der 8. (Oberschlesisch-sudetendeutschen) Infanterie-Jäger-Division.* N.p.: self-published, 1979.

Kameradschaftsbund 16. Panzer- und Infanterie-Division. *Bildband der 16. Panzer-Division.* N.p.: self-published, 1956.

Kameradschaftsdienst 35. Infanterie-Division. *Die 35. Infanterie-Division, 1935–1945, Deutsche Infanterie-Divisionen im Bild.* N.p.: self-published, 1980.

Kardel, Hennecke. *Die Geschichte der 179. Infanterie-Division, 1939–1945.* Bad Nauheim, Germany: H. H. Podzun, 1953.

Keegan, John. *Waffen SS: The Asphalt Soldiers.* New York: Ballantine Books, 1970.

Keilig, Wolf. *Die Generale des Heeres.* Friedberg, Germany: Podzun-Pallas-Verlag, 1983.

Kemp, Anthony. *The Unknown Battle: Metz, 1944.* New York: Stein and Day, 1981.

Kennedy, Robert M. *The German Campaign in Poland (1939).* United States Department of the Army *Pamphlet 20-255.* 1956.

Kesselring, Albert. *Kesselring: A Soldier's Record.* Westport, Conn.: Greenwood Press, 1970.

Kilgast, Emil. *Rückblick auf die Geschichte der 302. Infanterie-Division.* Hamburg, Germany: self-published, 1976.

Kissel, Hans. *Vom Dnjepr zum Dnjestr.* Freiburg, Germany: Rombach, 1970.

Klatt, Paul. *Die 3. Gebirgs-Division.* Bad Nauheim, Germany: Verlag Hans-Henning Podzun, 1958.

Knobelsdorf, Otto von. *Geschichte der niedersächsischen 19. Panzer-Division.* Friedberg, Germany: Podzun-Pallas Verlag, 1958.

Knoblauch, K. *Kampf und Untergang einer Infanterie-Division: Die 95. Infanterie-Division.* 2 vols. N.p.: n.p., 1991.

Koch, Horst-Adalbert. *Die Geschichte der deutschen Flakartillerie, 1935–1945.* Bad Nauheim, Germany: H. H. Podzun, 1955.

Kräutler, Matthias, and Karl Springenschmid. *Schicksal und Weg der 2. Gebirgs-Division.* Stuttgart, Germany: Leopold Stocker Verlag, 1962.

Kriegstagebuch des Oberkommando der Wehrmacht (Wehrmachtführungsstab) 1940–1945. 8 vols. Frankfurt am Main, Germany: Bernard & Graefe, 1961.

Krüger, Heinz F. *Bildband der rheinisch-pfälzischen 263. Infanterie-Division, 1939–1945.* Bad Nauheim, Germany: H. H. Podzun, 1962.

Kueppers, F. W. *Taten und Schicksal der mittelrheinisch-hessisch-saarpfaelzischen 197. Infanterie-Division.* Wiesbaden, Germany: self-published, 1969.

Kurowski, Frank. *Panzer Aces: German Tank Commanders of World War II.* Translated by David Johnston. Paperback edition. Mechanicsburg, PA: Stackpole Books, 2004.

Kursietis, Andris J. *Wehrmacht at War, 1939–1945.* Soesterberg, The Netherlands: Aspekt, 1998.

Lamey, Hubert. *Der Weg der 118. Jäger-Division.* Augsburg-Hochzoll, Germany: self-published, 1954.

Landwehr, Richard. *Charlemagne's Legionnaires: French Volunteers of the Waffen SS, 1943–1945.* Silver Spring, Md.: Bibliophile Legion Books, 1989.

———. *Fighting for Freedom: The Ukrainian Volunteer Division of the Waffen-SS.* Silver Spring, Md.: Bibliophile Legion Books, 1985.

———. "The Waffen-SS and the Crushing of the Slovak Military Mutiny." *Siegrunen* 5, no. 6: 23-30.

Lange, Wolfgang. *Korpsabteilung C von Dnjeper bis nach Polen: (November 1943 bis Juli 1944): Kampf einer Infanterie-Division auf breiter Front gegen grosse Übermacht, Kampf im Kessel und Ausbruch.* Neckargemünd, Germany: K. Vowinckel, 1961.

Lanz, Hubert. *Gebirgsjäger Die 1. Gebirgsdivision, 1935–1945.* Bad Nauheim, Germany: H. H. Podzun, 1954.

Law, Richard D., and Craig W. H. Luther. *Rommel.* San Jose, Calif.: R. J. Bender Publishers, 1980.

Lemelsen, Joachim. *29. Division: 29. Infanteriedivision, 29. Infanteriedivision, mot, 29. Panzergreandier-Division: das Buch der Falke-Division.* Bad Nauheim, Germany: Podzun-Verlag, 1960.

Lewin, Ronald. *Rommel as a Military Commander.* Princeton, N.J.: Van Nostrand, 1968.

Löser, Jochen. *Bittere Pflicht: Kampf und Untergang der 76. Berlin-Brandenburgischen Infanterie-Division.* Osnabrück, Germany: Biblio Verlag, 1986.

Lohse, Gerhard. *Geschichte der rheinisch-westfälischen 126. Infanterie-Division.* Bad Nauheim, Germany: Podzun-Pallas Verlag, 1957.

Lucas, James. *Alpine Elite: German Mountain Troops in World War II.* New York: Jane's, 1980.

———. *Germany's Elite Panzer Force: Grossdeutschland.* London: Macdonald and Jane's, 1978.

———. *Hitler's Enforcers: Leaders of the German War Machine, 1939–1945.* London: Cassell, 2000.

———. *War on the Eastern Front, 1941–1945: The German Soldier in Russia.* New York: Stein and Day, 1979.

Luck, Hans von. *Panzer Commander.* New York: Praeger, 1989.

Luther, Craig W. H. *Blood and Honor: The History of the 12th SS Panzer Division "Hitler Youth," 1943–1945.* San Jose, Calif.: Bender Publishing, 1987.

MacDonald, Charles B. *The Last Offensive.* Washington, DC: Office of the Chief of Military History, United States Army, 1973.

———. *The Siegfried Line Campaign.* Washington, DC: Center of Military History, United States Army, 1963.

Manstein, Erich von. *Lost Victories.* Edited and translated by Anthony G. Powell. Chicago: Regnery, 1958.

Manteuffel, Hasso von. *Die 7. Panzer-Division im Zweiten Weltkrieg: Einsatz und Kampf der "Gespenster-Division" 1939–1945*. Friedberg, Germany: Podzun-Pallas-Verlag, 1986.

Mayrhofer, Franz. *Geschichte des Grenadier-Regiment 315 der bayrischen 167. Infanterie-Division-Almhütten-Division—1939–1945*. Munich, Germany: Kameradschaft ehemaligen Grenadier-Regiment 315, 1975.

Mehner, Kurt, ed. *Die Geheimen Tagesberichte der deutschen Wehrmachtführung im Zweiten Weltkrieg, 1939–1945*. 12 vols. Osnabrück, Germany: Biblio Verlag, 1984–1995.

Mehrle, Hans and Walter Schelm. *Von den Kämpfen der 215. württembergisch-badischen Infanterie-Division: ein Erinnerungsbuch* Stuttgart, Germany: Kameradenhilfswerk und Traditionsverband der ehemaligen 215. I.D.e.V., 1954.

Mellenthin, F. W. von. *German Generals of World War II: As I Saw Them*. Norman, Okla.: University of Oklahoma Press, 1977.

———. *Panzer Battles: A Study in the Employment of Armor in the Second World War*. Translated by H. Betzler. Norman, OK: University of Oklahoma Press, 1956.

Melzer, Walther. *Geschichte der 252. Infanterie-Division, 1939–1945*. Bad Nauheim, Germany: H. H. Podzun, 1960.

Memminger, Fritz. *Die Kriegsgeschichte der Windhund-Division—16. Infanterie-Division (mot.), 16. Panzergrenadier-Division, 116. Panzer-Division*. 3 vols. Bochum, Germany: Pöppinghaus, 1962.

Metzsch, Friedrich-August. *Die Geschichte der 22. Infanterie-Division, 1939–1945*. Kiel, Germany: H. H. Podzun, 1952.

Meyer, Franz. *Tapfere Schlesier: Mit der 102. Infanterie-Division im Russland*. Mönchengladbach, Germany: self-published, 1983.

Meyer-Detring, Wilhelm. *Die 137. Infanterie-Division im Mittelabschnitt der Ostfront*. Petzenkirchen, Germany: Kameradschaft der Bergmann-Division (137 I.D.), 1962.

Miehe, Walter. *Der Weg der 225. Infanterie-Division*. Hamburg, Germany: Patzwall Militärverlag, 1980.

Military Intelligence Division, U.S. War Department. "The German Replacement Army (Ersatzheer)." 1945. On file at the U.S. Army War College, Carlisle Barracks, Pennsylvania.

Mitcham, Samuel W., Jr. *The Panzer Legions: A Guide to the German Army Tank Divisions of World War II and Their Commanders*. Paperback edition. Mechanicsburg, PA: Stackpole Books, 2007.

———. *Rommel's Desert Commanders*. Westport, CT: Greenwood, 2007.

———. *Rommel's Desert War: The Life and Death of the Afrika Korps*. Mechanicsburg, PA: Stackpole Books, 2007.

———. *Rommel's Last Battle: The Desert Fox and the Normandy Campaign*. New York: Stein and Day, 1983.

Mitcham, Samuel W., Jr., and Friedrich von Stauffenberg. *The Battle of Sicily: How the Allies Lost Their Chance for Total Victory*. Paperback edition. Mechanicsburg, PA: Stackpole Books, 2007.

Moll, Otto E. *Die deutschen Generalfeldmarshaelle, 1939–1945*. Rastatt, Germany: E. Pabel, 1961.

Munzel, Oskar. *Die deutschen Panzer Truppen bis 1945.* Herford, Germany: Maximilian-Verlag, 1965.

Nafziger, George F. *The German Order of Battle.* 3 vols. London: Greenhill Books, 1999–2000.

Neidhardt, Hanns. *Mit Tanne und Eichenlaub: Kriegschronik der 100. Jäger-Division, vormals 100. leichte Infanterie-Division.* Graz, Austria: L. Stocker, 1981.

Neumann, Peter. *The Black March.* New York: Bantam, 1960.

Nitz, Guenther. *Die 292. Infanterie-Division.* Berlin, Germany: Bernhard & Graefe, 1957.

Nölke, Hans, ed., *Die 71. Infanterie-Division im Zweiten Weltkrieg, 1939–1945.* Hannover, Germany: Druckhaus Pinkvoß, 1984.

Ott, Ernst-Ludwig. *Jäger am Feind: Geschichte und Opfergang der 97. Jäger-Division 1940–1945.* Munich, Germany: Kameradschaft der Spielhahnjäger e.V., 1966.

———. *Die Spielhahnjäger, 1940–1945: Bilddokumentation der 97. Jäger-Division, 1940–1945.* Friedberg, Germany: Podzun-Pallas-Verlag, 1982.

Paul, Wolfgang. *Geschichte der 18. Panzer-Division, 1940–1943: mit Geschichte der 18. Artillerie-Division 1943–1944: Anhang, Heeresartillerie-Brigade 88 1944–1945.* Reutlingen, Germany: Preussischer Militär-Verlag, 1989.

———. *Die Truppengeschichte der 18. Panzer-Division, 1940–1943 (mit 18. Artillerie-Division, 1943–44 und Heeres-Artillerie Brigade 88, 1944–1945.* Reutlingen, Germany: Preußischer Militärverlag, 1989.

Payk, Ernst. *Die Geschichte der 206. Infanterie-Division, 1939–1944.* Bad Nauheim: H. H. Podzun, 1952.

Pesch, Franz, et al. *Die 72. Infanterie-Division, 1939–1945.* Bad Nauheim, Germany: Podzun-Pallas-Verlag, 1982.

Playfair, I. S. O. *The Mediterranean and Middle East.* 6 vols. London: H.M. Stationery Office, 1954–1988.

Plocher, Hermann. "The German Air Force Versus Russia, 1941. United States Air Force Historical Studies *Number 153.* United States Air Force Historical Division, Aerospace Studies Institute, Maxwell Air Force Base, Alabama: 1965. On file in the Air University archives.

Podzun, H. H. *Weg und Schicksal der 21. Infanterie-Division.* Kiel, Germany: Remember-Verlag, 1951.

Pohlmann, Hartwig. *Geschichte der 96. Infanterie-Division, 1939–1945.* Bad Nauheim, Germany: Podzun Verlag, 1959.

Polach, Berndt von Bock und, and Hans Grene. *Weg und Schicksal der bespannten 290. Infanterie-Division.* Bad Nauheim, Germany: Podzun-Pallas-Verlag, 1986.

Quarrie, Bruce. *Panzer-Grenadier-Division "Grossdeutschland".* London: Osprey Publishing, 1977.

Rebentisch, Ernst. *Zum Kaukasus und zu den Tauern: Die Geschichte der 23. Panzer-Division, 1941–1945.* Esslingen, Germany: self-published, 1963.

Rehm, W. *Jassy: Schicksal einer Division oder einer Armee.* Neckargemünd, Germany: K. Vowinckel, 1959.

Reinicke, Adolf, H. G. Hermann and Friedrich Kittel, *Die 62. Infanterie-Division, 1938–1944/Die 62. Volks-Grenadier-Division, 1944–1945.* Fulda, Germany: Kameradenhilfswerk der ehemaligen 62. Division, 1968.

Reinicke, Adolf. *Die 5. Jaeger Division, 1939–1945.* Bad Nauheim, Germany: Podzun, 1962.

Rendulic, Lothar. *Gekämpft, Gesiegt, Geschlagen.* Heidelberg, Germany: Wels, 1957.

Riebenstahl, Horst. *The 1st Panzer Division: A Pictorial History, 1935–1945.* Translated by Edward Force. West Cheser, PA: Schiffer, 1990.

Riedel, Hermann. *Aasen/Schicksal einer Division (352. Volks-Grenadier Division).* Villingen, Germany: n.p., 1969.

Ringel, Julius. *Hurra die Gams: Ein Gedenkbuch für die Solaten der 5. Gebirgsdivision.* Graz, Austria: L. Stocker, n.d.

Ritgen, Helmut. *Die Geschichte der Panzer-Lehr-Division im Westen, 1944–1945.* Stuttgart, Germany: Motorbuch-Verlag, 1979.

———. *The 6th Panzer Division, 1937–45.* London: Osprey, 1982.

Roemhild, Helmut. *Geschichte der 269. Infanterie-Division.* Bad Nauheim, Germany: Podzun-Verlag, 1967.

Rommel, Erwin. *The Rommel Papers.* Edited by B. H. Liddell Hart and translated by Paul Findlay. New York: Harcourt, Brace, 1953.

Rowe, Vivian. *The Great Wall of France: The Triumph of the Maginot Line.* New York: Putnam, 1961.

Ruef, Karl. *Gebirgsjäger zwischen Kreta und Murmansk: Die Schicksale der 6. Gebirgs-Division ein Gedenkbuch.* Graz, Austria: L. Stocker, 1976.

Ruge, Friedrich. *Rommel in Normandy: Reminiscences.* Translated by Ursula R. Moessner. San Rafael, Calif.: Presidio Press, 1979.

Ryan, Cornelius. *The Last Battle.* New York: Simon & Schuster, 1966.

Sajer, Guy. *The Forgotten Soldier.* Translated by Lily Emmet. Baltimore, Md.: Nautical & Aviation Publishers, 1971.

Salisbury, Harrison E. *The 900 Days: The Siege of Leningrad.* New York: Harper & Row, 1969.

Scheibert, Horst. *Bildband der 6. Panzer-Division, 1939–1945.* Bad Nauheim, Germany: Podzun Verlag, 1958.

———. *Die Träger des deutschen Kreuzes in Gold: Das Heer.* Friedberg, Germany: Podzun-Pallas-Verlag, 1983.

Scheiderbauer, Armin. *Adventures in My Youth: A German Soldier on the Eastern Front, 1941–1945.* Translated by C. F. Colton. Solihull, West Midlands, England: Helion, 2003.

Schick, Albert. *Die Geschichte der 10. Panzer-Division, 1939–1943.* Cologne, Germany: Trad. Gem. Der ehem. 10. Pz. Div., 1993.

Schimak, Anton, et al. *Die 44. Infanterie-Division: Tagebuch der Hoch- und Deutschmeister.* Vienna, Austria: Austria Press, 1969.

Schmidt, August. *Geschichte der 10. Division, 10. Infanterie-Division (mot.), 10. Panzergrenadier-Division, 1935–1945.* Bad Nauheim, Germany: Podzun Verlag, 1963.

Schmitz, Peter, Klaus-Juergen Thies, Guenter Wegmann and Christian Zweng, *Die deutschen Divisionen, 1939–1945.* 3 vols. Osnabrück, Germany: Biblio Verlag, 1993–1997.

Schnabel, Ernst. *Weg und Schicksal der 183. Infanterie-Division. Geschichte der fränkisch-sudetendeutschen 183. Infanterie-Division. Divisiongruppe 183 in der Korps-Abteilung C. 183. Volks-Grenadier-Division, 1939–1945.* Nuremberg, Germany: Kameradschaft der ehemaligen 183. Infanterie-Division, 1988.

Schraml, Franz. *Kriegsschauplatz Kroatien: Die deutsch-kroatischen Legions-Divisionen—369., 373., 392. Infanterie-Division (kroat.) ihre Ausbildungs- und Ersatzformationen.* Neckargemünd, Germany: 1962.

Schrodek, G. W. *Die 11. Panzer-Division "Gespenster-Division"—Bilddokumente, 1940–1945.* Friedberg, Germany: Podzun-Pallas-Verlag, 1984.

Schroeder, Juergen, and Joachim Schultz-Naumann. *Die Geschichte der pommerschen 32. Infanterie-Division, 1935–1945.* Bad Nauheim, Germany: Podzun-Verlag, 1962.

Seaton, Albert. *The Russo-German War, 1941–45.* New York: Praeger, 1971.

Seemen, Gerhard von. *Die Ritterkreuzträger, 1938–1945.* Friedberg, Germany: Podzun-Verlag, 1976.

Senger und Etterlin, Frido von. *Neither Fear Nor Hope: The Wartime Career of General Frido von Senger und Etterlin, Defender of Cassino.* Translated by George Malcolm. 1963. Reprint, Novato, Calif.: Presidio, 1989.

Senger und Etterlin, Dr. F. M. von. *Die 24. Panzer-Division, vormals 1. Kavallerie-Division, 1939–1945.* Neckargemünd, Germany: Vowinckel, 1962.

Shirer, William L. *The Rise and Fall of the Third Reich: A History of Nazi Germany.* New York: Simon and Schuster, 1960.

Silgailis, Arthur. *Latvian Legion.* San Jose, Calif.: R. J. Bender, 1986.

Snyder, Louis L. *Encyclopedia of the Third Reich.* New York: McGraw-Hill, 1976.

Snydor, Charles W., Jr. *Soldiers of Destruction: The SS Death's Head Division, 1933–1945.* Princeton, N.J.: Princeton University Press, 1977.

Spaeter, Helmuth. *Panzerkorps Grossdeutschland: Panzergrenadier-Division Grossdeutschland, Panzergrenadier-Division Brandenburg und seine Schwesterverbände, Führer-Grenadier-Division, Führer-Begleit-Division, Panzergrenadier-Division Kurmark und ihre 108 Träger des Ritterkreuzes: Bilddokumentation.* Friedberg, Germany: Podzun-Pallas-Verlag, 1984.

Speidel, Hans. *Invasion 1944: Rommel and the Normandy Campaign.* 1949. Reprint, Chicago: Regnery, 1950.

Stahl, Friedrich Christian, et al. *Geschichte der 121. Ostpreussischen Infanterie-Division, 1940–1945.* N.p.: self-published, 1970.

Staiger, Georg. *26. Panzer-Division: Ihr Werden und Einsatz 1942 bis 1945.* Bad Nauheim, Germany: H. H. Podzun, 1957.

Stauffenberg, Friedrich von. "Panzer Commanders of the Western Front." Unpublished manuscript in the possession of the author.

———. "Papers." Unpublished papers in the possession of the author.

Stein, George. *The Waffen-SS: Hitler's Elite Guard at War, 1939–1945.* Ithaca, N.Y.: Cornell University Press, 1966.

Stoeber, Hans. *Die Eiserne Faust—Bildband der 17. SS-Panzergrenadier-Division "Goetz von Berlichingen"* Neckargemünd, Germany: Vowinckel, 1966.

Stoves, Rolf O. G. *Die gepanzerten und motorisierten deutschen Grossverbände: Divisionen und selbständige Brigaden 1935–1945.* Friedberg, Germany: Podzun-Pallas-Verlag, 1986.

———. *Die 1. Panzerdivision, 1935–1945: ihre Aufstellung, die Bewaffnung, der Einsatz, ihre Männer.* Dorheim, Germany: Podzun-Verlag, 1976.

———. *Die 22. Panzer-Division, 25. Panzer-Division, 27. Panzer-Division und 233. Reserve-Panzer-Division: Aufstellung, Gliederung, Einsatz.* Friedberg, Germany: Podzun-Pallas-Verlag, 1985.

Strassner, Peter. *Europäische Freiwillige: Die Geschichte der 5. SS-Panzer-Division "Wiking"* Osnabrück, Germany: Munin Verlag, 1968.
Tettau, Hans von, and Kurt Versock. *Geschichte der 24. Infanterie-Division, 1935–1945.* Stolberg, Germany: self-published, 1956.
Tessin, Georg. *Verbände und Truppen der deutschen Wehrmacht und Waffen-SS im Zweiten Weltkrieg 1939–1945.* 14 vols. Osnabrück: Biblio-Verlag, 1978–1989.
Thomas, Franz. *Die Eichenlaubträger, 1940–1945.* 2 vols. Osnabrück, Germany: Biblio, 1997–1998.
Thorwald, Jürgen. *Defeat in the East.* New York: Bantam, 1980.
Thumm, Helmut. *Der Weg der 5. Infanterie-und-Jäger Division, 1921–1945.* Friedberg, G ermany: Podzun-Pallas-Verlag, 1976.
Tiemann, Reinhard. *Geschichte der 83. Infanterie-Division, 1939–1945.* Bad Nauheim, Germany: Podzun, 1960.
Treffer, Rudolf. *Geschichte des Artillerie-Regiment 193 im Verband der 93. Infanterie-Division, 1939–1945.* Euskirchen, Germany: self-published, 1988.
Ullrich, Karl. *Wie ein Fels im Meer: Kriegsgeschichte der 3. SS-Panzer-Division "Totenkopf".* 2 vols. Osnabrück, Germany: Munin Verlag, 1984–1987.
United States Department of the Army. *Pamphlet 20-260.* "The German Campaign in the Balkans (Spring, 1941)." 1953.
United States Military Intelligence Service. "Order of Battle of the German Army, 1942." 1942.
———. "Order of Battle of the German Army, 1943." 1943.
———. "Order of Battle of the German Army, 1944." 1944.
———. "Order of Battle of the German Army, 1945." 1945.
United States War Department. Technical Manual *TM-E 30-451*, "Handbook on German Military Forces." 1945.
Velten, Wilhelm. *Vom Kugelbaum zur Handgranate: Der Weg der 65. Infanterie-Division.* Neckargemünd, Germany: Vowinckel, 1974.
Vetter, Fritz. *Die 78. Infanterie- und Sturmdivision, 1938–1945: Eine Dokumentation in Bildern.* Friedberg, Germany: Podzun-Pallas-Verlag, 1981.
Voss, Klaus, and Paul Kehlenbeck. *Letzte Divisionen—Die Panzerdivision Clausewitz und die Infanteriedivision Schill.* Schleusingen, Germany: Amun, 2000.
Weidinger, Division Das Reich: *Der Weg der 2. SS-Panzer-Division "Das Reich"* 5 vols. Osnabrück, Germany: Munin Verlag, 1967–1982.
———. *Division Das Reich in Bild.* Osnabrück, Germany: Munin Verlag, 1981.
Werthen, Wolfgang. *Geschichte der 16. Panzer-Division, 1939–1945.* Bad Nauheim, Germany: Hans-Henning Podzun, 1958.
Whiting, Charles. *Bloody Aachen.* New York: Stein and Day, 1976.
Windrow, Martin. *The Panzer Divisions.* Reading, England: Osprey Publishing, 1973.
Wistrich, Robert. *Who's Who in Nazi Germany.* New York: Macmillan, 1982.
Witte, Hans Joachim, and Peter Offermann. *Die Böselagerschen Reiter: Das Kavallerie-Regiment Mitte und die aus ihm hervorgegangene 3. Kavallerie-Brigade/ Division.* Munich, Germany: Schild-Verlag, 1998.
Yerger, Mark C. *Waffen-SS Commanders: The Army, Corps and Divisional Leaders of a Legend.* 2 vols. Atglen, PA: Schiffer, 1997–1999.

Zeller, Konrad, et al. *Weg und Schicksal der 215. württembergisch-badischen Infanterie-Division, 1936–1945: Eine Dokumentation im Bildern.* Friedberg, Germany: Podzun-Pallas-Verlag, 1980.

Young, Desmond. *Rommel.* London: Collins, 1950.

Young, Peter, ed. *The Marshall Cavendish Illustrated Encyclopedia of World War II.* 12 vols. New York: Marshall Cavendish, 1985.

Ziemke, Earl F. *Stalingrad to Berlin: The German Defeat in the East.* Washington, DC: Office of the Chief of Military History, U.S. Army, 1968.

INTERNET SOURCES

www.diedeutschewehrmacht.de
en.wikipedia.org/wiki/Koszalin
www.feldgrau.com
www.forum.axishistory.com
www.gebirgsjaeger.4mg.com
www.lexikon.com
philosophy.elte.hu
www.das-ritterkreuz.de
www.ritterkreuztraeger-1939-45.de
spearhead1944.com/toe1.htm

Index

Stackpole Military History Series

Real battles. Real soldiers. Real stories.

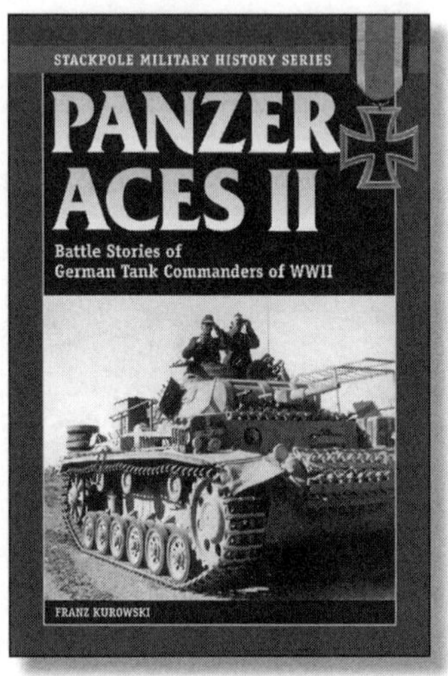
STACKPOLE MILITARY HISTORY SERIES
PANZER ACES II
Battle Stories of
German Tank Commanders of WWII
FRANZ KUROWSKI